*f*P

Also by Jonathan Stevenson for The Free Press

"We Wrecked the Place": Contemplating
an End to the Northern Irish Troubles

HARD MEN

HUMBLE

Vietnam Veterans
Who Wouldn't Come Home

JONATHAN STEVENSON

The Free Press
New York · London · Toronto · Sydney · Singapore

THE FREE PRESS
A Division of Simon & Schuster, Inc.
1230 Avenue of the Americas
New York, NY 10020

For information regarding special discounts for bulk purchases,
please contact Simon & Schuster Special Sales:
1-800-456-6798 or business@simonandschuster.com

Designed by Lauren Simonetti

Manufactured in the United States of America

1   3   5   7   9   10   8   6   4   2

Library of Congress Cataloging-in-Publication Data
is available.

ISBN 0-684-84264-5

For
Clay Burkhalter
and
Jeff Bartholet,

two more too young for the war
who may always wonder just what they escaped

We are made to persist, to complete the whole tour.
That's how we find out who we are.

—TOBIAS WOLFF
In Pharaoh's Army

One night in Bangkok makes a hard man humble.

—MURRAY HEAD
from the musical *Chess*

CONTENTS

THE VETERANS

Jim Agnew, a helicopter mechanic for the Army and later for Air America in Laos, elected not to return to his home in Miami, Florida, stayed in Southeast Asia to service the helicopters that the U.S. brought there during the Vietnam era, and never left.

Alan Dawson, from Ontario by way of Eugene, Oregon, was hooked on Asia and war as an Army journalist in Vietnam, covered the fall of Saigon as a civilian, and is now a senior reporter for the *Bangkok Post.*

Israel "Izzy" Freedman, from Willimantic, Connecticut, was a helicopter pilot for the Air Force in Vietnam and for Air America in both Laos and Vietnam, worked for oil exploration companies in Southeast Asia after the war, bought an interest in a Bangkok bar, and found no reason to leave.

Denis Gray, born in Czechoslovakia of refugee parents, graduated from Yale and became an Army intelligence officer in Vietnam, returning to Southeast Asia as Associated Press's long-time Bangkok bureau chief and chronicling Indochina's long-running strife.

Eric Herter, Boston-born, Harvard-educated, and the grandson of Secretary of State Christian A. Herter, started his tour as an Army photographer and ended it as a disaffected adviser to

USAID in the CIA-run counter-insurgency program, circling back to Hanoi as an Associated Press photographer out of a need to make restitution to the Vietnamese.

Glenn P. "Jeep" Holthaus, a decorated medic with a Marine Force Recon unit who was raised on military bases and attended the University of Nebraska, owns a burger joint in Pattaya, Thailand, suffers from post-traumatic stress, and runs a charity that refurbishes used computer equipment and donates it to Thai schools.

Jeff Johnson, born and raised in Worcester, Massachusetts, joined the Army Corps of Engineers and then Air America (for the latter building runways in Laos under the CIA's protection), and wended his way back to Thailand, where he has prospered as a consulting engineer.

Stan Karber of Fort Smith, Arkansas, a Green Beret during the war, to whom "nothing has ever seemed really important since the conflict," found contentment only upon returning to Vietnam to live.

Greg Kleven, an Oakland-born Force Recon Marine badly wounded in a firefight, lost faith in the war and in his country, descended into dissoluteness and self-destructive drinking, and believes that moving to Ho Chi Minh City saved his life.

L.C. Linder, from Columbia, South Carolina, was a Marine helicopter door-gunner during the war, drifted from job to job, and finally ended up in Lopburi, north of Bangkok, running a helicopter maintenance business.

Bill Maddox, a former helicopter pilot from Macon, Georgia, lived for eight years in Bangkok after retiring from the Army, selling military equipment to the Thai government.

Jeff McLaury, an Annapolis graduate from Denver who chose the Army and served two tours in Vietnam, found the U.S. post-Vietnam culture disenchanting, migrating first to Ho Chi Minh City and then to Bangkok in pursuit of various business opportunities—and lost youth.

Keith Mishne, a Cleveland-born former interrogator for Army intelligence, joined the antiwar movement after his tour and returned to Vietnam because "Vietnam's a trip."

Douglas "Pete" Peterson, who was born in Omaha, Nebraska, and grew up in Milton, Iowa, became an F-4 pilot, a six-year POW at the Hanoi Hilton, and a three-term Florida congressman, and served as the United States conciliation-minded ambassador to Vietnam from 1997 to 2001.

Ken Richter, once a Jersey City tough, discovered discipline and honor in Special Forces during two tours in Vietnam and success in stateside entrepreneurship, which gave him the freedom to relocate to Bangkok and donate much of his earnings as a manufacturer's representative to Southeast Asian charities.

André Sauvageot, from Akron, Ohio, spent the better part of eight years in Vietnam as an Army officer and came to love the Vietnamese in spite of his anticommunist convictions, returning to Hanoi as General Electric's in-country representative.

Chuck Searcy of Athens, Georgia, an Army intelligence officer based near Saigon during the war, joined Vietnam Veterans Against the War and now runs the Hanoi office of the Vietnam Veterans of America Foundation, operating clinics for crippled children and raising money for hospitals.

Major Mark Smith, from Lima, Ohio, by way of Torrance, California, is a much bemedaled winner of the Distinguished Service Cross and former prisoner of war who works out of Bangkok relentlessly to track down MIAs.

Les Strouse, who is from Doylestown, Pennsylvania, served in the Air Force but did not see Vietnam and Laos until he flew planes for Air America; warm weather and Asia's beauty have kept him in Thailand, where he was chief pilot of Bangkok Airways until his retirement several years ago.

Robert Taylor, who grew up in Fairbanks, Alaska, became a Green Beret and formed a bond with the Lao tribe with which he worked, coming to Thailand in the early 1980s and establishing a medical charity that ventures where he once fought.

Mac Thompson, an Army veteran from Portland, Oregon, who served with the U.S. Agency for International Development in Laos alongside Agnew, Freedman, Johnson, and Strouse, had a full career with AID before retiring to Bangkok and a steady stream of Air America reunions and on-line debates about the Indochina wars.

1
HOME ALONE

You couldn't easily find a more marginalized group of men. Even many of their former comrades dismiss them as "the losers of the lunatic fringe." "What makes you think that the overwhelming majority of Vietnam veterans share anything with the misfits and malcontents who decided that they couldn't cope with life in America and choose instead to live in a third-world country where the women are subservient and the work ethic is virtually nonexistent?" So asks a former Vietnam tank commander.

There are close to a thousand expatriate veterans living in Southeast Asia. If their brethren disdain them, the rest of their countrymen simply do not care about them. They constitute an awkward, out-of-the-way fringe group of veterans of a war that most of us would just as soon forget. As a student put it to her professor, "I had the feeling you weren't supposed to ask questions about Vietnam. It's like some dark family secret that nobody wants to talk about around the children."

Certainly there are moments that force us to remember. Bob

Kerrey talks of a long-ago mission that went awry. Robert McNamara offers an apology twenty-five years after the fact. Although the Reagan and Bush (senior) administrations engineered an apparent national reconciliation between the public and the veterans, in retrospect it may have been cynically aimed at galvanizing support for military interventions that carried the whiff of Vietnam. Whatever its purpose, it had that effect. Endorsed by two-thirds of Americans a year after it ended, the Gulf War was still deemed worthwhile by a statistically identical proportion on the tenth anniversary of the coalition victory in February 2001. Yet many Vietnam veterans felt slighted yet again when soldiers of the Gulf War—an incomparably less bloody engagement—received the festive homecoming and won the vicarious esteem that the Vietnam vets were denied.

For them the home front of cultural memory remains one of domestic betrayal lamented. Soldiers were castigated upon returning home in the sixties and seventies, and that was only the beginning. When they went to a movie theater or read a novel, they saw themselves depicted as sad sacks or nut cases. If they had few job skills, they found traditional heavy industries depressed and jobs hard to come by. The counterpoise of strife and respite—a comfort, if not a salvation, for a generation of British men after the Great War and American men after the Second World War—was rendered difficult by the roiling protest at home, then by the cultural amnesia that healing was deemed to require.

Vietnam has become the antihero's war. Having served there confers not so much a patina of dutifulness as the unhealable scars that come from staring into a moral abyss. For some men on the edges of society, lying about soldiering in Vietnam has become a popular way to glom the prestige of hard experience, made all the more credible by the fact that it was not necessarily even something to be proud of. In the 1998 book *Stolen Valor: How the Vietnam Generation Was Robbed of Its Heroes and Its History,* B. G.

Burkett and Glenna Whitley compiled thousands of instances of homeless men and others purporting to be Vietnam veterans traumatized by the war. They turned out never to have set foot in-country at all, lied about their experience to get government benefits, or were never even in the military. A guy in Central Park wearing a fatigue jacket tells you he's a Nam vet and asks you for subway fare; you flip him a token before you realize he couldn't have been more than two years old when Saigon was evacuated. A convict on death row for murder convinces three networks and a parole board that Vietnam War trauma made him do it when he was never in combat. Acclaimed historian Joseph Ellis lies to students and journalists about having served in Vietnam and then protested the war, apparently to enhance his claim to have participated in history. These anecdotes, more than any admirable exploits of actual Vietnam soldiers, have bored deeply into public consciousness.

There were, of course, plenty of American heroes in the Vietnam War. Will they ever get their due? Hundreds of expat vets have given up hoping. Some of their stateside fellows have simply stopped talking about the war, and have reached an uneasy truce with the hostile attitudes that pop up unbidden from even the kindest of strangers. For those several hundred expats, however, such obscure and unanswered doubts are unacceptable.

◦◦◦◦

Strategically dubious and morally ambiguous, Vietnam remains the hard case. Whereas World War II made the twentieth "the American century," Vietnam jeopardized that tribute. Intervention in Vietnam did not clearly enable either Americans or Vietnamese to live better lives. As a consequence, nobody's "good life" can vindicate the deaths of those who perished. Perhaps World War II has forced an unfair burden on Vietnam veterans. After all, murky moral purpose and senseless violence have been the rule of war, not the exception. Slightly redrafting the map of Europe hardly justified the idiotic carnage of the First World War. The U.S. Civil War was organized suicide. From the Iran-Iraq War back to the Hundred Years War, millions of men have died for dubious reasons. With Vietnam, war merely reverted to moral ambiguity. The Cold War geopolitics underlying the Vietnam War was far harder to understand than Hitler's evil.

THE WORST WAR IN HISTORY?

In his classic study *The Great War and Modern Memory,* Paul Fussell traces much of modern Western society's—especially Britain's—collective sense of irony to the immense discrepancy between what was expected of World War I (glory and heroism) and what actually emerged from the trenches (morbid attrition and anonymous death). On this criterion, Vietnam should be a comparably rich source of irony for Americans: they anticipated a military cakewalk and in fact got an agonizing defeat.

For Americans Vietnam marked the decisive termination of the tradition of romanticizing battle, the end of war's status as "the great adventure." In Europe, this cultural watershed occurred earlier, after the First World War. But during that war, nationalism, brotherhood, and perhaps a tinge of homoeroticism flourished, and perfumed the incomparable terror of trench warfare. The Great War in Britain's modern memory has remained an inspirational source of strength through another devastating world war and beyond. To this day nearly everyone in Great Britain wears a red paper poppy during the week of Veterans' Day, remembering Flanders fields. British television news broadcasts celebrate events that do not qualify as triumphs, like the evacuation of British troops from Dunkirk in May 1940. Not so with Vietnam. It produced no Blundens and no Graveses, no Owens and no Sassoons, to memorialize the finer aspects of national service in a cynical war.

This departure had plenty to do with the rise of realism in general, and with the trend, during the war-ridden twentieth century, toward de-romanticizing war, which is quite independent of what happened in Vietnam. The war also coincided with the dramatization of violence via the television camera. The result is that Americans regard Vietnam as uniquely tainted. While some (mostly veterans) respectfully affix Stars-and-Stripes pins to their lapels, they offer no gestures comparable to the reverence of the British for valor in victory and defeat alike. Any war is hell. Vietnam was not the first war in which the indigenous population, putative benefactor of the foreigners' intervention, in fact resented them. And Vietnam certainly was not the only war in which expeditionary combatants found conditions less than ideal.

Atrocities occurred in Vietnam, as they do in all wars. But thanks perhaps to the My Lai massacre in March 1968, when a U.S. army company killed 504 unarmed Vietnamese civilians in South Vietnam, as well as unprecedented television coverage, atrocity as an idiom of combat is peculiarly associated with the Vietnam War. Just ask Bob Kerrey. The picture of the crazed GI exterminating "gooks" has reached mythical proportions, and the imagery to emerge from Vietnam establishes a visceral semicriminality rather than anything like good old-fashioned American heroism. As a group, Vietnam veterans are too often misremembered by sheepish contemporaries as drug-addled basket cases, shell-shocked baby killers, or treasonous "fraggers" who deserved the jeers and taunts that some received at Travis Air Force Base on their Date of Expected Return from Overseas—the once-cherished "DEROS."

A 1979 Harris survey conducted for the Veterans Administration indicated that 52.3 percent of Americans over eighteen believed that Vietnam veterans had more serious problems than those of other wars; among teachers and employers, the figures were 68.4 percent and 59.7 percent, respectively. In the twenty years since, public perceptions have softened little. Yet Department of Veterans Affairs statistical surveys completed in 1999 reveal that Vietnam veterans compare very favorably both with their nonveteran contemporaries and with younger veterans and nonveterans in terms of educational attainment and level of employment. The DVA also puts the number of suicides among Vietnam veterans—which other popular, professional, and clinical sources have pegged at 60,000 to 100,000—at no higher than 20,000.

Vietnam veterans haven't done so badly, but they did miss the parade. They remain frustrated that their fellow Americans seem not to understand that the futility of that war does not necessarily diminish every man who fought it. Americans yearn for moral clarity that the Vietnam War, like most wars, cannot provide. Signally lacking strategic coherence and logistical definition from the start, Vietnam presents an especially daunting narrative. Even veterans groups like the Veterans of Foreign Wars and the American Legion at times have derided Vietnam vets as "losers."

Succeeding generations of nonservers—at their most charitable—consign Vietnam veterans to victimhood. Rarely are soldiers of the Vietnam War deemed to have had The Right Stuff. Positive lessons are silenced by the sentiment: *never again.* The helicopter crew who courageously stopped the slaughter at My Lai were decorated for their valor only in 1998—thirty years after the fact. American culture, it seems, conditions Americans to regard Vietnam in its entirety as a crowning abomination.

For Americans in 1972 as well as Brits in 1918, a wasteful war did have spoils, but these did not usually include a greater love of country, fortified piety, or the glow of victory. Instead both groups of men, if they were lucky, carried away an intimate knowledge of camaraderie and how it worked—of what men can do to survive together when they have nobody to count on but one another. But in fact, in Vietnam the soldier's bond was at a premium. Says Nat Tripp in his Vietnam memoir *Father Soldier Son:* "In this murder-ous 'emperor-has-no-clothes' environment, soldiers made up their own rules, designed their own parameters of good and bad so that they could navigate through the jungle of conflicting experiences. Individual leadership, strength, courage, and humanity were more important than in any other war, because there was no guiding vision, no goal, no leadership at the top."

Given these handicaps, Vietnam veterans arguably should be appreciated all the more for their accomplishments as soldiers and as people. In Vietnam there was, observes novelist Tim O'Brien, "no valor to squander for things like country or honor or military objectives." Soldiers needed "the kind [of courage] you dredge up in the morning, knowing it will be a bad day." Such courage had no moral reward, no triumphant culmination. Per military convention, soldiers would develop from callow newbies into seasoned short-timers. They would learn how to save their own lives and to protect others, but also to be callous as required for battle. War, of necessity, makes you crazy. The pathological aspect of combat is not something that Vietnam inaugurated. Rather, the uniqueness of the Vietnam experience is captured in the mantra that grunts in Vietnam repeated more and more as they gained experience and got closer to DEROS. What they said—about death, about missions, about life—was: "Don't mean nothin'."

The phrase and its partners, "Ain't no big thing" and "Sorry about that," connoted precisely the opposite of what they denoted. In the immediate circumstances of life in the field, they were a soldier's ironical means of defusing tension, and of steeling himself to horrors. But as the underlying attitude insinuated itself into the soldier's worldview, it portended the disaffection he would feel when he returned home. This connection accurately reflects the singular, and singularly disturbing, feature of Vietnam: too many soldiers, once they got to Vietnam and registered both the ambivalence of the indigenous population and the hesitancy of the military strategy, were not sure what they were doing there.

WHITHER VALOR?

"It is too easy, as a part of the healing process, to look back with a sense of victory when all I really felt at the time was defeat," says Nat Tripp. "It is too easy to forget the incredible suffering inflicted on so many. It is too easy for fathers and sons to goad each other into war. . . . Our children speak to us in hushed tones about the war, and what it did to us. There is talk of redemption, of honor, of returning to Vietnam and finding something there, something beyond the shattered bone fragments and vertebrae, something that perhaps might still be alive, that could even speak and say, 'Thank God you came back for me, now there can be peace, now justice is done.'"

Simple valor, then, does not seem enough to vindicate one's participation in Vietnam. Vets no longer press the case. They have grown tired of repeating that they won the war on the battlefield, that they fought bravely, that the politicians didn't allow them to finish the job. Vietnam vets are denied the traditional payoff of military service: the alluring posterity of a middle-aged war hero, who no longer had to prove himself and could live the rest of his life securely bolted to a venerable past. Despite that privation, they have a psychological need to fashion their war experience into something acceptable. To do so, the vets have several options. They can turn their valor in a bedeviled war into something better. Or they can deny it altogether. They can admit it had no place. Or they can simply ignore the war. The fifth alternative is to defend their part in the war and damn those who disagree.

Compromises though these are, the historical stigma that Americans attach to Vietnam makes any of these dispensations an extraordinary intellectual and emotional challenge. According to a November 2000 Gallup Poll prompted by Bill Clinton's official visit to Vietnam—the first by a sitting U.S. president since 1975—69 percent of the American people still believe that sending troops to Vietnam was a mistake (compared to only 34 percent with respect to Korea, America's other "limited war"). But only 60 percent, and less than half of those between eighteen and twenty-nine, know that the United States supported South Vietnam during the war.

Against this combination of disapproval, ignorance, and apathy, a fair number of veterans have chosen to forsake the United States in favor of the very scene of the controversy: Southeast Asia. Yet expatriate veterans face the same dilemmas as stateside vets about what to do with pride in service that is underappreciated, and have isolated the same set of options: to transform, deny, desert, ignore, or defend their valor.

The key difference between expat vets and their stateside counterparts lies in the enduring prominence of their Vietnam experiences in their contemporary lives. Those experiences have not been muted or diffused by the exigencies of living in a society that purposively wishes to forget about Vietnam. Memories remain closer to the surface of their lives. For that reason, their stories illuminate the grievances, demons, and virtues of the Vietnam veteran all the brighter. Now is a fitting moment to listen to those stories. Despite the generally low level of interest in the Vietnam War as history, the 2000 Gallup Poll also recorded that 72 percent of Americans acknowledge that the American people have not treated Vietnam veterans well since the war—up ever so slightly from 69 percent in 1990. A satisfying national reckoning is long overdue.

Robert Taylor, a Green
Beret in Vietnam,
with a Lao friend.
Courtesy Robert Taylor.

2
VALOR TRANSFORMED

There are at least six hundred veterans and retirees in Thailand, about two-thirds of them Vietnam veterans, and about two-thirds of those ex-Air Force. (The Department of Defense population report lists only about three hundred vets and retirees in Thailand, but this is because DoD counts those whose pension checks are sent to a U.S. address as U.S. residents even though many Thailand-based vets have their checks sent to a stateside address or bank. There is also no legal requirement that a U.S. citizen coming to live in Thailand inform the U.S. Consulate or the DoD.) Some vets in-country are "floaters," who come in for six months, then drift out for a few months, and so forth. Although there are some Vietnam veterans in Korea, perhaps an even greater

number of ex-Navy personnel in the Philippines, and now a smat-
tering of vets in Vietnam itself, among Asian countries Thailand
probably harbors the highest number of Vietnam-era vets who
were stationed in-country.

The vast majority of Vietnam vets in Thailand served in rear
areas—making them "rear-echelon motherfuckers," or REMFs—
and were not combat soldiers. Most Vietnam vets in Thailand
were Air Force ground crew who were never shot at. This feature
of Thailand's veteran population pretty much lays to rest the myth
that Thailand nests dozens of American mercenaries. Contrary to
another myth, very few veterans come to Thailand to evade trouble back home. According to the Retiree Affairs Office at the
Joint U.S. Military Assistance Group, Thailand—abbreviated and
known phonetically as "Jusmag"—of the thousands of vets that
have circulated through Thailand over the past twenty-seven
years, only two have been sought by U.S. authorities for criminal
offenses; both were returned stateside to serve prison sentences.
Only one expat veteran has done hard time (on narcotics charges)
in a Thai jail. There has been only one suicide. Deserters at large
number ten at most. For the most part, Vietnam veterans in Thailand live quiet lives married to younger Thai women who are
nonetheless now approaching middle age. Their $800-a-month
retirement pay buys less and less, and they are past the age for
marathon partying and womanizing.

That said, undeniably there are hedonistic attractions in Thailand that even aging vets indulge in. Bangkok's Washington
Square is an expatriate enclave of men's bars sequestered behind
not one but two *sois*—small streets—off Sukhumvit Road. On a
typical Saturday afternoon, the New Square One Pub might be
stone dead. Down Soi 22 a piece, the only expat in the New Cowboy Bar could be passed out in the crook of his elbow. Back in the
Square, there'd be no action in the Prince of Wales (a.k.a. POW)
Pub or Bourbon Street—just a terrace-scattering of tall, pale

drunks with bleeding tattoos groping Thai women. Two cul-de-sacs into the Square, the most promising sounds of community would probably come from the Texas Lone Staar Saloon, which would boast "Food Wimmen Likker" and a congenial brace of twenty or so happy, murmuring customers. All would be men, and all Caucasian. The five bartenders are all female, and all Thai, and food and likker revenues probably don't quite cover the payroll. According to regular patrons of the bar, for services after work, a woman could get about one-fifth of standard American daily wages, which is five times the Thai average.

The barroom of the Lone Staar is a dark varnished rectangle, flanked by six booths on either side and fronted with a dartboard. There's no "No Smoking" section. This day the stereo drawls country music in English, and the TV (by either tape or satellite) flickers *Monday Night Football.* A sweet almond-eyed girl of eighteen brings Bangkok's best product, a Singha Beer. It measures up to micro-brewed American lager or European thoroughbred, though Heineken is available and in fact preferred, probably because it enables Yanks to get into character. The footrail, the padded armrest, the towel under the beer, and the little wooden cup in which the bartender keeps each customer's tab become every patron's ecosystem. It is easy to settle in at the Lone Staar. Old soldiers on vacation wax rueful—"Hell, I haven't been supersonic since '65"—and eat free American food. Spareribs, beans, and greens are gratis as long as drinks are purchased as well.

On Thanksgiving Day, the bar is wall-to-wall people. The girls are decked out in tight, colorful dresses, too much makeup, and gold tiaras. It's a special day, so they are allowed to drink. They're drunk. Unfathomably, two lovely Thai women fight over a wizened septuagenarian white man with no teeth who has been buying them drinks and cadging tongue from each. One girl grabs the other's left tit and clenches. The other keens as they both fall to the ground. The crowd laughs. So do the women. The clenchee playfully flashes her pert, reddened breast. All crow's-feet, bowlegs, and chicken tracks, Charlie Brown—Korean War veteran, night manager of the Lone Staar, and permanent resident of the third floor of the building—captures the mood of the place. "When I die," he rasps, "I just want them to cremate me at Wat Tatong [a large Buddhist temple] and spread my ashes in front of every bar on Washington Square."

Notwithstanding its comely staff, the Lone Staar is technically a cocktail bar as opposed to a girly bar—meaning that its main purpose is to get people drunk rather than to get them horny. Reversing this emphasis are the girly bars of Patpong and Patpong II—the two *sois* in south Bangkok that harbor the most licentious, risqué establishments of Thailand's immense sex trade. Most of the women are from the poor Isaan province of northeast Thailand, and have been willingly relinquished to iniquity by their families for the sake of the money they send home. Despite rampant AIDS, the unenforceably illegal sex trade is one of the most efficient enterprises in Southeast Asia for redistributing income.

On either of the Patpongs, a man can go into any of a hundred bars, sit down on a stool or in a booth, and within seconds feel small but awkward Asian hands massaging his neck. Alternatively, a hostess will simply assign him a female companion at the door. As one Vietnam vet points out, "If you can't score in Thailand, you got a problem." The man need only acquiesce to a girl's attention—it starts at the shoulders, progresses to the thigh, then moves on to the crotch—to take her home. She will offer a standardized package of small talk that stretches her limited command of English to the maximum. *Where you from? What you do? You very handsome. You like Thai girl?* The vet adds, "They aren't real interested in where you went to school." Ignore them for a few minutes, of course, and they'll move on to the next guy.

Patpong girly bars tout live shows, which are usually free.

Totally naked girls get up on stage and do things like put eggs in their vaginas, dance around for a few minutes, then release the eggs unbroken into their hands. *Voilà.* Another favorite: a girl opens a bottle of beer with her cervix. And perhaps the biggest crowd-pleaser occurs when a girl puts a cheap plastic horn inside her and plays a crude tune on the thing. Physically, this feat requires her to bend over and spread her cheeks, so a fair number of patrons (most of them foreign) inevitably giggle in anticipation of a fart. It's rather demeaning, to put it mildly, but the girls seem to fend off embarrassment either by showing no interest whatso-ever in what they are doing or smiling sardonically as they per-form, as if the whole enterprise were a goof. Stay late enough, and a young Thai couple will come out and have sex on the stage.

The other central venue for sex-related fun in Bangkok is the Nana Entertainment Plaza, three stories of girly bars on Soi 4 Sukhumvit. It is marginally tamer than Patpong. Most of the dancers there too are completely nude, but instead of the live act with tricks one is more likely to see something like "The Shower Show"—a feature of a bar called The G-Spot in which three or four girls behind a glass partition take a shower and halfheartedly fondle and lick one another in every conceivable intimate place. Usually the girls are yukking it up as they "have sex," once in a while feigning an obligatory orgasm, so this gig has a more wholesome, jokey, burlesque feel than a squalid Patpong live show.

In terms of dramatic flair, the best performers are probably the so-called *katois:* male transvestites, many of them genuine psycho-logical transsexuals, who get hormone injections and breast implants, tape down their masculine equipment, and use makeup skillfully enough to fool drunken tourists. It is not uncommon to see an inebriated, gland-struck American walking arm in arm with a man he thinks is a woman. A legend has long circulated in the Bangkok expat vet community about an intoxicated Green

Beret on R-and-R from Vietnam who took home a *katoi,* had intercourse with "her," woke up to discover his mistake, and tossed *him* out of the window of his high-rise hotel to the poolside concrete below. As the story goes, he was never prosecuted.

Bangkok also has attractions other than its young flesh, attractions that partially redeem it despite its sleaziness. The cuisine is marvelous, the restaurants cheap, the informal family-style of many refreshing to a Westerner. Walk down Sukhumvit and look in the window of any of a hundred places, and you will see live fish, lobster, and crabs on display, offered for your dinner enjoyment. You choose the particular animals you want cooked, are escorted into a fairly earthy dining room, and are brought your drinks. The Thai proprietors then prepare your food, energizing it as only the Thais can with cilantro, lemon grass, lime leaf, Chinese chives, galangal, ginger, holy basil, dried shrimp, fresh turmeric, palm sugar, fish sauce, and five different kinds of incendiary peppers—for a start. They keep bringing you drinks until you've finished your food. With abundant potables, ten bucks a head.

Even hash houses have a grittily exotic other-worldliness. The New Light Coffee House is a sixties-esque joint with a long bar, low-slung booths, smoked glass windows, and soft green lighting, in the middle of a shabby grid of streets off Siam Square. The waitresses don't like Americans because they remind them that they can't speak English, but the manager speaks it very well. He looks and acts like a pit boss in a casino. He has the bad skin that comes with a subterranean urban existence, incongruously wears cheery baby-blue seersucker suits, and never shows emotion. The menu knows few bounds—a body can get a decent burger and fries, or traditionally prepared wild boar with peppercorns and perfectly steamed rice.

As a dining experience, the New Light is several shades more interesting than McDonald's, but there are at least forty of those in Bangkok, too. Likewise, Starbuck's coffee, designer clothes, and Saabs are available. Yanks *qua* consumers don't lose much in moving to Thailand, and they can exploit or decline local variations as they choose. But Bangkok is also ugly, dirty, polluted, and overcrowded. While the magnificent Grand Palace on the Chao Phraya River testifies to Thailand's admirable aesthetic heritage, it is more than offset by abandoned office buildings with filthy blue tarpaulins hanging like loincloths from their windows, open canals coursing with raw sewage, and chronic traffic jams. Symbolizing this urban squalor is a street population of pitiable mange-ridden dogs so depleted that the females leech milk from their teats and the males can't keep their penises in their sheaths. And save for meager, bulldozed Lumpini Park, public space has been relinquished to commerce.

In Thailand, though, American Vietnam veterans are, as Henry Hill said about *mafiosi,* like movie stars with muscle. One particular ex-Central Intelligence Agency case officer, a steward of the Lao war in the sixties and seventies, stayed on in Bangkok for twenty years. When he was about sixty, bald and paunchy, he returned to his home state of Texas for a visit. While drinking in a bar he went up to a couple of girls in their mid-twenties and asked them if he could buy them a drink. They looked at him and pointed across the room. "There are a couple of women about thirty years older than us sitting right over there," one said. "I'm sure they'd let you buy them a drink." According to the ex-CIA man, who tells the story with a self-deprecating smile, he called his travel agent the following day and said, "Put me on the next plane back to Thailand, in the smoking section if possible."

Most Thais would not characterize the American effort in Vietnam as a loss, but rather as a valiant stand against communism in Southeast Asia that—by raising the potential costs of insurgency—kept it from infesting Thailand, among other places. It's scarcely surprising, then, that some extended tourists lie about what they did during the war, and the phenomenon of *faux* vets has grown in Thailand since the 1980s, when Reagan's public-relations rehabilitation of Vietnam veterans improved their image. One guy who lives over the Lone Staar claims that he was given the choice of jail for "sowing his wild oats" or the service, joined the Marines in 1970, and wound up in-country in November of that year when he was eighteen—except he also notes that he was born in 1954, which would have made him sixteen. Supposedly he was assigned to "SOG," which he said stood for "Special Observations Group." He adds that he was in a Force Recon unit, part of a "five-man forward observation team" which took "orders from the boys in the suits" in the CIA (he mentions Pat Landry and Jack Shirley—both well-known Bangkok-based ex-spooks). Naturally, he worked around Saigon "and in countries where we should not have been," and was ordered to commit atrocities, though it was sometimes "my ass or yours." The one service friend who came to visit him in Thailand conveniently died of pancreatic cancer. *Agent Orange.* He conjures real tears when he talks about some of the things he saw and did for Uncle Sam during the war. Of course, "the things we did and the places we went as far as I know are still classified and probably will remain that way." He does allow that he did "two eighteen-month tours," and was awarded the Distinguished Service Cross, the Silver Star, and two Purple Hearts.

Unfortunately, this is mostly, if not all, easily detected bullshit. For starters, the acronym "SOG" originally signified "Special *Operations* Group," later "*Studies* and Observations Group," but never "*Special Observations* Group." Second, SOG's operational personnel were exclusively U.S. Army Special Forces—Green Berets. U.S. Marines in Force Recon were never detailed to SOG units. Third, after two eighteen-month tours in Vietnam, his DEROS would have been in September 1973; Military Assistance Command, Vietnam (MACV) SOG was inactive as of April 30, 1972. Fourth, most SOG operations were declassified after about twenty years. Fifth, if he'd been a Marine he would have received the Navy Cross, not the DSC. A Freedom of Information Act request for his service record (form DD–214) yielded nothing.

Why did he leave the United States? His answer is somehow unsurprising. For two years immediately following his discharge, he explains, this man rode around the United States on a Harley, too stressed to work. "I still wake up at night, just wringing wet." After fifteen years of working as a petroleum-drilling engineer in Texas (he says), he was given the opportunity to work in the Middle East and took it (he says). Ostensibly he was attracted to Bangkok because he had spent time here in the hospital during the war, recovering from shrapnel wounds. He was also losing faith in America. Casting the trauma of his wartime black ops as a springboard for his angst, he cites everything from unfair taxation to Rodney King to the inordinate power of Alan Greenspan, flaying whoever will listen with a rambling, incoherent neoliberal survivalist rap. Melodramatically he concludes: "The only way I will return to America is in a box."

Far more disappointing—and indeed psychologically more complicated—than the transparent fantasist is the studied dreamer, one of whom I encountered at the Sapa Restaurant in Ho Chi Minh City. He seemed to have cast himself as a living embodiment of all Vietnam ironies and to have mixed truth with fiction such that drawing a clear line between the two is impossible. Sitting on the patio of the bar, he starts his story by noting that he had little interest in going half a world away to fight a war that seemed to have minimal relevance to his way of life or any other American's. He was too busy breaking free of the shackles of his parents' Christian fundamentalist upbringing and racing Alfa Romeos to concern himself with Southeast Asia. When he received his first draft notice in 1964, he didn't even know where Vietnam was. "I just knew that Vietnam was a place far away where John Foster Dulles had decided to draw the line against communism," he recalled in a high, metallic voice that rings more cheerful than the man himself appears: a big guy, bald, with a whitish-gray goatee and gray, sober eyes, drinking rye at a table on the patio of the Sapa as music blares inside. The geopolitics, of course, was more than most early draftees knew. "I understood that there was this monolithic view of communism and this thing called the domino theory. And I believed it. I grew up in a very conservative family—religiously and politically."

An earnest cultural touch enriches his account of his prewar experience. His truest association with Asia, he says, was not geopolitical but romantic—and pre-Dien Bien Phu. "If someone had said, 'Indochina,' then I'd have said, 'Oh, okay, I can tell you where that is,' because when I was a kid I was very enthralled with listening to an old radio program called "Tales from the *Orient Express*." Until I was thirteen years old, 1953, you never had a television; the radio was the deal. This great program would start out with the sound of a railroad train, *chug-chug-chug,* and the people on board the *Orient Express* would be heading back to Paris or London from the Orient, telling about their experiences. I remember as a kid just being enthralled: Bangkok, Rangoon, Singapore, Hong Kong. I had no idea where those places were, but they sounded so exciting. Finally I went to a globe and I looked, and there was French Indochina. And I had an uncle who served with the Flying Tigers in China."

So Southeast Asia was to him a place of theoretical exotica, and it would retain its charm only by his leaving it that way. "I was a fuck-off in high school, and my grades were terrible," he confesses. He couldn't get into "any decent college," but on the strength of his parents' religious standing he was accepted into a religious college, where he "dicked off for a couple of years" and flunked out. He returned to his home in Maryland and enrolled in junior college. He soon dropped out and received that first draft notice. "I was not," he says, "militarily oriented at all, and I was pretty certain that somehow I was going to skate, that I was not going to get drafted. How I ended up in Vietnam, how I ended up in an infantry outfit—the whole deal—is a classic example of a snafu—you know, 'situation normal, all fucked up.'" Our new draftee says he was sent to Fort Holabird for induction, mumbling to himself, "Hey, man, I'm not ready for this, I'm having too much fun racing my little 1300-cc Alfa to go into the Army."

His account of how he tried to get out of military service may well be true. He'd heard, he says, about ways to beat the draft, but his feet weren't flat and his knees were strong. So, in filling out the mandatory forms at the induction interview, he checked the Yes box next to "homosexual tendencies." An embarrassed Army doctor subsequently held up the form and pointed to the relevant entry. "Is this true?" he asked, eyebrows peaked. The young man nodded. "Well, what do you mean?" queried the doctor. He offered the lame explanation that he always sat with the boys at mixers. The doctor, maybe still shaken by the Kinsey report, deferred his induction. After a couple of rounds of psychological tests, in December clinicians at Walter Reed Hospital determined that he was not, in fact, a homosexual. He was inducted into the U.S. Army. That much we know is true: a Freedom of Information Act request for this man did produce a service record indicating that he really did serve in the U.S. Army during the Vietnam War in the time frame he specified. Other key details of service from the rest of his story, though, are not on the DD-214 and appear to be in doubt.

Supposedly, a convoluted comedy of errors ensued from his induction, through which he, by virtue of his talent but against his preferences, wound up a combat soldier in the thick of the biggest, bloodiest battle of the Vietnam War: the Battle of the Ia Drang Valley in November 1965.

According to this vet, given his scholastic experience he didn't expect much of himself, but as it turned out, he was merely an underachiever. He scored extraordinarily high on the Army's IQ and aptitude tests, which earned him latitude in choosing his military occupational specialty. He opted for journalism and after basic training was sent to Defense Information School, a joint service institution. Finishing at the top of his class, the new PFC got his pick of all the open billets. He chose to be Information Specialist (essentially, an emcee and flack) for the Golden Knights, the Army's elite parachute team, which appeared at international air shows, exhibitions in Europe, county fairs, and the like. No combat, nothing but good times—or so he figured. But he had to be airborne-qualified. No problem. He went to jump school en route to the new assignment, got his wings, and was promoted to E-4, or corporal. Standing in line to receive orders, he remembers, "I'm telling my buddies, 'Shit, I've already *got* my orders, I'm going to the Golden Knights.'"

He gave the assignment officer his name, rank, and serial number, and the officer handed him the envelope containing his orders. Whoops. They specified that he would be an Information Specialist, not for the Golden Knights but in a unit called the Eleventh Air Assault Division (Test). While he was in jump school—and then a private—a sergeant first-class had been approved for the Golden Knights job. He protested to the personnel officer that his second and third choices—the U.S. Army booth at the New York World's Fair and Cameron Station in Alexandria, Virginia—had been ignored. The alleged response: "All that shit's done, Bud Roe. *You* are back in the pipeline, and right now there is a levy by the Eleventh Air Assault for every airborne-qualified person." *The Army owns your ass.* "So what's this Eleventh Air Assault?" he asked in resignation. "Ah, it's just this helicopter outfit," the officer answered obscurely. "They're just practicing, they're testing out this concept."

After the Battle of Ap Bac, the army had realized that to expect success in a complex air-mobile infantry assault that had not been refined or tested was rash. So by coincidence, our man says, he became a member of a test team, through which the army was developing the idea of conducting a war by inserting and extracting combat troops into battle areas via helicopter. That, of course, ended up being the way the Americans fought the Vietnam War. Now a corporal, he found himself caught in the slipstream of military history. The color he provides again adds credibility: in June 1965, at Camp Stewart, Georgia, where the Eleventh trained, the quartermaster for clothing collected the troops' shorts, skivvies, and towels, which then were all white. A couple of days later they got back their laundry, which now was olive-drab.

A few weeks later they crossed the state back to Fort Benning and received new orders. His, he says, indicated "30 days' leave en route to 1st Cav Division, RVN." The Eleventh Air Assault Division (Test) had become, on July 3, 1965, the First Cavalry Division, the vanguard unit for U.S. air-mobile operations in Vietnam, and he was bound for Vietnam. He was to report to Travis Air Force Base. On account of his boyhood experience as a surveyor working for his father, a mechanical engineer, he was also ordered to ship out as part of the advance party that would build the First Cav's base camp at An Khe, Camp Radcliffe, in Binh Dinh province. He arrived in-country in late August 1965, that famous yellow-and-black patch with the horse head silhouette sewn on the shoulder of his uniform, landing at Tan Son Nhat Air Base in Saigon, then flying to Qui Nhon, and finally traveling overland to An Khe. When asked what his military occupational specialty was, he answered, "71Q20. I'm an Information Specialist." *We don't have any need for anybody like that. What else can you do?* He says he ended up in a Pathfinder unit, whose job is to be first in a landing zone to prepare and secure it for additional troops and to provide terminal air control during combat. The rest of the division deployed in late September, and he was at last assigned to an administrative company as a public information officer. But the division started to take heavy casualties virtually from the outset, and he was shifted into a line company—Alpha Company, Second Battalion of the Third Brigade (Seventh Cavalry Regiment). In early November, he says he made buck sergeant (E-5) and became a squad leader.

On November 16, 1965, in Pleiku province during Operation Silver Bayonet—better known as the Battle of the Ia Drang Valley—his Second of the Seventh relieved the decimated First of the Seventh at Landing Zone X-Ray, which by then, after thirty-six hours of vicious fighting in which NVA outnumbered Americans by three to one, roughly a regiment to a battalion, was cold. Despite 79 American dead and 121 wounded, Westmoreland refused to authorize a large-scale helicopter extraction on the grounds that it would play in the press like a retreat. In the foothills of the central highlands, from the base of the Chu Prong massif, the unit he claims he was in marched in a column two and a half miles north to LZ Albany and was ambushed.

His account: "The center element of this march, C Company, got virtually annihilated. I was on the lead end, in A Company. We were already on Albany when C Company got ambushed. But then Albany came under heavy attack, and that was my first experience in a major firefight." In fact, the Second Battalion lost 155 men killed in action and 121 wounded in less than twenty hours. Dien Bien Phu had been, in the estimation of Bernard Fall—the French-born American Vietnam scholar, killed by a booby trap in South Vietnam in 1967—"hell in a very small place." And LZ Albany, according to Lieutenant General Harold Moore (retired), who as a lieutenant colonel commanded the First Battalion of the Seventh Cavalry Regiment at LZ X-Ray, warranted the same description.

Alpha Company did come under heavy fire, and he maintains that he himself killed a large number of NVA soldiers. Two and a half months later, to the east in Binh Dinh province, he says he

saw more heavy combat, "another ass-kicking" (150 U.S. KIA) at
Bong Song, which, unlike the Ia Drang Valley, was delta country.
During these two engagements, he says that his squad and platoon were badly depleted, and that he was wounded twice—once
in the head, where he points to a visible scar. He claims to have
been awarded a Bronze Star with a "V" for his performance at LZ
Albany, as well as three Army Commendation Medals with "V,"
the Combat Infantryman's Badge, and two Purple Hearts overall.
In his mind, at least, combat was the biggest adrenaline rush he
had ever had (after LZ Albany, he says, he didn't sleep for days)
and, in the poignant camaraderie of fighting for and with his
friends, the most meaningful experience of his life.

But seeing body bags being loaded onto aircraft at An Khe
never left him either. "There were more than you could count,
lined up like cordwood," he recalls. "Pretty fucking serious."
Afterward, he and other grunts would practice denial. "From your
tents you could see helicopters come in, and you'd see wounded
come in and maybe one or two body bags. You'd just look the
other way—you know, 'Hey, man, you got a cigarette?'—and just
try to ignore it." After R-and-R in Bangkok in February 1966, he
says he extended on condition that his final year in Vietnam would
not involve combat. And he finally got his old wish: he served as
an REMF in the Joint U.S. Public Affairs Office (JUSPAO) with
MACV at Tan Son Nhat.

In the postwar phase of his autobiography, the ironies mush-
room. As he arrived, he seems to recall, the Army's Vietnam
"information doctrine" was being upgraded and expanded. "'Maximum disclosure with minimum delay, except . . .' and then you'd
get fifty exceptions. That's when I really started to question the
war. The policy said that if a unit in the field is rendered incapable
of engaging in and sustaining combat with the enemy, then it has
suffered 'heavy casualties.' If a unit's ability to fight was reduced
or diminished, that unit was said to have 'moderate casualties.'

And if the unit was neither rendered ineffective nor its capacity to fight diminished, then it was 'light casualties.' The real tricky part of the deal was that you always reported in terms of the largest element in the field. What I'm saying is that you could have a major task force operation—a reinforced battalion, six-, eight hundred guys out in the field, four to six companies—and if one company gets annihilated, that's very heavy casualties, but you didn't report about company so-and-so because it was part of the reinforced battalion. If you lost one company out of six, it did not render the task force incapable of sustaining combat and did not diminish the task force's capability. So always the report was 'light casualties.' I said, 'This is pretty bullshit.'"

He was required to apply spin to news out of Vietnam: actual numbers of casualties were no longer given; instead, the only descriptions were those questionable modifiers "light," "moderate," or "heavy." From this he inferred that American GIs were being sacrificed for show by the government. By his lights, he had gotten a taste of it the year before; in four days in the Ia Drang Valley, 234 American soldiers died—far more than died in combat during the entire Gulf War—but NVA casualties were multiples heavier, so the brass played the engagement like a successful experiment in air-mobile infantry operations. "Infantry guys love to make you think that the infantry whipped them, but really at Ia Drang it was that the infantry saved its ass up close. The infantry was able to defend the perimeter, but it was artillery and air support that accounted for the greatest number of enemy casualties." He knew that there was too much ground fire for the choppers, courageous as the pilots were, to generate much air mobility. He knew it was, as far as morale went, an ass-kicking. "Heavy casualties" didn't tell the story. He DEROSed in December 1966 and immediately left the Army.

This guy even evinces some symptoms of post-traumatic stress. He says that under pressure, he gets angry easily, and that he sometimes wakes up at night shaking, imagining that the butt of a firing M-16 is rattling against his shoulder. During periods of strain, he drinks too much. And when he gets exercised about a subject he's talking about, particularly combat, he becomes increasingly animated and expresses himself with his hands. As we talked, every few minutes he pointedly and eccentrically moved the tape recorder a few centimeters away or to the side, as if diverting the barrel of a gun.

The remainder of his story seems to extend a rich archetype: He put the war behind him and quietly earned a degree in civil engineering. When the Kent State incident occurred in May 1970, the social gravity of the war hit home: something was wrong if the military was killing its own people. He joined Vietnam Veterans Against the War and with hundreds of other veterans threw his medals and ribbons over a wire fence in front of the Capitol. In the fullness of time, he decided that the war "wasn't right, it wasn't wrong, it was circumstantial." Neil Sheehan's *A Bright Shining Lie,* a "terrific" book, helped him decide for himself what the war was about, which he takes to be a misguided attempt to fight a civil war in place of the people who should have been fighting it themselves. Having saved some money and buried his parents, he went to Bangkok and Phuket to "go whoring in Asia" in January 1994. When the Vietnam embargo was lifted a month later, he headed there for a couple of exploratory months. He revisited An Khe and Pleiku, finding the experience mildly therapeutic insofar as the evidence of the American war was scant. "Finally I could say, 'Well, I guess it really is over.'" The crowning irony was certainly true: in November 1998 he was supervising the building of the new U.S. consulate in Ho Chi Minh City, which opened the following summer.

According to his DD-214, he did have a military occupational specialty as an information specialist, but he did not make E-5 until September 1966. While he might have seen some combat, his service record indicates that he received no medals for valor and no Purple Hearts. According to Joseph Galloway—coauthor with General Moore of *We Were Soldiers Once . . . and Young,* a moving and painfully meticulous account of Ia Drang—the man's name does not appear on the November 1, 1965, monthly company roster for Alpha Company, Second Battalion, Seventh Cavalry, or in the company daily reports (which include men absent on leave, due to illness or wounds, or on account of detached duty) for each day of the month thereafter. Further, S. Lawrence Gwin, who was executive officer of Alpha Company from August 1965 to August 1966, kept personal records on his unit, and they do not include my interviewee. Gwin also does not recall any such person. His memory on this matter is especially sharp, since between Ia Drang and the end of Gwin's tour, all but fifteen of the original members of Alpha Company were killed or wounded. (Two entire platoons were wiped out at LZ Albany, and the mortar platoon, which survived it intact, was killed to a man in a C-130 crash in the An Khe pass in January 1966.) While the veteran I spoke with did command authentic and detailed facts about the evolution of the First Cavalry Division from the Eleventh Air Assault (Test) Division, the Ia Drang battle, and the events at LZ Albany, they are widely available—in particular, from Moore and Galloway's book, a veritable primer.

So it appears possible that the man I interviewed may have been, in fact, merely an REMF. In any event, it seems likely that he was not at LZ Albany and was not decorated. On the other hand, the sight of body bags being loaded onto aircraft, and the requirement that he as an information officer launder casualty reports, may well have anguished him. Though his apparent embellishment dishonors those who really did participate in combat, it is worth noting that if he were the real thing, he would make a fitting and articulate spokesman for Vietnam veterans. "People who served here in combat," he says, "either went home stronger or weaker, and it had to do with their personal constitution coming in. Strong people went home stronger, weak people went home weaker. Nothing I've ever done in my life will ever be more pivotal or meaningful than having served in the U.S. Army and having served in Vietnam. The very thing I wanted least to do was one of the things I was the best at." The "saddest commentary" on his life, he says, is that despite a "pivotal" experience as a combat soldier that made him a better man, knowing what he knows now back in 1965 he "might have been off to Sweden or Canada." If that experience was in fact genuine, its juxtaposition with the retrospective sentiment would almost be profound: he would be a hero of a war he knows was pointless.

Certainly that is the image he wishes to convey. After more than two hours pass on the patio of the Sapa, I ask him whether there is anything he wants to add. "No," he barks with confident finality, "that's all." Each of us has had three drinks—rye for him, beer for me. He pushes my money away and shakes his head vigorously. "Absolutely not. This is on me, *Bud Roe,*" he says, using the generic name that grunts called each other back then. He bows and salutes and, his crinkled eyes lifting that saturnine goatee, cracks the warmest smile of the night. Then he turns and walks back into the Sapa. Perhaps he wishes he'd exploited his opportunity to be a hero, and can't stand the fact that he was just another pogue.

There are a fair few ersatz heroes in Southeast Asia, as there are legions of them in the United States. But the fact remains that there are far more genuine expatriate veterans who neither fabricate nor celebrate their war experiences. Most of them have opaque reasons for being in Thailand. It is not just a matter of weighing practicalities, of measuring the opportunities for indulgence and status against a longing for home. There are some who were profoundly changed by the war, and are driven by the past—not into the ground, but to greater heights than they'd have expected of themselves when they DEROSed thirty-some years ago.

"JEEP"

Glenn P. Holthaus was a Navy medic assigned to Marine Force Reconnaissance, and did two tours in "the Nam." Most guys who were really in the shit don't talk about it, he said at first, but he hemmed and hawed and finally agreed. He lives in Pattaya, the low-rent (i.e., not Phuket) beach resort that GIs on R-and-R from Vietnam fertilized decades ago, and owns "Jeep's Joint," a burger bar his Thai wife Lek runs with his backing. She gives me a Coke with a straw and calls on the phone to their apartment upstairs to tell him I'm here. On the wall there are, among other typical barroom memorabilia, an autographed picture of Mel Gibson and a picture of a handsome young man in a uniform with a Bronze Star and a Purple Heart underneath it. He materializes in a dark room behind the bar, turns on the air-conditioning, and invites me to sit down. At fifty-three, Holthaus still sports a USMC buzz cut. He wears an olive-drab T-shirt with a sleeve pocket for cigarettes. Depicted on the chest are crossed M-16s and four grinning skulls wearing green berets and soft guerrilla camo-hats. Beneath them is printed: "Vietnam—good soldiers, gutless politicians." On the back: "DMZ Bar, Angeles City, Philippines." Holthaus—called "Jeep" for the initials "G.P." and because his mother drove for General Patton as a WAC—explains that he saved the DMZ Bar owner's life and later helped him open the establishment. He has a potbelly and favors one leg, but at full height still has a threatening countenance. His grainy face and obdurate expression intimate: you may think you can but you can't. Secreted in the wrinkles, the age-freckles, and the capillaries, perceptible but just barely, is the decorated young man in the picture. After a while he beckons Lek and quietly demands a drink. She brings him a Coke laced with Sangthip—cheap Thai liquor that tastes something like a cross between rum and bourbon. He sips his drink and drags on an Asian Marlboro knockoff.

At first, Jeep seems to epitomize the grizzled, bitter expatriate barfly wearing half a uniform. He is charming in his vintage charmlessness—menstruation makes for lousy Marines, blacks in the Corps have gotten too touchy. Yet he doesn't grumble about what a raw deal he got from the U.S. government, and despite the stock diatribe against the unmanly nineties, his swagger fades as he approaches the psychic wall he has built to sequester his memories of the Vietnam War. Jeep operates on a thin edge between resignation and resilience, remorse and defiance, cynicism and sympathy. He is too contradictory to be trite. The paradox, the abrupt changes in his demeanor, suggest an overload of harsh episodes.

Son of a Marine Corps officer, Jeep was born in Hawaii and grew up on military bases. He spent some time in reform school after stealing a car and rat-racing a policeman who chased him into a tree, but a decent brain got him to the University of Nebraska. He took a semester of pre-med before becoming one of less than a thousand young men drafted into the Navy in 1965, which used the draft to troll for medics at the start of the escalation for Vietnam. Holthaus hadn't heard a thing about Vietnam and couldn't locate it on a map, and had seen "only English books" in his six months of pre-med. He was not pleased to receive his induction notice—partly because he considered his father "an asshole" and didn't want to follow in his straightlaced military footsteps, partly because he had native problems with authority. A rebel without a cause, Holthaus set fire to the post office that issued the notice, then swaggered down to a filling station and picked a fight. Nobody bothered to press charges since the judge, adhering to the popular judicial policy for putting a young man's mind right, would have given him a choice of jail time or military service anyhow. Holthaus reported for boot camp with two broken wrists.

Notwithstanding his initial reluctance, with Marine bases and reform school behind him, he was not a complete stranger to regimentation. He had also been an all-state football player, so the gung-ho mentality, though so far unchanneled, came easily. Once Holthaus resigned himself to a hitch in the service, he volunteered to serve as a corpsman in an elite Marine Force Reconnaissance unit. Force Recon pulled arguably the toughest infantry duty of any American troops in Vietnam, penetrating deep into enemy territory, usually in free-fire zones. Jeep holds several combat distinctions for Navy corpsmen in Vietnam. War stories, though, do not surface comfortably.

"Most of the guys who were really on the pointy end don't talk about it much," Jeep growls, spitting out words like a broken chain saw. In this remark he is repeating himself, but the comment was of a piece with something dark and telling. "We leave that to the REMFs and the Air Force assholes who sat in bars and drew combat pay, and just walk away from them. *We don't talk about it.*" But, to let other troubled *combat* vets know they're neither alone nor hopeless, he pulls down the wall to revisit his first recon patrol, when a Marine two feet from him had his chest blown away. "I'd only known him for four days. We hadn't met too many times. For that reason—you just didn't want to get tied up with them." Yet the anonymous Marine's untimely death was traumatic to Jeep, and forged a lifelong connection. He excuses himself to cry, retreating to the bathroom to blow his nose and wash his face.

He breaks down a little later as he summons other grisly operational details, and again as he plummets from pride in his autographed copy of *Fortunate Son* from Lewis B. Puller, Jr.—who followed his legendary father "Chesty" Puller into the Marine Corps, only to lose his legs to a mine shortly after arriving in-country—to the somber remembrance of the author's suicide, then still further to tearful existential remorse. "Bummed me out when he fucking killed himself, but I can see why he did that, too. A lot of times I kind of think about, I should check out. It just seems like uh, I'm just not supposed to be alive still. Why them, not me? It doesn't piss me off too much except when the other guys brag about, 'I was in combat,' during the war and shit. I mean, the only reason I'm talking to you is because there might be some other asshole like me out there. He might just say, well, I'm not alone instead of. . . ." Instead of killing himself, is the implication. "Because we're very few. Maybe somebody else will read it and say, hey, there's another asshole out there who's fucked up too."

Still coveting Marine-toughness, Jeep gruffly apologizes after each bout of emotion and proceeds matter-of-factly to life and death "in the shit": seeing that Marine cut down; watching a pal lose his weapon and defiantly flip the bird and bellow "Fuck you, gook!" to NVA troops before they shredded him with a machine gun; saving a blinded Marine in a landing zone under close enemy ground fire. His account of the latter incident, for which he earned that Bronze Star with a combat "V" for valor, and the Purple Heart, has an air of self-deprecation, as though the damage that the war caused his psyche had devalued even the most noble of his deeds. "It was a small knoll, probably not any bigger than three times the size of this building. The reason we had even stopped there is to try to get a medevac in for one guy from Texas who had heatstroke, went down. I was trying to treat him, and still try to keep where we're going so nobody knows where we're at of course, clandestinely. Without making no noise because there were gooks following us. They came in from above us in the tree-line, so they were shooting down at us—which was probably the only thing that saved a lot of our asses, because when they're shooting down-hill they always tend to miss you. I don't know why, but they do. And the first guy got hit in the eyes, way up on the left, closest to the gooks. I don't know how far up, but it seemed like a long way to go at the time. Uphill, about thirty-five yards probably. He just started hollering, 'Doc, I'm blind.' I just said, 'Shit, I've got to go get him.' That's just automatic, that's no thinking, too, you just go. Corpsmen have done that notoriously through the centuries. You just go. I ran out and treated him under fire. It was stupid, but I didn't think about it as though I did anything good. I still don't think I did anything good. Ran in the wrong direction, is basically what I did."

Jeep doesn't admit to having post-traumatic stress, but plainly he does. At least he survived it to make his twenty and retired in 1986 as a Senior Chief Navy Hospital Corpsman. For a year he worked for Vinell Corporation in Oman, helping to set up facilities for the U.S. Rapid Deployment Force. Then he came to Pattaya, which owes its growth and raunchiness to carousing GIs, a town that Jeep extols as "one of the raise-hell capitals of the world," where he'd never had a chance to come while in Vietnam because, he says, Army personnel got priority on R-and-R destinations. He came to coast and forget. Over time, his pride in his combat record soured. For a few years he sat on the patio of Jeep's Joint, sipped Santhip, and watched the more decadent incarnations of the Thai/expat world go by. He opened a bar on Pattaya's waterfront strip called the TCF, for Two Camels Fucking, which sported an illustrative cartoon logo drawn from a well-known postcard photograph of a pair of dromedaries locked in heavenly transport. He gained a reputation as a local tough guy. He drank too much, still does. He wired the town, made it his own. During the Gulf War he decided to tweak a local Arab who came to his bar.

"I had a big pig on my bar labeled 'Saudi' with a slish-slash over his head and all that," he recalls. "This one Saudi kept trying to get in, and I tell him he ain't allowed in here. He kept pushing, pushing. He made a mistake. See, his heels were downhill from me, so I just smacked him out in the god damn street. Cops came and took him away on a motorcycle, laid him on the back like a dead Indian on a horse. They come back about a half-hour later with the guy on the back. Same Thai, same raghead. Cop's saying, hey Jeep, better take down that pig, it's offending this Saudi guy, you know. I said, okay, so I took it down. Soon as he goes away I put it back up again. The bar was pretty full that day. Here he comes again, same raghead on the back. Comes up, hey, Jeep, you have to take that down, it's offending this guy from Saudi. Okay. So I said to myself, well, the guy's going to bug me all night, I'll leave it down. About two hours later the cop comes back alone, and he says, where's the pig? I says, you stupid bastard—this is all in Thai—you told me to take it down twice, so I took it down. He says, well please, put it back up because every time I come around here the Saudi guy gives me 500 baht."

Willfully, then, Jeep is a bit of an asshole. His quality of life improved when he started to hire out as an adviser on Vietnam War movies made in Thailand, including *Air America*. He was even an extra in the scene in which the CIA officer slaps the Vietnamese woman in Oliver Stone's *Heaven and Earth*. These were his claims to fame until he got serious about life in Southeast Asia.

The charity work started out as a Vietnam thing. Thirty years ago, while radioing enemy positions from a listening post, he was captured by a Vietcong patrol. They beat him senseless with rifle butts, then tied him up and began marching him to either imprisonment or execution. A B-52 strike interrupted their plans. As the Vietcong scattered, Jeep bolted. A unit of hill-tribe Montagnards, American allies, saved Jeep and took care of him for several days.

About five years ago, he started making routine trips to the homeland of the Akha hill tribes, which are related to the Vietnamese Montagnards, in northern Thailand to deliver and administer medicines and medical treatment on a self-appointed "sick call." He befriended a former Miss Thailand and enlisted her help. He considers these efforts compensation rather than generosity. "I don't see myself as charitable, big-hearted, at all. It's got something to do with the hill tribes' helping me in 'Nam."

That hardly explains the metamorphosis of the Pattaya Computer Club. A self-taught computer expert, Jeep started the club simply to cultivate a hobby and built it to over one hundred members. Then, in late 1997, he and Lek went to a Sunday softball game at a local primary school. "Three little kids walked by, and I asked them, did you guys ever see a computer? And they told me, no, we wish we were orphans so we could have everything. And I went, whoa! Those orphans down here, they got everything they ever wanted. I said, all right, I'm going to help you. These little bastards, they ain't done a thing wrong, they're not drug addicts, they're not cripples, they're not orphans, they're just plain old poor kids."

When Jeep broached the idea of salvaging old computers from local businesses and donating them to Thai schools, most club members balked. Within a few months, he had banished "the guys who want to draw flowers and shit on computers and don't care anything about my projects helping Thai kids" to another club. Jeep and his team of expatriate "hardware gurus" then rebuilt over twenty laptops and desktops and gave them to underfunded Pattaya schools.

A cultural problem arose: For fear of losing face, Thai teachers would neither allow others to instruct their pupils, nor instruct the children themselves unless they had gained command of the subject. Jeep's Thai isn't good enough for pedagogy, so he enlisted several handicapped Thais to whom he had earlier taught computer basics, and Lek as well, to help him train seventeen Thai schoolteachers over seventeen weeks.

Pattaya Primary School No. 4 now has a policy of ensuring that all of its students are computer literate. The teachers have lightened up, and allow Jeep and Lek to provide some direct instruction. Further, the two have instituted a program whereby Lek assesses students from indigent families for educational advancement on the basis of their computer acumen, then recommends them to an association of local charities (also Jeep's brainchild) as candidates for further educational funding. As of January 1999, the association had agreed to provide tuition for 173 kids for three more years of school. Without Jeep, those children would have hit a dead end at sixth grade. Publicity in Thailand has yielded more donations and volunteer instructors, enabling Jeep to expand the existing program and set up similar ones in three northern Thai cities.

All told, Holthaus spends a third of his retirement pay helping Thais in need. "Maybe that has something to do with the Nam," says Jeep, quizzically. "I'm not sure, but it has something to do with something, because I don't even like kids." This appears to be a bit of a pose. He also likes to say he married Lek as a matter of convenience, calls her Dracula on account of her big crooked teeth, but treats her with respect and concern and vaunts her work ethic over that of Thai men every chance he gets. Maybe he has engaged in too much war to think of himself as a Good Samaritan. But moments after his W.C. Fields act Jeep pointed exuberantly to a framed photograph of two Thai girls sitting in front of a computer screen, with Jeep at their sides. "Look at their eyes. A light bulb just went on. 'Wow! We're not just poor kids. We got a chance.' That's all I can give them. The Thais don't do anything, but somebody is." Several times his good works have been written up in the *Bangkok Post.*

Over four hours, the conversation meanders from K-bar knives to Pattaya's hookers to why he does what he does. In a moment of recognition, Jeep barks: "I didn't have any choice in anything I did, basically, except now helping the kids. That's the only choice I got. The rest was mandatory, either through peer pressure or parental pressure or government pressure. The whole time I never did nothing that I wanted to do."

The involuntary experiences he reports are haunting. He watched askari worms slither out of the carotid artery of an NVA whose throat had just been cut. During a prisoner-snatch snafu, he saw a female NVA soldier shot in each breast and left hanging dead upside-down in a tree. He witnessed his Force Recon unit cut down three Green Berets accidentally in a free-fire zone. Even discounting his remembrances for retrospective embroidery, Holthaus's service record supports his claim that he has been through much of the archetypal terror chronicled in the books and the movies about the Vietnam War. He understands why Puller killed himself, and says he frequently contemplated suicide, agonizing over why he's here and other Force Recon Marines aren't. He allows that he felt "pissed off when Calley got burned," referring to Lieutenant William Calley and the infamous massacre at My Lai. Holthaus understands the dementing anguish of taking casualties from an unseen enemy. Even in Pattaya he has woken up in a vacant field across the street, imagining that VC are in the shadows.

But Holthaus thought he might yet venture back in-country—"just to see what I'd do, just to see whether I could take it." Like any good Marine, Jeep is stoic and counterphobic. He apologizes "for being so damn much of a wimp." Glenn Holthaus is a trainwreck of a man, but he still rolls down the line and hopes to add value along the way. "Maybe it'll help some other crazy fucker to know he's as fucked up as I am. That he's not alone. Maybe."

You couldn't write the tortured, enigmatic vet part much better. Ostensibly, he came to Southeast Asia to forget Vietnam, yet intuitively it makes little sense to get closer to the scene of trauma in order to get it out of your system. In any case, he can't—"the Nam" is still in him. He still calls Vietnamese "gooks" and "dinks." His experiences far beyond the pale appear to preclude his former enemies' rehumanization in his gut, though in more reflective moments he does regard them as people in his head. Holthaus is not a politically sophisticated man, but he does not believe a people's hearts and minds can be won by confiscating their land and ridiculing their political or religious beliefs, as the Americans did to the Vietnamese.

Still he accepts no blame for following orders, and resents the way in which Americans have disowned Vietnam veterans. He remembers bitterly how his neighbors wouldn't talk to him when he got back, on the assumption that Vietnam had twisted him beyond sociability. He still has a problem with Americans. In the early nineties he returned to the States for a visit. "I went back to see my ex-kids. I landed at LAX International Airport, laying over to go to Phoenix. I had time, a three-hour layover, so I was sitting in the bar. These guys at the international airport, sitting around, wouldn't look at you, couldn't talk to nobody, so I started talking about Thailand. They said, 'Oh, we know, that's out in China there'—Taiwan, that's what they were thinking. No, no, I said. They said, 'What's it like?' So I started talking about blow-jobs. All of a sudden these guys just started ignoring me completely and talking to each other. The biggest problem was that one guy's supervisor didn't like him, and another guy just bought a brand-new lawnmower, another guy just built a new garage. I said, man, I don't need this kind of fucking bullshit. Life's too short. I didn't even go to Phoenix. I went right back downstairs and asked for a ticket on anything that was going west. It just wasn't my world."

Jeep's world has since become even more distant from the increasingly precious United States. As self-admitted "poor white trash," he figures he might fit in at a trailer park, but not in many other places. Jeep will most likely die in Southeast Asia. The image of him sitting in front of Jeep's Joint, saluting me with his Santhip and Coke as I head back to the bus station on the back of a Thai teenager's dirt-bike in the hazy Thai twilight, is a durable one. He had just urged me to stay because it was the day of the Buddhist festival, Loi Krathong, and the fireworks were exploding, and the girls were dressed to the nines and drunk and even looser than usual and I should have been taking advantage of his experience and raising some hell. He left his mother and his two children in the States and may never see them again, or the American ex-wife he claims to despise. It may seem pitiable, but it's important to remember what he said about choice. He didn't come to Thailand only to die.

∞∞

"BRU"

As Jeep Holthaus left Vietnam for the last time as a soldier in 1969, Robert Taylor was starting his tour as a radioman and weapons expert in Military Assistance Command, Vietnam, Studies and Observations Group. MACV SOG—bland bureaucratese for U.S. Army Special Forces' storied (and then classified) cross-border strategic reconnaissance troops in Vietnam. Bob was a Green Beret. He got that way improbably. As he was raised in Alaska, he was imbued with a rugged individualist attitude, which, despite a period in high school when he used drugs and acquiesced to antiwar rhetoric that went along with the drug culture, suited him well to soldiering. He did not keep the antiwar attitude, and being from a conservative background generally agreed that communism should be opposed. After tasting adventure vicariously as a ham radio operator, then operationally as a young helicopter-borne firefighter, in 1967 he joined the Army for more.

Now a born-again Christian, he was then an irreverent wiseass. Friction with superiors got him dismissed from helicopter school for "lack of military development." "I wasn't strak enough," he shrugs, using military parlance for straight-laced and squared away. But he aced the Special Forces aptitude test and joined them, managing to elude the swimming requirement; anchored down in Fairbanks, he'd never learned. Once steeped in

40

army culture, Taylor assumed he would go to Vietnam and became reflexively pro-war. "You become a product of your culture," he shrugs. The remark is a telling indicator of a simple but sometimes overlooked truth about the Vietnam generation as well as any other: that most young men and women are not philosophers. Rather, they are looking for a home, a group to join. Their sense of adventure may vary—in the military, they might settle for being REMFs, or might ascend to Special Forces—but on the ideological level they tend to "go with the flow." Down to fifty-eight days in his first Army hitch and still stateside, Taylor re-upped. "I'm thinking, this is like training to be a brain surgeon and not doing an operation. This is not good. I'll never know what combat is like. I wanted to know. It'd be like training to be a lawyer and never arguing a case before a court. You've got to know if you can do it. And I had to know whether I could step out in the open and get shot at. I had to know what it was like. I had to know whether I could go through combat. Was I a coward? You know, you have to know these things."

Like Jeep, Taylor belonged to a combat elite. Like Jeep, he volunteered. He went on deep recon patrols, frequently engaged the NVA in firefights, and suffered for the experience. But Jeep's epiphany came late. Bob's began in Vietnam. He operated mainly in Laos (one operation took him into North Vietnam) and fought side-by-side with the Bru tribe. Taylor made frequent contact with the enemy and killed quite a few. He became fond of the Bru people, learning their tribal language and acquiring the nickname "Bru" from his fellow SOG soldiers. But a year in-country and intimate knowledge of how the war was being fought gave Taylor little hope that the Americans would deliver the Bru and other native allies from North Vietnamese communism.

"We were trained to do guerrilla warfare. But guerrilla warfare had ceased in Vietnam in about '64, '65—it had certainly ceased by the time the first Marines landed. We were fighting hard-core

NVA in main-force units, using conventional infantry tactics, in a war of attrition. Forget that guerrilla bullshit. That didn't exist. But what the NVA did have was very good intelligence support within the population, which was merely ambivalent to them and in some cases preferred them over us—enough to support them. The war ended up being a war of punishment against North Vietnam for the things Hanoi was doing in South Vietnam." Punishment, of course, is not a proper military objective, and the effort, Taylor believes, was neither sufficiently focused nor sufficiently committed to bring victory. "I told my Montagnards, get all the guns you can get, learn everything you can learn, get all the ammunition you can, steal everything. We'd 'lose' stuff, we'd give them all we could. We told them we're leaving. The handwriting's on the wall. We're pulling out. We're gonna leave you hanging. We knew that in '69. To be very frank with you, the United States is a country that doesn't always have much honor."

For Taylor, the question of whether it was right for the United States to be in Vietnam is too simple to be constructive. "I look at it at different levels. There were many Vietnams, not just one. After World War II, we took a man [Ho Chi Minh] that was a communist, no doubt, but a nationalist and controllable, and turned him into a hard-liner. We could have avoided all of this and ended up with a very close relationship with Indochina when we could have bought it for almost nothing: just tell the French, 'You're not coming back here and re-colonizing, these people need to have their freedom,' and establish some economic ties. I look at that, and I consider it a mistake, okay. When I look at the things that the communists did later in Vietnam to poor villagers, I think that fighting against them in any form was good. When I look at the 'Yards, fighting for them was good. If I look at what I did in the war, it was fine. I was a professional soldier, and I'm not afraid to tell any Vietnamese, north or south, today, that that's what I did."

Some historians do not regard placating the French during the early part of the Cold War as unimportant, but it is difficult to fault Taylor's view that once Ho Chi Minh had turned ideologue—whether by necessity or by choice is beside the point—the U.S. decision to intervene had valid moral and geopolitical justification. And Taylor's idea was to continue the war as a civilian. Though he loved Special Forces and agonized over leaving—"I cried when I left Vietnam in 1970"—he had spoken with CIA people operating in Laos who expressed enthusiasm for his services. He wed Prayud, nicknamed Toi, a Thai girl he had met on R-and-R while she was a waitress at an NCO club. He left the Army as a buck sergeant (having earned his Combat Infantryman's Badge and several other decorations) and applied to the Agency, only to be rejected on the ground that he was married to a foreign national.

He is still married to her today. It is easy to assume that Taylor—a short, broad-shouldered, muscular man, now bald, bearded, and agreeably fat—is a quiet Bible thumper who has blithely whitewashed the stains of combat with the broad brush of evangelical Christianity. Wrong. Taylor is a salt-of-the-earth—religious, yes, but with a very sharp edge, long honed by a refusal to capitulate to the quiet, insular lot of the troubled vet that American society seemed to prescribe as the only available cure for psychic ailments caught in Southeast Asia.

It took a couple of probationary meetings before Taylor agreed to talk to me on the record. First I had a couple of beers with him at the Indra Regent Hotel in central Bangkok. We twisted on barstools to face each other as we talked. His sleepy blue eyes verged, when the conversation ran to the treachery of wannabes and critics of Special Forces like those who formerly worked for CNN, on baleful. He made sure that I concurred that *faux* vet liars are lame players, that I meant this book to be more about the hard-earned successes of the better class of vet than the abject failures of the vet underclass. He and other Special Forces alumni might "knock on the door" of someone who misrepresented himself. He consented to an appointment a week later.

We convene at his office, a couple of short blocks from his bungalow. I get a staccato Special Forces history lesson. In the Vietnam War they had to function under secrecy because in entering Laos—nominally a neutral country—they violated the Geneva Convention. All told, only thirty-six Special Forces POWs escaped their North Vietnamese captors. All of their names are known, so false claimants are easily identified; one guy recently got a knock on the door. Many SF soldiers lamented getting green berets because it made them easier to identify. And many "hibernated" after the war. They have resurfaced recently on the Internet, and in an anonymously produced newsletter called the *SF Resistor.*

SF people are often libertarians, and take seriously the theory behind the Old West's *posse comitatus* ("power of the county" in Latin) that proper law enforcement is local, and military forces ought not be deployed against other Americans. Taylor mentions the Posse Comitatus Act of 1878, which states that "it shall not be lawful to employ any part of the Army of the United States, as a *posse comitatus,* or otherwise, for the purpose of executing the laws, except in such cases and under such circumstances as such employment of said force may be expressly authorized by the Constitution or by act of Congress." The theory has eroded. The Marines are exempt, and by executive order so is Delta Force. A 1981 federal law permits the government to use the Army and Air Force for drug interdiction. Special Forces could be next. Waco and Ruby Ridge are ominous portents of the improper uses of special operations. Timothy McVeigh was an evil misfit but his concerns can't be dismissed as altogether freaky.

We are interrupted by three Thais seeking Taylor's help in drafting an application for a grant for their community charity. He excuses himself and confers with them for forty-five minutes.

They are anxious, needy, and impatient. Taylor never raises his voice, never condescends. When they complete the application, they stand and bow. Taylor offers me a perfunctory apology, but I am left in no doubt as to what comes first for him.

All this talk about the Branch Davidians and Oklahoma City should not give one too much pause about Bob Taylor. He goes to Las Vegas every year to the SOG Convention. Otherwise, he's in Thailand helping people, not in Montana target-shooting at militia barbecue-retreats. On the other hand, although there have been more malevolent ideas than restricting domestic law enforcement to civilian bodies, the term *posse comitatus* does raise a few red flags. An eponymous Christian white supremacist movement was founded in the 1970s, and McVeigh is believed to have had ties with its 1980s offshoot, the Arizona Patriots. Such "marching militias" have arisen in virtually every state and have become violent. But they espouse policies far more reactionary than those that Taylor would entertain: they reject any form of government above the county level, and oppose all income taxes, the existence of the Federal Reserve System (not to mention the United Nations), and the subordination of state courts to the federal judiciary.

Anyway, on the subject of Vietnam, Taylor the hard-ass gives way to a more searching man. This one was traumatized by "a wounded spirit" as much as by combat, and suffered post-traumatic stress in varying degrees of intensity. "Post-traumatic stress comes from bitterness and rejection. Combat? I enjoyed it once the first shot was fired. Once I got off that first magazine and lit up that cigarette, we were having a pretty good time. The terror of getting up to that point weighs on your psyche a little bit, but the shooting was a relief. So I don't have any problems about seeing my enemies in dreams, or having killed them."

He also felt unfairly rejected by the CIA—his own government—and unappreciated by his noncombatant countrymen. One of Taylor's first post-service jobs was a lowly one, with an airline. "My boss gave me a cash box with about fifty bucks in it. The guy says, 'Do you think you can be responsible for this?' I almost hit him. I said, 'I've just been responsible for people's lives, I don't think this cash box is going to prove too difficult.' I had a little problem decompressing." There was also in Taylor an element of derision toward some fellow vets. He avoided the local Veterans Administration vet center because he "didn't want to go down there and listen to any war stories from any of these wannabes, guys half-drunk talking about 'how I won the war.'" Instead Taylor began studying the Bible. Eventually, he established a "personal relationship with God," which he is quick to distinguish from the "rule-based relationship to churches"—which can be "hiding places for hypocrites"—that he rejected as a teenager.

During those dark seventies, Taylor tried going into business with a friend, and when the venture failed worked on the Alaska Pipeline to pay off the start-up debts. Though he eventually landed a $72,000-a-year job as a power plant supervisor in Fairbanks, and "life was pretty good," Toi and the Bru connected him intimately to Southeast Asia. A series of religious revelations (he does not elaborate on their precise nature because he believes they will seem silly to one who has not had such experiences) convinced Taylor next to visit Thailand with an eye toward missionary work. During a seven-week trial run in 1981, he and Toi managed to convert their neighbors—thirteen young prostitutes—to Christianity and wean them from the sex trade. "It was like a suckerpunch from God," he laughs. He came back to Alaska, sold everything he had, paid his now considerable bills, and climbed with Toi on an airplane to Thailand with $250 and a one-way ticket.

Starting life lean in Thailand in 1982, Taylor taught English and Bible at a poor evangelical church in Bangkok while Toi ran a ministry on Patpong to help more Thai prostitutes escape the life.

Over the past fifteen years, the Taylors have sheltered, fed, and clothed about one hundred Thai children—most of them from the poor Isaan province and border areas—and funded their schooling. His bungalow became a veritable refugee center, housing as many as fifteen kids at a time. But Taylor itched to do more. After attending and teaching at Wycliffe Bible Translators School campuses in Texas and Oklahoma, in 1989 he began providing medical relief, largely on his own, in border areas and in Laos. Then he and two other Vietnam combat veterans founded World Aid, Inc., which the Laos Ministry of Health hired under contract in 1990 to provide a range of medical relief services through volunteers whom Taylor recruits. The contract has been continually renewed and remains in force.

Taylor's initial return to Laos was testing. At the Thai-Lao border, he and the Montagnard border guards enjoyed some genial banter. Their commander, however, was Vietnamese. "He'd heard about 'this foreigner' up there talking to his boys. I remember watching him come up the path in his bedroom slippers and thinking, ten years ago, bud, and you would have never made it. It's like God talked to me then and said, 'You know, I'm going to send you back over to this country, and if you have anger in your heart you won't be able to stay.' Anger and bitterness—up until that point I still had a lot of it." Even now, he says, "I'm amazed I don't want to kill people more often."

In targeting which part of Laos to serve first, Taylor did not make his psychological journey easier. He went east to Sepone, which is right on the Vietnamese border, 85 percent Bru—and the location of most of his missions with Special Forces. "The Bru were always big in my heart. I had learned the jungle from them, and when we got into fights they saved my butt, so I figured I owed them quite a bit." Sepone was also where he was most needed: at the time more than 50 percent of the children born there died before their first birthdays, and the average life expectancy was forty-three. Eighty percent of the population suffered from malaria. Polio, tuberculosis, diphtheria, and even smallpox were all killers.

"The first night I got to Sepone," Taylor says in a soft voice, "I went to this decrepit, broken down, piece-of-shit hospital out in the middle of nowhere. The doctor had a six-month-old baby there that had died of malaria. That seriously affected me. I prayed that night and asked God that if I were to come there to help me really make a difference. From that day on, whenever I stayed in that area [one to two weeks per month for three-and-a-half years], no one died in that hospital. I always thought that was pretty nice of God."

Taylor brought in medical teams and launched a mobile child vaccination and tetanus immunization drive, covering a village a week over the course of a year. His volunteers rebuilt the hospital, imported new equipment and medical supplies, and provided training for doctors, village health workers, and midwives. They dug water wells. They treated malaria. Infant mortality went way down, the child survival rate and life expectancy way up. World-Aid, usually with four volunteers in Laos, sustained this level of achievement. Later, after Taylor learned that Laotian doctors used razor blades to remove cataracts, the organization pioneered ophthalmologic services in Laos, supplying corneas for transplants through U.S. eye banks, procuring new equipment, recruiting surgeons, and providing support medical training.

He produced World Aid's most innovative and far-reaching accomplishment by orchestrating the translation of a comprehensive medical dictionary into Lao, which the organization initiated, financed, and pushed to completion. Doctors in Laos had been trained by American, French, and Russian doctors, and Laotian medical schools were operating on handwritten notes. At the Minister of Health's prompting, in 1993 Taylor borrowed a translator from Wycliffe Bible Translators and brought in an American missionary expert in Lao to advise on the project. The missionary, John Durdin, received a medal from the Lao government. The dictionary, published in 1997, is 817 pages long and contains over 60,000 entries. "If there's a legacy I've left in Laos, it is this," says Taylor serenely. "This will be there for a hundred years."

Over the course of ten years, he has drawn hundreds of volunteers to Thailand, Laos, and Burma, including dozens of Vietnam veterans. The work has turned many of them around. By Taylor's account, Dennis "Doc" Paterson—in the war a Navy medic assigned to a Marine unit, like Holthaus—lost his leg, survived on disability payments for twenty years, drank too much, and carried his service Colt .45 under his stump. Taylor met Doc at a retreat and suggested that he come to Laos to work for World Aid. Doc's immediate response was roughly, "I didn't leave anything there that I've gotta go back and get!" A year later, the amputee medic asked to go.

To cross into Laos by wooden ferryboat, Doc had to descend and climb the rugged clay bank of the Mekong River on crutches while Taylor carried his wheelchair. Doc became Sepone's pharmacist. He returned for three more stints with World Aid, the last helping the Karen in Burma, in a village that government troops later burned to the ground, and where he contracted both malaria and dysentery. "Here's a guy hanging onto a tree limb by one hand, suspended above the ground [shitting], still going on," marvels Taylor. "This is from a guy who was so bitter he could hardly talk to his kids. Now his kids have become missionaries."

While Taylor does endeavor to educate local Christian clerics and teachers about Christianity, he emphatically does not condition aid on conversion or worship, nor does he require World Aid volunteers to be Christians. "World Aid is not a Christian evangelical organization," he explains. "It is a medical relief organization that has a lot of Christians in it. My director of ophthalmology was an atheist. Most people that we render aid to have no concept of who we are, where we've come from, or what we're doing. They just know somebody brought medicine." Besides, he adds, Christ didn't force people to sign anything before he fed them.

World Aid consists of Taylor, two unpaid administrators who raise funds and handle paperwork out of a one-room office in Seattle, and a stream of volunteer field workers who cover their own expenses. Taylor has frequently taken extra jobs—in 1999, he designed an inventory control computer network for a Thai compact disk manufacturer—to fund World Aid's $15,000 annual operating budget. Pretty lean, but the organization's principal assets are people who work for free and Taylor's extraordinary ability to attract them.

Several of Taylor's imports have been ex-Special Forces soldiers. That they excel at rendering aid in the third world is no surprise to him. Special Forces' unsung achievements in Vietnam include thousands of wells dug and hundreds of hospitals, dispensaries, and churches built. "In both sorts of work," Taylor points out, "you have to be resourceful, you never have what you need, you have to think of ways to get the job done. You have to be able to live with anybody, eat anything, understand where people are, understand their culture, understand what's important and what's not important. When we went to 'Nam they told us, 'if you go over there and at the end of your year you get people to dig a latrine and use it, you've just changed ten thousand years of their history.' That's not a small thing."

But the inclination of some to return to Southeast Asia has less to do with guilt than with pride. "There's a tremendous misunderstanding on the part of the American public about the feelings of Vietnam veterans about Vietnam, Laos, et cetera. I think most of us really loved Vietnam and the Vietnamese. We liked helping people. In fact, there was always a lot of kindness going on that never made the papers. Civic action was a big part of what we did.

And people didn't do civic action just because it was a great deal, they did it because they really wanted to do something for people. Here's what the [South] Vietnamese government said about SF [reading from an official citation]: 49,902 instances of economic aid between 1964 and 1970. We dug 6,436 wells, and built 1,900 kilometers of road, 129 churches, 272 markets, 110 hospitals, 398 dispensaries, 1,000 classrooms, 670 bridges. That's all done by Special Forces. Now, I don't know which part of this was done by John Rambo. Our mission was to kill the enemy, but also to help the people. Of course, Asia was also a place of extreme trauma for these men when they were young, so there's a lot of apprehension about coming back to this area and they've got to deal with that ghost, too. But Special Forces was still the best missionary training in the world."

At the outset of American involvement in Vietnam, President Kennedy took an interest in counterinsurgency and unconventional warfare in general and Special Forces in particular. He authorized them to wear their distinctive green berets, and viewed them as a promising mechanism for nation-building. The main idea was to make a strategic impact in a given conflict by training and working with sympathetic locals to help stabilize a society against an insurgency or outside intervention, and to take direct military action if necessary. As Taylor sees it, both Special Forces and World Aid do earthy work of lofty purpose. "You're a change agent and that's not bad, but you have to be able to separate out what's good and bad about your own culture, about what you're bringing with you. Not everything we have is good, and not everything we have is proper—even in terms of religion." Green Beret pedigree notwithstanding, Taylor does not want to force anything down anybody's throat. "Special Forces doesn't want Rambo and muscles so much. They want a body capable enough to deliver the mind to the target. God wants to deliver the heart to the target as well."

"SNAKE"

Most of the American veterans in Thailand are neither techno-philanthropists like Holthaus nor medical relief workers like Taylor. But it's not strange for a vet privately to support a Thai child or family, and each VFW post raises money for charity. The Udorn Thani post in northeast Thailand, for example, has heavily supported the Thare Orphanage and the Khon Kaen Blind School for years. Bob Taylor doesn't do bars, but Jeep Holthaus does and in fact has arranged for the Bourbon Street restaurant, on Washington Square, to be his Bangkok drop-off point for donated computers. It's a good choice. He's collected a lot of hardware.

Judging by Holthaus and Taylor, and by Taylor's roster of volunteers, those most deeply involved in charity do tend to be combat veterans. Motivations vary, but they invariably relate back to the war. Jeep Holthaus got sick of taking orders to fight Asians and found a measure of liberation by doing something decent for them on his own terms. Bob Taylor discovered that cause coalesced with duty in his wartime work with the Bru, witnessed his efforts undone by America's ultimate failure in Vietnam, but returned to offset the losses.

Ken Richter is a rough-hewn American classic. Unlike Taylor, he looks the part of an old Green Beret. He's about five-foot-nine, with slicked-back blond hair and blue eyes, a square jaw and a cleft chin. The fact that he is missing his right index finger tantalizes the imagination. Though he has a slight roll around the middle, he remains in good shape and "can still hump a rucksack." Richter sports a large gold ruby-and-diamond ring on his left ring finger, and a sapphire-and-diamond ring on his right pinky. He's strak as ever. Special Forces were his salvation, Vietnam the only disappointment in the package.

Richter's taxi-driver father, an alcoholic, died when he was eight. He was raised with three sisters in Jersey City by an alcoholic mother and a series of stepfathers. In 1954, when he was fourteen, he opened the door to find the current man of the house punching his mother. "I had a big Garrison belt that had a bunch of license-plate bolts on it. They called me 'Studs' back in those days. I took that belt off and beat him pretty good, to the extent that they took him to the hospital and me to jail. They let me go when they'd seen that my mother had been hit and I was defending her, but I made up my mind then that as soon as I could I was going to get out." He lied about his age and joined the Army at sixteen in 1956 to escape his turbulent family and teen years that would have been spent in a street gang. His was the Wolverines, and, he remembers, "they ended up writing a book about them."

He was attracted first to the 82nd Airborne Division "by a camaraderie I had never seen except in a street gang." He tested well at everything the Army threw at him, frequently earning the accolade of "Soldier of the Month." After nine months in Korea, he went to Japan as a motor sergeant with the 549th Quartermaster Aero-Delivery Company, then the only American airborne unit in Japan. In true fifties fashion, Richter was a gear-head, raced motorcycles and cars in Japan, and would later win a record four consecutive Houston Autorama first places for custom cars and trucks. In Japan, he married a Japanese woman, and got his first exposure to Southeast Asia when he helped Special Forces fly supplies into the Hmong at the beginning of U.S. involvement in 1960–61, in Operation White Star.

The United States, he figured, was right to intervene in Laos because communists were repressive and the Hmong were genuinely opposed to them "and were willing to do what it took." His exposure to Special Forces in Laos enamored Richter of unconventional warfare: he no longer wanted to be in a line company. He did well in the SF aptitude exams, and implored an assignments major in Washington to override his orders to report to the 101st Airborne Division in Fort Campbell, Kentucky. As a new Green Beret in the Third Special Forces Group at Fort Bragg, he says, "I believed I was with and amongst the very best." He fit in well, acquiring the nickname "Snake" on account of the culinary fare he arranged during survival training—a merely typical example, he notes, of SF resourcefulness and toughness.

More significantly, in Special Forces he found the family he never had. "If I, as a kid, could have designed what family life could have been like, this is what my brothers would have been like. My team sergeant—that was what my father would have been like. I gave my all to it. Anything that came up I would do." And he always excelled. Richter ended up being chosen for "The Gabriel Team," named for the first Special Forces casualty in Vietnam: a touring group of twelve select Green Berets who stoked patriotism by showing the public what Special Forces could do. A black-and-white publicity photograph hangs on the wall of his home office. Immediately after he completed his training, he volunteered for Vietnam.

Richter lived primarily to serve with honor in the small military world—Special Forces—that he had come to cherish, which is precisely the mind-set that is prescribed for the best soldiers. He therefore cared little about larger political questions. As an incidental matter, he did believe that the South Vietnamese were indeed committed to thwarting communism, if generally "lousy soldiers," and continued to hold these views after his first tour in Vietnam in 1963–64. He earned a Bronze Star with a "V," working in II Corps with the Montagnards, whom he came to like and admire. "If a guy didn't gravitate to the Montagnards, he was a shithead. It was his problem, it wasn't theirs."

During his last combat tour in 1965, when he was with the Mike Force (Special Forces' in-house reactionary force) in Third Special Forces' in II Corps near Pleiku, he earned another Bronze Star and a Purple Heart (there went the index finger) but grew dismayed with the way the war was being fought. He thought that Special Forces and similar deep-penetration groups should be exploited more to distract NVA troops from moving south, which might lead to victory without escalation. The only "mistake," he believed, was a lack of full commitment on the part of policymakers and brass; the decision to support the South Vietnamese was still the right one.

After returning from Vietnam, he took a highly sensitive job as the chief NCO in Special Forces' Special Atomic Demolition Munitions (SADM) unit: elite soldiers charged with delivering low-yield nuclear bombs—sometimes known as "backpack nukes" or "suitcase nukes"—in small infantry teams in hypothetical circumstances that most of them would have considered suicide missions. He was able to choose his own men, but the bombs were of course never used in actual combat. And although Special Forces was "the family he would have liked to have," and he believes Forces literally saved his life, Richter was discouraged about the standing of the armed forces in American society. He had been strafed by the usual antiwar epithets at Travis Air Force Base and in San Francisco, and foresaw U.S. involvement in Vietnam ending ingloriously. In 1970, after fourteen years in the Army, he declined to reenlist and was discharged. Many career NCOs, equally disaffected, followed suit during the early 1970s.

Richter knows that Vietnam veterans were unappreciated, and comes equipped with a cinematic-caliber anecdote that happens to be true. Disneyland offered free admission to men in uniform during the war. In 1968, after his second tour in Vietnam, he took his wife to the theme park. He was in uniform. "We were standing in line for a ride and these two hippie types were behind us, and they began to chant some anti-Vietnam slogans. I ignored them. Finally they started yelling, 'Hey, look at this Green Beret baby-killer! You kill babies—you think you're tough enough to kill me?' This guy was pretty big, and really mouthy. I had a Disneyland program, with all the rides and a map, in my hand. At that time, I don't know if it was *Life* magazine, but something had published an article that said Green Berets were trained to kill people with a newspaper. He said, 'Hey, tough guy, I heard you could kill a guy with a newspaper, blah, blah, blah!' And he looked at this program. 'Could you kill me with that? How many ways could you kill me?' I just rolled this ten-page brochure up, and I guess he saw something in my face because he started back-tracking. There was a big crowd. And I blew it. He again said, 'You're not as tough as you'd like me to believe. Without that beret you ain't shit.' And I hit him in the forehead with that rolled up brochure. Blood spurted out, I cut him. When he went down on his knees, I kicked him in the balls. Guy probably never did have kids. His friend tried to jump me and I beat the shit out of him, too. Well, the crowd that was there started applauding. It was one of the most moving experiences I think I ever had, because all I'd heard was a bunch of shit about baby-killers. And now the crowd got behind me."

The exhilaration was fleeting, though, and the experience ulti-mately alienating. "I wasn't really particularly proud of myself. I hurt those guys pretty bad. There were no charges, but I was asked to leave the park." The lasting memory was of an afternoon spoiled and a country divided against its armed forces.

The sting wore off as the years went by and was salved by the enduring brotherhood of Special Forces. At one recent reunion he attended, following a "static (i.e., in-place) display," staged by serving Green Berets, Richter and "other old-timers" in atten-dance clambered back into the bus that was ferrying them around the base. After they were seated, a squared-away young Special Forces sergeant snapped off a sharp, solemn salute and paid trib-ute to them: "You guys are our heritage, you are where we come from, and we strive to be what you were and are." Says Richter: "He spoke from his heart. All the times that I was called a baby-killer and a war criminal were negated by that one moment." Richter gets tears in his eyes then, and more tears come when he recalls the moment.

He enjoyed great success as a businessman (dive schools and shops) and salesman (home exercise equipment, hardware) in California, the Midwest, and Texas after the service. In the late seventies, having divorced and started drinking more than he knew he should, Richter became a Christian and started a Christian toy company called WeeWin. In the early eighties he sold the company and became independently wealthy. Then he started his own manufacturing consulting firm, which took him to Asia for more than half the year through November 1996. He then became sales manager for Asia and the South Pacific of Generon, a German-owned maker of nitrogen generators, at an annual salary of $250,000. He had his choice of cities, and, remembering R-and-Rs during his Japan and Vietnam tours, chose to live permanently in Bangkok.

Richter remains an uncomplicated man with straightforward American beliefs and values. He got to know John Wayne when he came to Vietnam to research the movie *The Green Berets,* and, improbably, considers it a good and reasonably accurate film. Because he was on an elite team—Special Forces—Richter manages to be both proud and modest. He believes that Special Forces saved his life, and that to protect SF's legacy he should do the right thing in what's left of that life.

While he is a self-described "achiever" and enjoys the frontier atmosphere and the challenge of free enterprise in Asia, he was drawn back mainly due to a sense of unfinished business. Though he thinks the Americans could have won and he left the Army quite disillusioned, he knows we can't fight the war over again. Yet he believes the cause was good, and therefore would like to find other ways of helping Asians. He lives one street down from Bob Taylor. Though not as religious as he once was—he is no longer "a zealot"—Richter takes his moral cue from Taylor. Thus, he gives over $50,000 a year to charitable causes in Asia, including World Aid and a local school for ministers, and to Thai families for the support of children and teenagers. After he retires, he wants to finance labor-intensive enterprises in Vietnam's central highlands, where he soldiered, and train Montagnards to run them. "I don't wake up feeling sorry for me or anybody else. I did what I could when I could, and I'm doing what I can when I can now. When I stop believing that I'm making an impact, then I'll change. But I expect that I will spend the rest of my life in Southeast Asia."

Hard-bitten as he is, Richter freely admits that he has suffered from post-traumatic stress. If his troubles were rooted in guilt, though, it was over what he didn't do for Americans rather than what he did to Vietnamese. "I went through a period when I first got out of the service when I carried a weapon all the time, I slept with a gun under my pillow, fought a lot. I would go into a bar and pick the biggest guy to fight, knowing that if I beat him or not, nobody would screw with me again. I was always bruised and black-and-blue. It's easy to say you're chasing a ghost. That's a way of saying, 'I don't understand what the hell it is that's bothering me.' I felt and still feel a certain amount of guilt that I maybe didn't do everything that I could have done to save or help somebody. Because sometimes survival instincts make you hunker down. I'm not saying I was a coward. I wasn't. But I think that anybody who's ever been in extended combat and has lost some people—those are the ghosts that they haven't recognized."

Though he occasionally has a nightmare, Richter's anger has subsided. "I think part of that is because I'm here and doing something. Today I could point you to a hundred men whose biggest fantasy is to come over here, but they want to go back to where they were [during the Vietnam War] and they can't. I think when I recognized that, things changed for me." He can't save fellow soldiers who died, and can't beat an enemy that is no longer. With that self-revelation, he may have captured the essential reason for the combat vet's resort to helping Asians. "A large number of veterans feel like when they left Southeast Asia, they didn't complete the job. There's an emptiness there. We can't win back Vietnam, and I don't expect to, and I don't want to come over here and have another war. But there were people left behind that needed our help, and although at that time it was out of my control to help, it's not now."

Even for the guys who saw real combat, "on the pointy end," winning hearts alone now seems enough. But it is not personal guilt over what they did in the war that moves these men to help Asians now. They are not trying to conquer demons, and it would be presumptuous to suggest as much. On the other hand, they would not be as happy helping Americans in America because doing so would not be intimately connected to the paramount event in their lives— the Vietnam War. While their altruism might be equally, indeed more, celebrated back home, their Vietnam background would be recognized only in passing and perhaps dismissively, in that off-key tone of foreboding or disingenuousness that the term "Vietnam veteran" so often produces in the United States.

Thailand, though not a warrior nation, is certainly pro-American, and during the war got $30 billion in infrastructure out of Washington that helped pave the way to economic success. The Thais had a full division in Vietnam, and quietly acknowledge that the United States stanched the flow of communism. From the Thais, then, Vietnam veterans get credit for being Vietnam veterans. While it may be an exaggeration to say that they were pushed back to Southeast Asia by a sense of America's betrayal of veterans, it is fair to say that they were drawn back there by its people's relative lack of apathy about the war and, in Thailand, the Thais' greater acceptance of the American role in it. Transforming Vietnam-vintage valor into something more useful is hard enough anywhere—particularly in the United States, where it is barely considered good raw material. There is little doubt that Holthaus, Taylor, and Richter could have toughed it out stateside, but they might have done so sullenly, with no ready outlet for their better instincts. Surely their successes in Thailand vindicate their choice of venue.

Mark Smith, left, receiving
the Distinguished Service
Cross from Major General
Tom Tarpley at Fort Ben-
ning, Georgia, in 1974 and,
right, with the Laotian
resistance forces in 1989,
monitoring the Vietnamese.
Courtesy Mark Smith.

3
VALOR DENIED

Thailand's constant assault on the physical and aesthetic senses is leavened by the gentleness and friendliness of the Thai people. They volunteer help to confused foreigners, invariably with a smile. Practically speaking, Buddhism is a sensible and civilizing religion: there's no way of telling about an afterlife, it seems to hold, but just in case let's not upset anybody's ancestors. Buddhists also believe in reincarnation, and seek to "make merit" through charity and generosity in the conviction that doing so will earn them a better life next time around. Beggars rarely go hungry in Thailand. The linchpin of the religion is the principle that suffering comes from desire, so Buddhists aspire not to desire much. In the face of burgeoning capitalism, of course, they have found Western-style materialism and acquisitiveness difficult to resist: the key to making headway in Bangkok's horrendous traffic is to cut in front of the Mercedes because its owner is so terrified of damaging his precious car. Nevertheless, smart-looking girls in miniskirts carrying cell phones take a moment to bow and pray to the Buddhist shrines that are found large and small, in reserved areas as well as gas stations, all over Bangkok.

The casual terminology of the Thais reflects a carefree attitude that is no doubt seductive to expats: *chip joi* (small problem that keeps getting smaller); *mai pen lai* (you're welcome, never mind); *alai kadai* (it doesn't matter). At the same time, they are fiercely proud of their mensch of a king, Bhumibol Adulyadej, now in his seventies. He devotes most of his time to charity, and his tolerance for corruption is sufficiently finite to have helped stabilize Thailand politically. A recent biography by William Stevenson, in whom the king willingly confided, was nonetheless banned by Thai censors for revealing a few royal foibles, and *The King and I* and all its cognates have long been disallowed on account of their earthy portrayal of Rama IV, the present king's great-great-great grandfather. Thais also treasure the fact that Thailand is the only country in Southeast Asia never to have been conquered by a colonial power. In school, it's true, they are taught that they are racially superior, and the Thais' grinning, nonconfrontational style doesn't mean that an individual won't stab you in the back instead of the chest. But the fact remains that most Thais are easy to deal with casually from day to day.

Not so in the case of some Vietnam veterans there. Bernie Newson, an Australian veteran of the Vietnam War, shares a house in suburban Bangkok with a shadowy retired U.S. Army major named Mark Smith. Bernie handles Smith's communications, and himself claims to be the first recognized Agent Orange victim. An Asian answered their phone. "You wait." Someone trudged toward the phone and in short order an Australian said hello and nasally slurred apologies for his "niggers." Commonwealth folks use that term to disparage all nonwhites. Major Smith was in Cambodia doing something that couldn't be divulged. Bernie seemed to be intoxicated. It was nine o'clock in the morning.

The next time, Major Smith himself answers the phone. He has a high, regimented voice with military bearing. The major is obviously sober. It is an opportune time for an interview, he says. He has been to Cambodia and completed negotiations with the Khmer Rouge, and the Army has just informed him that it will consider upgrading his Distinguished Service Cross, the United States' second-highest decoration for gallantry, to the Medal of Honor. Impressive, and, after Bernie, something of a relief. The first interview takes place on Sunday at noon at the Coffee Bean at the Thai Panit shopping center in Viphavadi, the area of greater Bangkok where Major Smith lives.

Smith's reedy voice rises improbably above those of the other patrons of the restaurant. Smith is talking to a Thai about what happened in Cambodia. He stands up to shake hands. He is about six-foot-one, with close-cropped iron gray hair and a gunfighter mustache. His mud-brown eyes are baleful, though often softened by classic aviator sunglasses that would tend to signify, to an American, The Right Stuff. Smith chain-smokes Salem Light menthols in a cigarette holder, a habit he picked up during his ten-month imprisonment in Kratie, Cambodia in 1972–73 after the Battle of Loc Ninh. He's a nonstop coffee drinker (at the Coffee Bean, cappuccino). He's got a paunch and is running to fat, but is heavily muscled and well-built. He has a bad back (two vertebrae were crushed in battle and went untreated for twenty-five years) and walks pitched forward—the result of shrapnel still lodged in his back. From the outset Mark Smith seems too eccentric not to be authentic.

In a minor way he is world-famous—for his remarkably bemedaled military career in Vietnam, for his unrelenting insistence that there are American prisoners of war and soldiers "missing in action" who are in fact alive and should be retrieved, for his lawsuit against President Reagan seeking to compel official efforts to do so. No journalist need fumble for words with Mark Smith because he fills in all the white noise. He is the star of the patio, the cock of the walk; he'd just as soon hang out all day. He wants to tell his story, to hold court on himself.

Most apparent negatives having to do with Mark Smith have explanations. Bernie is not a libertine redneck drunk after all. He doesn't even imbibe. He uses morphine because he has cancer of the liver and without the morphine would be in constant and excruciating pain. According to Major Smith as well as Newson, Agent Orange is the culprit.

Mark Smith is from central casting. Born in Lima, Ohio, Smith talks in a nasal midwestern twang. His stock verbal filler expression is, "You know?" It is uttered in a minor key, imparting resignation and muted disgust. When he recalls talking tough to someone in need of Mark Smith's guidance, he begins, "Listen here, Willis!" Who the hell is "Willis"? Smith shrugs. It's just a name, like Joe Blow, that he uses when he wants to make a point. It has become a trademark. Trademarks transmit character—in spaghetti westerns, in life.

Smith gives the impression of being a lovable rake and, more substantively, a cagey operator. He engaged, so he says, in at least two mercenary operations since coming to Bangkok at the Thai government's request in 1985 to consult on counterterrorist operations. And he professed to have too much local clout to have to worry about parading his status. "The Thais owe me," he smiles. He is vague about the intent and consequences of the ops. He styles himself the protector of a timid, self-deluding people. "They don't know whether they want to be boys or girls," he cracks. As for all that pride in not having been colonized, Smith says it's a little misplaced. "The Japanese occupied Thailand during World War II and a day later the Thais declared war on the United States. After the war, the British wanted to punish them but the Americans decided to ignore the collaboration." Cuttingly but succinctly true: the bridge on the River Kwai was built in Thailand.

On the half-mile walk from the Thai Panit shopping center to his bungalow, a Thai waves and salutes "Major Mark." He murmurs that this man is King Bhumibol Adulyadej's spy, and that he taps Smith for intelligence on the clandestine politics of Bangkok. So do the Thai police. In fact, Smith was instrumental in gaining William Stevenson access to the king. And evidently the Thais give Smith wide latitude as a political player—especially in Cambodia, where he has quietly tried to broker deals to bring recalcitrant Khmer Rouge leaders to trial and to check Hun Sen's power—and still consult him on certain security matters.

Why did so many vets wind up in Thailand? "Pussy," says Smith resolutely. Smith amplified the point by noting that Bangkok is an ugly man's paradise. Take a look, he said, at the fat middle-aged white goons sashaying around the city with slim, hard-bodied Thai babes on their arms. For the woman a white man is a meal ticket; it doesn't matter what he looks like. He ingenuously notes that he has a thirty-year-old Thai wife and six children by three other women—three by an American wife, two by a Vietnamese wife, and one by a Korean girlfriend. Five children live in the United States. His son was murdered in 2001.

The Major lives around the corner from two other ex-Green Berets: Bob Taylor, who is also his landlord, and Ken Richter. Smith's household is positively Casablancan: Valeeporn Nilnoy (nicknamed "Noc," meaning "The Bird"), the Major's Thai wife; Bernie Newson, the cancer-afflicted Australian ex-sergeant; Claude Clement, a half-breed French/Vietnamese Montagnard ex-captain Smith rescued from Cambodians who were attempting to sell him as an American POW; Chet Sourisak, former colonel in the Laotian Air Force and ex-commander of Savannaket Air Force Base in Laos; Sourisak's teenage son, who functions as a houseboy; and Milo, an affectionate female St. Bernard named after a Thai chocolate soft drink. The men call one another "the Major," "the Sergeant," "the Colonel," and "the Captain." Major Smith runs the house like a military unit. The Colonel answers the phone and does the copying. The Captain buys the groceries. The Sergeant, Bernie, handles electronic communications. The Major gets the air-conditioned master bedroom.

Still he treats his people with respect and affection. The Colonel—a robust, perpetually shirtless sixty or so—trained with the U.S. Air Force in San Antonio in the early sixties, and he gets full credit for that and the fact that even nearing his golden years he's still an insatiable hit with the ladies. Cancer has whittled Bernie, who is six-foot-four, down to a frail 130 pounds, but the Major was quick to note that the Sergeant boxed for the Australian Army and was in the Australian Special Air Service.

Smith weighed in Claude the Captain as a legendary killer of Vietcong and as a staunch ally of U.S. Special Forces—as indeed many Montagnards were throughout the war. Claude was imprisoned in Vietnam in a "re-education camp" from 1975 to 1981 and fled to Cambodia after his release due to the vindictiveness of Vietnamese authorities. Though his mother was a Vietnamese Montagnard, his father was French, and Claude looks more like a Gallic Caucasian—with a long, straight nose and receding chin, a bit like Yves Montand, actually—than an Asian. It was for this reason that the Cambodians claimed he was a U.S. POW and tried to peddle him as such. He is a Southeast Asian version of Joe Christmas, the tortured mulatto of William Faulkner's *Light in August,* and Smith makes a strong argument that Claude should be entitled to permanent U.S. residence, though the State Department has told him instead to seek repatriation in Vietnam.

"I don't accumulate memories," says Smith, "I accumulate people." They are a family. The price for Smith's fatherhood is unwavering personal loyalty and the moral servicing of grievances that hearken back to the Vietnam War. Bernie vilifies anyone who is not foursquare with Mark Smith on all issues Vietnam to a degree that embarrasses even the Major. At Smith's prompting, Claude says he wishes the United States won the war, and theatrically refuses to call Saigon "Ho Chi Minh City." Smith is an arrogant, exclusionary man. He leaves others little room to disagree without pitched confrontation, and rarely concedes the possibility that he may be wrong. Like a pampered professional athlete, he often refers to himself in the third person: *Mark Smith* this, *Mark Smith* that. Yet it is testimony to his self-confidence and, in a way, an incongruous humility, that when he first came to Thailand and needed money he literally "sang for his supper" at the Indra Regent Hotel and the El Gordo Canteen in central Bangkok. (When he was a boy, Mark's parents had traditionally asked him to stand up on the piano bench and croon. He thrived on the attention then as now and continued to enjoy singing in the Army and after. His specialty is country western music, in particular "Jambalaya" and Willie Nelson's "You Were Always on My Mind.")

Singing is just a hobby. Smith's vocation in Thailand for the past fifteen years has been fighting the Vietnam War. He is still preoccupied with that long stretch of his adult life. Mark Smith's five-odd tours in Southeast Asia amounted to a sinecure of unrequited patriotism. After being expelled from a Christian fundamentalist boarding school in Kentucky, young Mark was awed by a uniformed 101st Airborne Division soldier at the bus depot as he waited for transport back to his family's home in California. In 1963 he joined up at age seventeen, and killed his first man in combat on the streets of San Salvador, the Dominican Republic, during President Johnson's brief intervention in 1965. Later that year he went to Vietnam a gung-ho soldier. His uniform was already stitched with a Combat Infantryman's Badge by 1966. He was there on and off for seven years. During this period he became fluent in Vietnamese, made staff sergeant at twenty, and won a battlefield direct commission as a first lieutenant at twenty-two. "I had found myself a home," he remembers. Eventually he would serve in Vietnam with the 101st Airborne.

In April 1972 Captain Mark Smith, then Senior U.S. Battalion Liaison Officer to the Ninth Army of the Republic of Vietnam Infantry Regiment, commanded ARVN (Army of the Republic of Vietnam) troops in the Battle of Loc Ninh, one of the first major tank incursions launched by the NVA, which ultimately overran Smith's ARVN soldiers. Smith himself directed more than two days of nonstop heavy combat in which he killed numerous NVA soldiers and disabled several tanks (one single-handedly), was wounded thirty-eight times and temporarily blinded, and refused to surrender. Attempting to evade advancing NVA troops, Smith was knocked unconscious by the concussion of a rocket-propelled grenade (RPG) against a rubber tree, inches from his head, and captured. These were the defining moments of his life.

THE BATTLE OF LOC NINH

In early 1972 the town of Loc Ninh, capital of the Loc Ninh District in northern Long Binh province in the so-called "Iron Triangle" north of Saigon, was ARVN's regimental headquarters in III Corps. Though Loc Ninh's population numbered only about three thousand, mainly Montagnards, it was strategically significant: about sixty kilometers due north of Saigon and ten miles east and south of the Cambodian border, not far from the Ho Chi Minh Trail, a few miles southeast of a river with a secret bridge made of submerged stones that provided access for troops and vehicles to points south, most importantly Saigon. And ARVN's control of the town was a pet peeve of Ho Chi Minh's, the town's rubber plantations once having constituted virtual French penal colonies in which Vietminh had been enslaved. Mark Smith had fought battles in or near Loc Ninh in 1966, 1967, and 1968. The village also housed ammunition and ordnance for the regimental-strength ARVN units deployed in the area.

"Vietnamization"—the United States' program shifting primary responsibility for defending South Vietnam to ARVN—had been under way for a couple of years. It was not working. Virtually the same problems of fatuous, politicized leadership and operational immobility that haunted ARVN in 1962 haunted it in 1972. Holding Loc Ninh was crucial to defending the provincial capital of An Loc ten miles to the south. An Loc's military importance, like that of Khe Sanh and other U.S./South Vietnamese outposts earlier in the war, was overrated: even if the NVA took the city, the American B-52 onslaught would render holding it infeasible. On the other hand, because An Loc was only fifty miles northwest of Saigon, its fall would have symbolic significance. Taking a provincial capital could damage the United States' bargaining position in the Paris peace talks, and maximize Hanoi's territorial advantage once an accord was reached.

Thus, An Loc's defense would, as a *Washington Daily News* headline put it, conclusively "test the mettle of Vietnamization." Serious doubt had already been cast on the program a year earlier. In February and March of 1971, ARVN's limited invasion of Laos in Operation Lam Son 19, aimed at cutting the Ho Chi Minh trail, though momentarily successful and highly damaging to the NVA, had resulted in nine thousand ARVN casualties (more than 50 percent of its attacking force), the loss of two hundred American helicopters, and an abrupt, bloody withdrawal. The operation had shown, among other untoward things, that the South Vietnamese could not do without U.S. advisers on the battlefield.

After a comfortable stint as an instructor at the Ranger Training School in Fort Benning, Georgia, Captain Mark Smith was in Vietnam for a final tour at his own request. He had no illusions about the dubious will of most ARVN soldiers to fight, but believed they, like most line soldiers, were as good as their leaders made them. His optimism, then, resided in his egotism. In addition, in his opinion the VC guerrillas were spent after the Tet Offensive, so that after 1968 the war had become the kind of conventional engagement that Americans know how to fight. Shake these realities together and what poured out was the fact that Mark Smith and those of his military persuasion were America's last best hope in Vietnam. The defeat at Loc Ninh in 1972, the evacuation of Saigon in 1975—they don't change that. The consensus is that his performance at Loc Ninh had strategic consequences: that it bought ARVN precious time to regroup and withstand the NVA's siege of An Loc—the largest of the war— and substantially delayed the fall of Saigon. But nearly thirty years later, the situation does not strike him as any less depressing than it did in the moment.

Smith's superiors in the chain of command were Major General James Hollingsworth, commander of the Third Regional Assistance Command, and Lieutenant Colonel Richard Schott, commander of the Ninth ARVN Infantry Regimental Advisory Team. "It was supposed to be just like a speed-bump once the battle developed, but General Hollingsworth said, 'Try to buy us some time.' I said, 'I'll give you two days at least, and I'll try to give you some more. That was on the fourth of April. Colonel Schott also asked that the ARVN pull their First Squadron, First Cavalry, back to Loc Ninh, and then we'd put them around the airfield. But Colonel [Nguyen Cong] Vinh and Major General [Le Van] Hung, who was President Thieu's brother-in-law, wanted to give the NVA a variety of targets, so that they'd hit a number of places and wouldn't mass up and get all the way to Saigon. Everyone's sitting there on the Fourth, waiting for them to come storming out of Tay Ninh province." Everybody except Smith. "I think they hit Tan Le Shanh over in Tay Ninh, but I knew it was just a feint. They always came down Highway Thirteen—it was a straight shot to Saigon, plus the rubber plantations gave them high-speed avenues of approach with good cover and concealment, all the way to at least Binh Long. The Montagnards knew they were coming because they had built an underwater bridge and made the Montagnards participate up on the [Cambodian] border. This was written off down at MACV [U.S. Military Assistance Command—Vietnam, based in Saigon] headquarters when Colonel Schott and I went down there. I mean, they laughed. 'Offensive? Where'd you get this guy?' I said, 'They're coming, they're going to come in a big way.'"

As the Battle of Loc Ninh loomed, Hanoi had begun its Easter offensive, the primary thrust of which was well north of Loc Ninh in I Corps. ARVN troops in III Corps were roundly defeatist, and would engage the NVA and Vietcong only when led by American officers. Colonel Vinh, the ARVN commanding officer, had demonstrated his lethargy a couple of weeks earlier by refusing to order the underwater bridge destroyed, dismissing its tactical role. The bridge, he rationalized, was probably used by Montagnards to smuggle exotic wood to Cambodia. In general, Vinh made it clear that he preferred capture to combat and repeatedly evaded his duty to engage the enemy by operating exclusively within the confines of a rubber plantation managed by a Frenchman who had bribed the NVA and VC not to initiate hostilities there. Between the Cambodian border to the west and Loc Ninh itself, therefore, the North Vietnamese had nearly complete freedom of movement. On March 30, when news that NVA divisions had begun their onslaught in northern I Corps, even as he read an issue of *Stars and Stripes* showing photographs of NVA-manned Soviet T-54 tanks moving south on the Ho Chi Minh trail, Vinh was in cowardly denial. He convinced himself that the Ninth ARVN Regiment would have to face only armored personnel carriers (APCs), and contented himself with a single recoilless rifle, six antitank rounds, and fifty rounds of canister ammunition in the regimental ammunition dump.

The day before the battle began, the few ARVN soldiers left at Loc Ninh were gathered at a local bar, drunk. When Smith dressed them down, they explained to Smith that tomorrow they would die. Colonel Vinh had divided the bulk of his remaining forces. A cavalry squadron and two infantry companies (Task Force 1-5) were deployed to Fire Support Base Alpha northwest of town, while a small force of five APCs and a lone M-41 tank were left at the junction of Highways 13 and 14, about three miles due north of Loc Ninh. This arrangement conveniently ignored Loc Ninh's left flank. Against American advice, Colonel Vinh declined to fortify Loc Ninh. His theory? Leaving a southern route intact for the enemy and avoiding tactical confrontation would encourage the enemy to bypass Loc Ninh and spare his regimental headquarters and ARVN soldiers. In the event of capture, he could argue that he had helped the NVA and VC. His verbiage was peppered with the phrase "when we surrender."

On the afternoon of April 4, NVA tank units advancing from the west wiped out most of an ARVN reconnaissance company. A survivor was able to radio headquarters that the tanks were proceeding "in large numbers" toward Loc Ninh. Later the same day nearer Loc Ninh, ARVN units ambushed a squad from the 272nd NVA Regiment and took several prisoners. They revealed that the Ninth NVA Division would bypass Loc Ninh and hit An Loc, but that the 272nd was assigned to block a southward withdrawal by the Ninth ARVN Regiment while the Fifth Vietcong Division attacked Loc Ninh. So much for Colonel Vinh's wishful thinking.

In the wee hours of the morning of April 5, the Fifth VC Division launched a coordinated ground and rocket attack on Loc Ninh. Now that it was too late for reinforcements, Colonel Vinh, again contrary to American advice, ordered the men assigned to FSB Alpha to return to Loc Ninh—not, it transpired, to reinforce it but to surrender to the NVA. Almost as soon as it left the firebase, Task Force 1-5 was confronted by a far bigger enemy force and, with Vinh's blessing, was planning to surrender without a fight. Disgusted, Captain Smith promptly relieved him of command and ordered the regimental commander to resist. The cavalry squadron gave up and in fact moved west *with* the NVA into Cambodia, voluntarily driving enemy APCs and tanks. But the two infantry companies advanced to the intersection of Highways Thirteen and Fourteen, boarded the tank and five APCs there, and proceeded toward Loc Ninh with air cover from an AC-130 Spectre gunship called in by Captain Smith. These units would be of minimal help.

The Fifth Vietcong Division was reinforced by tanks, artillery, and surface-to-air missiles, while the Ninth ARVN Regiment had minimal artillery and no tank support and was outnumbered by ten to one. Beyond his reluctant and under-strength infantry, Smith's only resort was tactical support from American carrier- and land-based helicopters and airplanes. Over the next sixty hours, Captain Smith would not sleep. From a bunker on Loc Ninh's perimeter, he directed ARVN movements and U.S. tactical air strikes against enemy positions, holding NVA tanks at bay in the tree line ringing Loc Ninh and thus depriving enemy infantry of the armored punch necessary to breach the perimeter.

The NVA's indirect artillery assault on Loc Ninh continued for a day. When NVA T-54 tanks massed in the woodline outside Loc Ninh's perimeter began to advance across the airfield, Smith called in cluster bombs and napalm, which repelled them. Enemy artillery and mortar fire remained a problem. An American adviser holed up in the north compound reported to Smith that mortar crews were firing from the swimming pool on the rubber plantation. Smith summoned an AC-130 Spectre gunship—capable of covering every square inch of a football field with fire in less than a minute—to get rid of these irritants, which it did. The U.S. adviser also noticed that an NVA forward artillery spotter was positioned on top of the plantation house. General Hung, however, was monitoring radio traffic and countermanded a Spectre strike on the house. Using a recoilless rifle, Captain Smith hit the position with 106-millimeter canisters, spraying the house with flechette rounds. The forward observer was silenced and enemy fire abated.

On the evening of April 5, Colonel Vinh had his bodyguards open the gates of Loc Ninh "so," as he explained to Smith, "we can run out easier." Smith considered shooting the man on the spot but decided there was no point. At first light on the morning of April 6, the NVA forced South Vietnamese women and children carrying American flags to march toward the perimeter. Captain Smith laid down fire in front of the civilians, giving them no option except to retreat to safety.

In preparation for a ground attack, on the morning of April 6 Captain Smith placed Claymore mines and white phosphorous grenades behind gas drums lining the west perimeter and attached them to a blasting machine with communications wire. By five o'clock the NVA regimental-strength tanks and infantry advancing from the west approached Loc Ninh. A Spectre gunship forced the tanks to return to the forest, but an infantry battalion reached the perimeter and stood in the wire facing ARVN soldiers positioned on the other side. From a bunker Captain Smith detonated the explosives, whereupon the ARVN soldiers opened fire. The NVA battalion was decimated. By late evening, ARVN and NVA infantry engaged in the barbed wire and trench lines outside Loc Ninh; ultimately the fighting was hand-to-hand.

The air and ground onslaught continued, ARVN taking over two hundred casualties. That night, in a bizarre display of "leadership," Colonel Vinh distributed all remaining soft drinks to the ARVN troops. Grasping his own bottle of warm soda, he then stripped down to his white undershorts and T-shirt, advising officers to surrender and enlisted men to run or face execution by the NVA. The NVA stepped up artillery attacks during the night and incinerated Loc Ninh's infantry and artillery compounds, including the ammunition dump. Hundreds of ARVN soldiers died in a nuke-like fireball. ARVN's artillery was wiped out, leaving Smith completely dependent on aircraft for fire support. At about 7:00 A.M. on April 7, T-54 tanks penetrated Loc Ninh's perimeter from the north and southwest. As one of them chased Captain Smith, an American helicopter swooped in low to draw fire off Smith. He maneuvered to the rear of the tank, where it was most vulnerable, and destroyed it with an M-72 light antitank weapon.

An hour later Colonel Vinh and his bodyguards surrendered at the front gate of Loc Ninh. Vinh's executive officer then ran from a bunker to the inner perimeter to lower the Republic of Vietnam flag and replace it with his white T-shirt. Other ARVN soldiers watched and peeled off their T-shirts. Captain Smith shot the executive officer dead and hauled down the T-shirt of surrender, prompting the ARVN soldiers to put their shirts back on rather hurriedly. In short order, over the objections of the forward air controllers, U.S. tactical air support was withdrawn from Loc Ninh to permit B-52s to strike to the west. NVA tanks rolled into the compounds near the airfields without resistance.

American A-37 Dragonfly attack planes reappeared at 10:00 A.M., but they were too late to save Loc Ninh. Captain Smith called for bombs and napalm strikes to destroy the camp. The air strikes drove out most of the tanks, but by noon only fifty soldiers from the Ninth ARVN Regiment remained at their posts in the south compound, a mere thirty district militiamen in the north compound. Some 1,300 South Vietnamese troops, of whom 1,000 had merely surrendered, had been captured. Loc Ninh had fallen. Audible in Smith's final radio transmission was a baby in the bunker, the child of an ARVN soldier, crying.

As NVA flung satchel charges in the door of the bunker, Smith advised his two fellow American soldiers that they must fight their way out. One, Lieutenant Colonel Richard Schott, had a serious head wound, could not move quickly, and ordered the others to leave without him. Captain Smith decided to stand by him and ordered the other American, a sergeant, to stay put as well. In Smith's opinion, Schott was unwilling to hinder the escape of his two comrades and behaved heroically. Schott raised his service Colt .45 and shot himself between the eyes, dying instantly. To debunk the skepticism of other officers, Smith in his after-action report defended Schott: "On the best day of your life, you should be half as brave as LTC Richard Schott. His was an act of sacrifice, not personal desperation. He died for me."

For Mark Smith, Loc Ninh enshrined soldierliness in all of its forms. "Let me tell you what: this was the greatest battle I was ever in. And I was in a lot of big battles. The battle where [Lieutenant Colonel] Terry Allen died in 1967 was a regimental horseshoe ambush. That was a big battle. All of the previous battles at Loc Ninh [were substantial]. In November of 1967, eight hundred NVA died in the airfield at Loc Ninh. I was attempting to relieve Fire Base Ripcord in I Corps when [Lieutenant] Colonel [André] Lucas got the Medal of Honor, and the second of the 506th got flat whacked. I fought in the A Shau Valley, I was in the Battle of Bu Prangh, which was a big battle in II Corps with the [South] Vietnamese Rangers. Fire Base Dodd in III Corps. I mean, I was in a lot of big battles, but there was never any of them that approached this. Ten thousand rounds of indirect fire a day for two and a half days."

After Schott's suicide, Smith went to the roof of the bunker and tried to rally the three South Vietnamese infantrymen who remained there, but they simply kept yelling, *"may bay,"* the Vietnamese term for "helicopter." He tried to call for air support, but NVA sniper fire destroyed his radio, then penetrated his backpack, and finally entered his back and lodged in his left lung. Immediately after he was shot, a U.S. helicopter did descend into the town to rescue friendly personnel. During the attempted extraction, while the U.S. sergeant and twelve ARVN soldiers remained in the bunker and played dead, Captain Smith emerged from the bunker to cover the ARVN men with an M-60 machine gun. As the chopper swooped in from the west to extract him and the other friendlies, Smith noticed NVA coming out of the bunker line and preparing to fire on the chopper. Now without a radio, Smith tried unavailingly to wave the pilot off, then resorted to shooting out the chopper's windshield with his M-16 to impel the pilot to abort the rescue and avoid NVA gunfire. It worked. The pilot withdrew to the south.

Smith reentered the bunker and, firing his M-16 from the hip, killed three NVA soldiers. Having already removed Lieutenant Colonel Schott's collar and nametag, they were about to decapitate him. The somnolent friendlies sprang to life, and with Smith they retook two bunkers and held them for seven hours, then behind a curtain of Spectre fire made their way across a minefield to the southwest. As they crossed the perimeter road at twilight, an NVA squad ambushed them. Smith and his men returned fire and killed all five NVA, but several of the South Vietnamese soldiers were shot dead as well and Captain Smith took a pistol round in the groin and shrapnel in his lower abdomen. His bowels filled with blood. To empty them he dropped his pants. Smith's bodyguard and the regimental surgeon stuck with him. Just after midnight, the American sergeant and ten of the ARVN men abandoned Smith and ran up a hill.

Nearly incapacitated and emotionally drained, Captain Smith could only cry. He believes that that night the sergeant and his ARVN contingent perished in a massive U.S. air strike. A South Vietnamese doctor reported that he linked up with the sergeant alone, and that NVA executed him six miles north of An Loc and buried him on the spot. In any case, neither the American sergeant nor his ARVN cohort were ever seen again. After they departed Captain Smith, he regained some strength and with his two South Vietnamese comrades began to march. About five hundred yards to the southwest they came to a dry streambed. A reinforced ARVN company had tried to dig in to the streambed to elude an American cluster-bomb and napalm attack. Almost all of them were dead, but the few that weren't gaped pleadingly at Smith and his men. They could do nothing to help and proceeded past the scene in a similarly horrified miasma. No one from either party uttered a word.

Over several kilometers Smith and the ARVN soldiers engaged the NVA three more times. Again he was wounded, as were the others. Exhaustion and injury reduced them to crawling through an area rife with NVA. At 8:00 on the morning of April 8, Smith spotted a forward air controller droning several thousand feet overhead and signaled him with a mirror. Two American fighters moved in with cluster-bombs; the NVA took casualties and scattered, but yet again Smith was wounded. As best they could, he and his men fled up a hill toward some rubber trees. Just as Captain Smith shot dead an NVA soldier with his .45, he was knocked unconscious by an RPG round, wounded one more time. When he awoke, a North Vietnamese soldier was standing on Smith's head. Smith helplessly watched NVA execute his bodyguard, but convinced the North Vietnamese to spare the surgeon. They were taken to a prison camp in Kratie, Cambodia, crossing en route the underwater rock bridge that, according to Colonel Vinh, had no military utility.

FROM DESIGNATED HERO TO EMBITTERED VET

Smith was imprisoned for ten months. Initially he was singled out for abuse when the NVA learned (through an inadvertent remark by the doctor) that he was "Zippo," who they knew had been their tormentor from the frenzied radio traffic at Loc Ninh. Along with about twenty other POWs Smith, though sick and wounded, was chained inside a cage made of logs. He refused to spew any anti-American propaganda for his captors and consequently was denied medical treatment for the shrapnel wounds in his bowel. He didn't shit for forty-five days. When it became apparent that he would die of septic infection unless treated, the camp doctor scraped hardened feces from his rectum with a nail, then gave Smith an enema and some penicillin. He got better. The NVA never broke his resolve to deny them fodder for propaganda. On the radio he heard others who provided it voluntarily—among them Jane Fonda and Ramsey Clark. He also heard POWs in Hanoi spouting what he considered treasonous bilge. He angrily commited their names to memory. The NVA permitted Smith and his men to have Christmas dinner together. The event was filmed for propaganda purposes. When the NVA guards ordered the POWs to stand and thank their captors for their compassion, Smith had them rise and clasp their hands and give thanks to God instead. His intent was to ruin the film for the godless communists. Before Smith and his fellow POWs were released on February 12, 1973, he stole his chain, his old POW clothes, and his rice bowl. He later donated these items to the National Infantry Museum at Fort Benning.

After ten months of imprisonment in Cambodia, Mark Smith returned to the States as one of the initial 591 prisoners of war released in February 1973 pursuant to the Paris Peace Accords. A designated hero, he snorts. The only official heroes of the Vietnam War, he spits. The *concluding* heroes. "This was it. The war was over. And the American people bought it. They gave us cars, trips. They put together a parade for returning POWs. I don't care where they stood, most Americans were not radical, and they came out and cried. Guys with hair down to their ass. They were happy to see you." So he harbors no grudge against the common man, only against people in government for closing the books prematurely, in embarrassment. Naturally he concedes that he was a hero, but not for getting captured. (Recall the movie *Patton:* "No son of a bitch ever won a war by dying for his country. He did it by making some other poor bastard die for his country.") Mark Smith was heavily decorated: that Distinguished Service Cross for Loc Ninh, a Silver Star, eight Bronze Stars (which might be some kind of Vietnam record), six Air Medals, six Army Commendation Medals with "V"s, four Purple Hearts.

In 1973, Mark Smith was twenty-seven years old. After the war he helped run the Army's program for settling South Vietnamese refugees in California, taught again at the Ranger school, and finally commanded the U.S. Army's Special Forces Detachment (Korea). From there Smith expected, with considerable justification given his record, to become a boy general, from lowly private to the top, like James Gavin, who commanded the 82nd Airborne Division in World War II. This was not to be. Smith retired in 1985. He was bitter, and remains so. He misses the Army every day, yet he also professes to have the most interesting life of anyone he knows.

Depending on who tells the story—Smith himself or more line-toeing soldiers and ex-soldiers—he was (1) forced to retire for political reasons after futilely insisting that the Army act on evidence he had gathered that the Vietnamese government was holding live American POWs in Laos, or (2) simply a casualty of the Army's need to trim personnel to correct a peacetime surplus of officers left over from the Vietnam era. Major Smith's ego is too robust to permit anyone to take all that he says as the unalloyed truth. Yet it is difficult to dismiss too readily a sane man who took fire and came back for more, and more, and still more. The explanation for Smith's career problems appears to be more complicated than either of these two offerings.

Mark Smith is not West Point. He did not attend college. His commission was given on the battlefield during the peak of the Vietnam War, when peacetime rules didn't apply. In Vietnam he was more a military thrill-seeker than a careerist. He not only commanded a reconnaissance platoon and a rifle company but also "got it right" when on loan to the CIA's Phoenix Program, which targeted suspected Vietcong agents for elimination. As part of a "provincial reconnaissance unit," Smith oversaw the identification and neutralization (which sometimes meant assassination) of (he brags) 2,834 of them. Throughout his military career he wended his way between standard army and Special Forces, during a military epoch when top brass often scoffed at Green Berets. And of course, he did shoot that South Vietnamese XO in the head. . . .

He conducts his affairs with jaunty swagger. He is a tough guy, but he is too individualistic to be called "strak." During the war, in 1970, he was reprimanded for allegedly transporting the naked body of a North Vietnamese soldier from the field to his base camp tied to the hood of a truck and permitting his men to mutilate the corpse. Smith had sought out this particular man—the notorious battle-scarred commander of the Sixth NVA Regiment, allegedly responsible for killing three thousand civilians earlier in the war, known as the "One-eyed Jack" and the "Butcher of Hué"—and Smith's men had shot him and his bodyguards while he was "swinging in his hammock." He explains, deadpan, that he was required to verify kills when possible and had nowhere else to put the body. "I couldn't put him in the back of the truck with my troops because he stunk like shit," he pleads. A chaplain at Camp Evans filed a report stating that the One-eyed Jack was unclothed and that his ears and nose had been severed, and his genitals cut off and placed in his mouth. Smith protested then and insists now that this was untrue: the corpse was wrapped in a poncho and merely a little the worse for wear. He blames all the foofaraw on the Army's hypersensitivity to atrocities in the wake of My Lai. Major Smith was not formally disciplined, but was sent stateside to teach in the Ranger Department.

Behind all that, he was always a little undiplomatic.

In Vietnam, back in the days, he once pulled his .45 on an MP to get a drink.

When Smith stepped off the plane carrying him and his fellow POWs home wearing a green beret, he infuriated General Creighton Abrams—William Westmoreland's replacement in 1967 as commander of MACV, a World War II tank officer, and an old-fashioned devotee of the regular army who was particularly disdainful of Special Forces.

After he was released from the Cambodian prison camp, Smith impugned the battle performance of two higher-ranking officers involved in the defense of Loc Ninh and the conduct of one during imprisonment.

While he was teaching in the Ranger school at Fort Benning, a noncommissioned officer from Liberia—Africa's oldest independent state, founded by freed American slaves, and then a stable U.S. ally—was sent there for special training. The young man's name was Samuel Doe. He asked whether it was appropriate for a state's military forces to overthrow its civilian government if it was undemocratic. Smith answered as our founding fathers might have: "Theoretically." In April 1980, Samuel Doe and his fellow insurgents assassinated (and disemboweled) Liberian president William Tolbert, and ten days later tied thirteen of his cabinet members to electrical poles on the beach outside Monrovia and publicly shot them dead. The U.S. State Department asked for an explanation. Doe referred them to Major Smith. Did you tell Sergeant Doe that it was okay for him to stage a coup and assassinate Liberian civilian leaders, Mark? asked the Pentagon. "Well, I don't really think so, but. . . ." He tells the story coyly, self-amused.

When Defense Intelligence Agency officers debriefed him after his release, Smith told them that in fall 1972 B-52 strikes rained down all around the POW camp but never hit it; that an American forward air controller broadcast an audible message that the war would soon be over and played a Christmas carol; that the U.S. government obviously knew then precisely where Smith and other American soldiers were being held. The DIA men refused to confirm Smith's inference. This reticence pissed him off. It also planted in him a germinal suspicion that the 591 POWs released in February 1973 were not all there were. If the Pentagon would deny past knowledge of POWs already freed, it might also play dumb about those still in captivity.

Smith assumed command of the Special Forces Detachment (Korea) in 1981. By participating in joint U.S.-Thai parachuting exhibitions in Thailand (called Operation Meetrapop), Smith's men became the first Green Berets to touch Southeast Asian soil since the war. "Meetrapop" means "friendship" in Thai. Admission was charged and the proceeds were donated to charity. The program created substantial goodwill between the United States and Thailand, and constituted a first step in the United States' reopening of Southeast Asia—an effort which culminated in annual large-scale joint U.S.-Thai military exercises known as Operation Cobra Gold. Major Smith also used Meetrapop as cover for photographing sites in Laos where, based on information he gleaned from sources in Bangkok, he believed live POW/MIAs might be held. Smith recruited Thai soldiers to gather intelligence on POW/MIAs. He submitted his findings to his superiors. They were not pleased, as they had refused to authorize reconnaissance missions in Laos for purposes of detecting possible POW/MIAs, but Smith short-circuited straightforward disciplinary action by threatening to go public with the information. They warned him not to do so. He refused to back off and registered his intent to sue President Reagan, whom he considered "a god, a great guy" who merely wasn't paying attention.

Smith was passed over for promotion to lieutenant colonel for the second time. There may have been arguably good reasons. Smith's lack of a college degree made him ineligible for the Army's Command and General Staff College, for example, matriculation at which was preferred for promotion beyond major. His mandatory retirement due to "nonselection," after twenty years in, might also have been consistent with prevailing Army quality control measures.

Smith contends these arguments are nonsense. "Former prisoners of war, even without all these medals and all the rest, could sit in the corner and suck their thumbs and make lieutenant colonel in the United States Army. I'm no fool, I know that. It doesn't have anything to do with education, he didn't have a college degree, he wasn't a graduate of the Command and General Staff College, blah blah blah." Smith rants about another combat officer who fared better after the war. "He came back after nine years. They promoted him first to major, then to lieutenant colonel, then to full colonel. He also never went to any of those things. What happened in my case was that I chose not to be the fair-haired boy. I chose not to go to the trough and suck with the rest of the heroes, and spend my time getting a master's degree in whatever, preparing myself for a political career or sitting in the Pentagon currying favor. I stayed at the same level I had always been at— with the troops, with the soldiers. I know why the military felt so betrayed by my performance: it had been my opinion that there were no Americans left in Vietnam or Laos who didn't want to be there, I had been the proponent of the party line. Once I had proven myself wrong I was man enough to say so. The problem with a lot of my contemporaries was that none of them had been man enough to say it. Every one of them knows that there are 'people there,' but they're from this category, that category, that category."

In any event, Smith asked instead to be "retained in grade"— that is, at current rank. The request was denied. He left the army and followed through on his suit against Reagan to enjoin the government to act on evidence that POW/MIAs remained in Vietnam. *Smith* v. *Reagan* and the major's quest were featured on *60 Minutes, 20/20,* and the BBC. In 1988, however, a U.S. Court of Appeals dismissed the case as a nonjusticiable "political question." He was offered a number of "off-the-wall jobs"—advising Christian militias in Lebanon, protecting plantations as a mercenary in Papua New Guinea—but declined, somewhat offended that those who knew him by reputation seemed to think that he was in essence a professional murderer.

In 1986, Smith moved to Thailand. During his first few years there he continued undaunted his search for POW/MIAs and his attempts to secure their release. *Soldier of Fortune* magazine published a feature about and helped finance his efforts to gain public support for his cause. He declared, on the basis of Vietnamese Army and Cambodian sources, that there were 572 living soldiers held and never released by the Hanoi government in the 1970s. Many, he is sure, have died. In terms of incredibility this number did not rank with the palpably ridiculous claims, some of which exceeded five thousand. Such numbers are decisively proven untenable in several sources (nicely condensed in Arnold Isaacs's *Vietnam Shadows*), which show them to be the product of Defense Department double-counting and the military's unrealistic insistence on physical evidence for listing a soldier as killed in action. Smith does not believe such numbers. On balance, however, he has been unable to substantiate his more modest claims.

His motives for pursuing the matter are difficult to unpack. As a POW Smith heard about a Marine Corps private named Robert Garwood. The official government line on Garwood is as follows: he disappeared from the Da Nang Marine Base in South Vietnam in 1965. He lived with U.S. POWs in prison camps in South Vietnam, but not as a POW himself. Rather, he defected and collaborated with the communists. When U.S. POWs, including Smith, were released in 1973, Garwood stayed in Vietnam, where he lived freely until he had a change of heart and returned to the United States in 1979. He was convicted by a military court of collaborating with the enemy and striking an American POW.

Zalin Grant's 1975 book *Survivors,* which includes the recollections of several POWs held in the camp where Garwood lived, supports these verdicts. Some of the book's subjects testified at the court-martial. Smith himself was initially convinced of Garwood's singular guilt. Yet Grant's book also shows that other American POWs indulged in forms of collaboration which, if not as flagrant as Garwood's, were no less detrimental to POW morale or the war effort. Remembering the quisling radio voices of Hanoi Hilton POWs that his captors piped into the Kratie camp, Smith decided that Garwood had been made a scapegoat. Smith also developed the view that most POWs simply were not as tough as he was, that it was not within the capacity of most to resist breaking. The fact that he did, in his estimation, entitled him to judge the others. For some reason that remains opaque, Smith chose mercy over accountability. Bobby Garwood was a victim. When Garwood told of other American POWs still in Vietnam, Smith believed him. Under military regulations, Smith has pointed out, POWs are presumed to be under duress. The Army has a legal duty to rescue them. When the Army abdicated, Smith saw himself as filling a moral void. In doing so he vouchsafed his own abandonment.

The POW/MIA issue seems to shake out as a vehicle for self-made martyrdom. Perhaps it works better for Mark Smith than quiet, inglorious stateside retirement, which to him means "fat and fifty." There may be still more to it. In any case, now that he has backed off the POW/MIA issue to an extent, Smith comes off a more reasonable man than the fanatical crusader he has sometimes been portrayed to be. Although still convinced there are unrepatriated living POW/MIAs and unreturned remains thereof, and still proud of his lawsuit, these are not subjects that he brings up obsessively or irrationally. Of his brief celebrity a few years ago, he says he disliked the process of "becoming a personality" and simply glomming "face time." That is one reason he returned to

Thailand, and even there he could probably draw more attention to himself if he wanted to.

His opinions about the Vietnam War are not part of the pose. Mark Smith concedes that the war was badly executed on the part of the Americans, and he started to get an inkling of this after the Tet Offensive. But between August 1966 and February 1968, while leading a reconnaissance platoon in the First Infantry Division, Smith was an inspired soldier and saw many more like him. "I think being in a recon platoon helped me understand the American soldier—the motivated American soldier, the guy that wanted to be there. In 1966, we didn't have any antiwar types. Most incidents of people not wanting to fight involved older guys who thought they'd done their thing in Korea and should be in the rear and this, that, and the other thing. But we also had older NCOs who were standing in line to be platoon sergeants, really good soldiers. That's why I think the Army, when I first arrived in Vietnam, was in good shape. People were a little oriented toward a war that didn't exist there on a day-to-day basis, but could exist within thirty minutes."

In 1965, the Americans and ARVN were still up against mainly Vietcong, with their old M-1 carbines and Browning Automatic Rifles. After the Battle of the Ia Drang Valley in November 1965, Hanoi was emboldened and its commitment intensified. In 1966 and '67, the North Vietnamese Army began to pour into South Vietnam. It was much better equipped than the Vietcong had been, and Hanoi began to provide better equipment—AK-47's and RPGs—to the Vietcong too. ARVN simply was not ready for the challenge. Major Smith reasons that Vietnamization should have started in 1964, three years earlier than it actually did, when effectively probationary South Vietnamese troops had a less professional opposing force on which to cut their teeth.

But after Tet '68, in any event, the misguided American focus on body counts rather than territory, on superior force rather than superior tactics, was becoming entrenched. "By 1968 I'd gotten to know [William] Colby, and I'd gotten to know John Paul Vann. These were the philosophers of this war, and these also were the guys who didn't agree with the way it was being fought. I began to study, if there were people in a given area, an entire unit could go out and comb that area and not find them. It became obvious to me that it was because the entire unit went out to comb that area that they couldn't find them. They always knew we were coming because we always prepped the area with huge amounts of artillery and gunships and air strikes and this, that, and the other thing, to preclude being ambushed."

Whatever our war-fighting philosophy, adds Smith, our intentions were good and were, to an extent, vindicated by the communists' defeat in the Cold War. In a May 2000 letter to the *Bangkok Post* aimed at supporters of the Communist Party of Thailand, Smith defends the domino theory: "The war in Southeast Asia was not 'The American War.' It was a war waged not only to keep the communists out of Laos, Vietnam and Cambodia, but also Thailand, Malaysia, Singapore and the offshore nations. Australians, New Zealanders and Asians, including Thais, died in the thousands beside Americans to allow dupes and fools to hold up the enemy as 'heroes.' So write on in freedom, but at least take a moment to honor those who died so you would still have the right to do so. You'd never have that right in one of the 'liberated zones' of Southeast Asia." And Smith feels that in abandoning Vietnam, we left not only the South Vietnamese but also Laos and Cambodia in the lurch. These viewpoints are at once typical of career soldiers, superficially supportable, and rankly unpopular among people under fifty. Those ten months in the Kratie prison camp convinced him that the United States' overall decision to fight communism in Southeast Asia was the right one, and he remains inclined to characterize the causes of American failure in Vietnam as technocratic rather than sociologically or politically ordained.

Smith's chronological chart of South Vietnam's trajectory for winning the war is idiosyncratic. "By 1972 I was becoming fairly cynical about the war. Yet I think we nearly had it won in 1972. ARVN did it to them with U.S. air support. Then we just stopped and handed it to them. Congress modified the War Powers Act and denied the right to the president to supply anything to Vietnam, even though we had promised that we would. Anything that the North Vietnamese got, we were supposed to make sure ARVN had something to match it. It happened in even a bigger way in '75. They came in with artillery that the South Vietnamese couldn't range. Whoever has the artillery that shoots the farthest wins. That's just the way it is, because this was not guerrilla warfare now; in '72 it had become a conventional war. The NVA could engage the South Vietnamese reinforcements ten to twelve kilometers before they even got up to where they could shoot. And they came in with bigger and better tanks. The greatest myth of the Vietnam War was that the Vietnamese were happy to accept the communists if the war would just stop."

Thus is Smith a man who understands the relationship between violence and honor. In a letter to the fellow Loc Ninh combatants who supported his DSC upgrade to the Medal of Honor, Smith declared that he never hated his enemies but certainly hated what they stood for. He credited the NVA for being chivalrous on the battlefield in sparing women and children, and blamed "political types" in a sapper battalion—sappers were notoriously vicious and zealous grenade-wielding infantry—for the episode at Loc Ninh in which they were used as human shields.

His primary postwar mission now, as he has articulated it, has been to continue "the fight for freedom and democracy" in Southeast Asia that started with the Vietnam War. To him this means neutralizing the Khmer Rouge and bringing Pol Pot's former minions to justice. It is hard to argue with these objectives, though they are stated grandiosely. His means are of questionable effectiveness. On the day of our first meeting in late October he had just returned from a meeting with Khmer Rouge leaders in the Cambodian bush. Smith's standing claims were that there were some twenty thousand Khmer Rouge at large—not a mere four or five thousand as claimed by the U.S. State Department or the news media. He showed me a typed document signed by three putative Khmer Rouge leaders. In this document, they agreed to the disbandment of the Khmer Rouge and asked that its soldiers be retrained by U.S. military advisers so as to constitute "truly professional armed forces."

Smith notified journalists, but his initiative was overtaken by Hun Sen's agreeing to a coalition government with Prince Norodom Ranariddh, his decision to give the Khmer Rouge amnesty, and Washington's acquiescence thereto. While Smith may have the ear of Senator Jesse Helms and Congressman Dan Burton, the State Department, the Drug Enforcement Administration (DEA), and the CIA consider him a pain in the ass. He has written letters to *The Nation,* the more provocative of Bangkok's two English-language dailies, condemning what he considers the appeasement of Hun Sen in connection with the Khmer Rouge amnesty deal. Though fearful Thai interlocutors have accused him of "trying to start World War III," his view is far from indefensible.

If Major Smith is part charlatan, he still should not be consigned to the cadre of Vietnam "losers." For Mark Smith is also part career soldier, part loyal American, part Horatio Alger, and a large part war hero. What Smith did at Loc Ninh and thereafter was, for the most part, exemplary. He stayed put and stayed alive in a nearly hopeless situation and orchestrated the infliction of thousands of casualties on NVA and VC units. (Between April 1 and 25, 1972, the Fifth Vietcong Division that initiated the attack on Loc Ninh was 90 percent destroyed.) Smith hung tough in the prison camp. His accomplishments are real and considerable, and so therefore is his bitterness toward his detractors in the Army understandable. He *has* traveled into the Cambodian bush to meet with veterans of the most brutal regime of the twentieth century. He *does* try to do good. He *does* have balls. And he's aware of his egomania. "I figured the Army ought to put its best foot forward and I always thought that was me. That's why you'll hear, 'he's an arrogant son of a bitch.' Well, there's a lot of truth to that point."

The key to the no-bullshit facet of Mark Smith is his cigarette lighter. It is a talisman to him. Given to him by his men at his retirement in 1985, the lighter is of course a Zippo—standard issue in Vietnam. "Zippo" was also Smith's nickname, and his call sign at Loc Ninh, deriving, he says, from his much-admired practice of uncovering enemy soldiers hiding in tall fields of elephant grass and bamboo by blanketing the fields with a flamethrower. On one side is embossed "Loc Ninh" in oriental-style mock-bamboo metal letters. Below it is the insignia for Special Forces Detachment (Korea), his last command. On the other side, a parachute signifying Smith's airborne status and insignia for Special Forces, Distinguished Service Cross, Medical Corps, and Combat Infantryman's Badge.

Fifteen other American soldiers involved in the battle of Loc Ninh acknowledged, in writing, his performance as worthy of the Medal of Honor. These included a stolid, but nevertheless affirming, appraisal from a man (who retired from the Army only in the 1990s) whose own actions during the battle and in prison Smith denigrates. Some of the operative phrases, though true, were boilerplate: "bravery above and beyond the call of duty, against insurmountable odds," "heroism unsurpassed," "valorous leadership," "conspicuous gallantry," "gallant actions against overwhelming odds and with total disregard for personal safety." A few were a tad hackneyed, yet heartfelt: "the ultimate warrior cut from a piece of cloth woven of the finest fabric;" "it was a very big battle and Mark Smith has very big balls. Toughest man I ever met. I hope they don't throw away the mold." Other testimonials spoke directly and particularly to Smith's singular accomplishment: "extraordinary heroism unmatched by anyone I know"; "fearless, determined and fully in charge of his soul—from the sound of his voice he seemed to have enjoyed what he was destined to do"; "the bravest and most unselfish soldier that I have ever known"; "Mark Smith performed his duty just as Robert E. Lee had defined Duty as the most sublime word in the English language"; "I rate his performance as one of the two or three most heroic that I witnessed during my [two tours of] Vietnam service"; "I had a deep sense of another version of 'The Alamo' and a courageous last stand for freedom, God and country." All witnesses testified to Smith's preternatural calmness in the heat of battle. Bob Taylor points out that over a two-and-a-half-day period Smith continually committed acts of heroism any *one* of which might have earned someone else the U.S. military's highest award.

Nothing he has done or will do can erase Loc Ninh. To a person of Mark Smith's biases, the battle epitomized American involvement in Vietnam in its entirety. The incompetence and cowardice Major Smith witnessed in Colonel Vinh in 1972 echoed the same failings in South Vietnamese officers that daunted Lieutenant Colonel John Paul Vann in the Battle of Ap Bac almost a decade earlier, and fatefully persuaded Washington to shift the lead combat role to U.S. troops. The capacity of American firepower and military professionalism to exact immense costs on an enemy who nonetheless carried the battle salvaged that day for posterity. It is not hard to comprehend why Major Smith holds onto his commemorative Zippo, why he wants to feel it in his hand every time he lights a cigarette.

Major Mark Smith is a larger-than-life character, made larger still by his faults as well as his virtues. Patton-esque, he seemed destined to shine in combat, yet equally bound to trip over life's subtler obstacles. Whatever else, he is an authentic hero of the Vietnam War. He deserves to be honored for it.

Eric Herter with his wife Tran
Thi Hoa and daughter Saaran
Tha Tran Hoa Herter. A for-
mer Army photographer, Eric
has worked for the Associated
Press in Hanoi and is now a
freelance photographer there.
Photo by Geoffrey Clifford.
Courtesy Eric Herter.

4
VALOR IN PROTEST

It is one thing for a veteran to want to help the Vietnamese. It is quite another to live in Hanoi—the communist capital then and now; a durable source of anti-American propaganda; the victorious seat of a government that sent America packing. To be an American living in Hanoi requires a certain self-conscious defiance of history.

Surprisingly, officials at Hanoi's Noi Bai International Airport do not hassle Americans. American names and vocations are merely on the list at passport control, and briskly—if dourly—checked off. Noi Bai is separated from the city it serves by farmland and rice paddies. Along the two-lane highway, in a gauzy pre-twilight haze, men and women in conical bamboo hats stand

and bend in rice fields with water buffalo at their sides as the sun bleeds into yellow, orange, and red behind the mountains. The scene recalls many others from countless TV news spots and movies, as do the twenty-five-year-old bomb craters next to the road. "Vietnam, Vietnam, Vietnam, we've all been there," wrote Michael Herr in *Dispatches*. But the real thing begins a spiral of associations that a photograph might not: how disturbed these peasants would have felt had blade-slapping helicopters inserted a platoon of American soldiers, how nonplussed the GIs would have been if one of the peasants had ducked into the tall grass to be replaced by a sapper, how sordid a napalm strike on the Vietnamese would have seemed, or should have, to all involved. In their casual, primitive, pregnant beauty, those peasants serenely working their rice paddy evoke the strife of Americans only half a generation removed and the misfortune of a people caught in a snarl of history. It is a discomfiting sight, and weirdly an American one.

Hanoi itself is throwback quaint. Hoan Kiem Lake is opaque and a tad rank but nonetheless a decided bonus as an urban centerpiece. Skirting the water's edge are decently kept grassy park areas with shrubbery, winding pedestrian paths, and benches. A gently arcing footbridge connects to a Buddhist temple in the middle of the lake, where men practice *tai chi* and friends and lovers walk together. French colonialism survives, in harmless urbane fashion, in espresso and croissants and baguettes (better in Hanoi than in Saigon, and often up to the Parisian standard), and in old yellow houses and halls. Cyclo drivers congregate on corners and solicit fares, filling downtime by smoking and jawing. Some of the younger ones wear combat fatigues and gray caps with red stars on the front, or occasionally red-starred combat helmets: Vietminh stuff. There are trees on every street, some of which even have brick sidewalks. Otherwise the experienced pedestrian is advised to walk in the street with his back to oncoming traffic, which signals drivers that they alone are responsible for avoiding a collision with an effectively blind pedestrian. The practice bespeaks both a wantonness and a trustfulness in Vietnam's street culture.

Cabs don't cost much, and drivers take the long route to stretch the fare, but we aren't talking Nigeria here. When a driver offers his "sister," there's no hard sell. The ethic in Hanoi is more work than hustle. While café patrons sip espresso and eat brioches, preteen boys importune them to take off their shoes for a shine. If it's a go, they time the shine to coincide exactly with the customer's pleasure, and provide substitute plastic sandals while they buff. There is a decent performance standard in this.

Not everyone is employed, of course. On corners men drink beer, usually draft from a keg, or *bia hoi,* and piss obliviously in the street. They meander with their children, with whom they are unfailingly and demonstratively affectionate. It is a conspicuous quality—the Thais, for example, are very reserved in their public interactions with their children—and speaks perhaps to the Vietnamese determination to live well in avenging past hardship. To Western eyes boys are favored, and untoward attention is paid and drawn to their penises, which a doting relative will stroke until a boy is as old as five—a custom to which the misogynistic tendency of Vietnamese men might be credibly attributed.

Open-front stores full of cheap but serviceable stuff (often fictitiously labeled "Made in Germany" or "Made in USA") are generally staffed by women who buttonhole Western tourists to tempt them into a haggle, culminating, they hope, in a sale. Few speak passable English. The two parties communicate offers and counteroffers through pocket calculators. The starting price, usually quoted first in dollars, is never firm. The Vietnamese always begin the haggle with a smile, and vigilantly monitor their interlocutors for reciprocal good cheer, until the bidding process has bottomed out. Then their faces turn solemn, and they raise their hands and draw a line in the ether, and point terminally to the number on the display of the calculator. *You're in my town, I've been nice, now take it or leave it.* If the final terms are accepted, the smile reemerges instantaneously.

Where Saigon is jadedly commercial, its establishments enclosed, Hanoi is heartbreakingly primitive. Barbers set up stools on the sidewalk, place greasy mirrors on walls, and ply their trade skillfully with scissors and comb out of doors. Dentists pull teeth from groaning patients in open-air rooms set three feet back from the street. Old men reading books passively offer the use of bathroom scales placed next to them for 1,000 dong (about seven cents). Vietnamese are generally rail-thin and do not need to diet; the commercial enticement is the prospect that a customer has *gained* weight, as a little extra fat prestigiously indexes prosperity.

Government was substantially decentralized and commerce slowly privatized beginning in 1986 under the slogan *doi moi,* meaning renovation. While communist party conservatives have been reluctant to relinquish control—some inefficient state-owned and subsidized enterprises remain—they have been persuaded to do so for the sake of tangible economic benefits. The visible hand of communism, therefore, has well and truly atrophied. Vietnam has gone from Marxist-Leninism to "market-Leninism." In 1988, agriculture was de-collectivized, and the peasant household officially recognized as the basic unit of farm production. While peasants were not allowed to own land outright, they were granted long-term rights of access to land. Production increased markedly. Vietnam became the world's third-largest exporter of rice, which became the country's largest source of export revenues after oil. Between 1989 and 1992 there was major constitutional reform. The new constitution recognized five economic sectors including the private sector, expressly incorporated human rights and other freedoms, and replaced collective party responsibility for government with a ministerial system.

Thus, the forty-foot tall statue of Lenin, halfway between the bustling lake area and the somber citadel sector, seems almost tongue in cheek. His hand is emerging from his coat, and the standing Vietnamese joke is that Lenin is checking for his wallet after having been to Ho Chi Minh City. Still the authoritarian nature of Vietnamese government is far more evident in Hanoi, the nation's capital, than in Saigon. Policemen are pointedly unhelpful to Caucasians, and chastise visitors who dare to leave their sunglasses on while standing in the two-square-block promenade that surrounds Ho Chi Minh's huge mausoleum, where he lies, like Lenin, chemically preserved.

Beggars are earnestly forlorn rather than slickly guilt-tripping. The cripple who holds out his hand and says he is a war veteran actually looks the right age. Another, with no arms, simply lights a cigarette with his feet, earning a folded 5,000 dong note (the currency makes you feel rich) wedged between his toes and a knowing grimace. He might have got that way from the Christmas bombing in 1972, or he might have been born deformed. It doesn't matter. He's a metaphor.

America Contrite

Chuck Searcy, who runs charitable programs for the Vietnam Veterans of America Foundation (VVAF) in Hanoi, is known throughout the city as a friendly revisionist and reconciler. Searcy goes a step further in declaring unequivocally that the war was not only misconceived and mismanaged, but also essentially immoral.

His office, right on the lake, is a comfortable, air-conditioned ground-level suite in a villa near the opera house. Searcy is tall, thin, and loose-jointed, with watery blue eyes, a hawk-like nose, and thin lips. He looks like an elongated version of Robert Young who doesn't smile as much. In a beveled Georgia accent he speaks softly but with singular decisiveness. Vietnam and his time there have been and remain constant influences on his life: he has already carefully considered the content of every question long in advance.

Having dropped out of the University of Georgia and expecting to be drafted, Searcy enlisted in the Army in 1966. He went
to Vietnam in June 1967 not as a gung-ho patriot but as a politically conservative (Goldwater) American who grew up a strong
Presbyterian with a general sense of obligation to his country and
faith in its leaders. (Searcy's father, Hayes, fought in the Battle of
the Bulge and was a POW, liberated by Patton's army.) He viewed
communism as a "grave global threat" but "didn't have a well-for-
mulated view" about the war. "I certainly didn't know about the
war and our policy as Clinton did, for example, in his much-pub-
licized agonizing over that. Frankly, I have a lot of respect for that.
That was very unusual. Most of us didn't go to the lengths that he
did to examine the policy. So for me it was a very uninformed and
superficial attitude: somebody must know what we're doing or we
wouldn't be doing it."

En route to Vietnam, his dominant emotion was self-preserva-
tion. But the day he arrived in Saigon, after three days in Pleiku,
he was disconcerted by the fact that American transport vehicles
required protective chicken-wire over their windows to guard
against bombs launched by indigenous Vietnamese—that is, Vietcong. The distrust extended to ARVN. "The pervasive assumption was that anyone Vietnamese was the enemy. There was an
attitude of distrust, an attitude that [ARVN] was undependable,
that they either willfully or just because of incompetence endan-
gered the mission that we had assigned to them."

He was even more dismayed by the contempt—"from top to
bottom, almost institutionalized"—with which, as he perceived
it, Americans treated the Vietnamese. On his first day in-country
a seasoned enlistee drove him from Tan Son Nhat air base to his
unit. It was the rainy season. An old Vietnamese woman carrying
baskets of rice balanced on a *chogie* stick across her shoulders was
walking in the road. The driver hit a large puddle, drenching the

woman in a sheet of water. The move may or may not have been intentional. In any case, he paid her no mind. Searcy turned to look at her. She was standing in the road, wet and still, staring in soporific resignation, long beyond anger. The image stayed with Searcy, and to this day persists as his personal synecdoche for U.S. involvement in Vietnam.

Assigned to the 519th Military Intelligence Battalion, Searcy managed to avoid involvement in the Phoenix Program. He worked instead at the Combined Intelligence Center, Vietnam, which was responsible for material and document "exploitation" and for interrogation. Although military intelligence activities were formally joint American–South Vietnamese operations, most South Vietnamese intelligence personnel were not permitted to see classified materials and there was little functional interaction. Searcy was responsible for editing intelligence reports sent back to the Pentagon, and thus was able to see how facts were manipulated to cater to policymakers' wishes and biases. The job was relatively safe but certainly not hermetic. His two-hundred-strong unit, stationed in the Saigon suburb of Xao Ding, was cut off from MACV during the Tet offensive with just M-14s (REMFs sometimes weren't issued M-16s) and one M-60 machine gun. During the Vietcong withdrawal, they were surrounded by heavy action, but luckily the retreating VC had other things to worry about. Searcy did, however, lose some buddies. A close friend, Rick Ohler, had one leg blown off in "friendly fire" and later died at Walter Reed Hospital, just before he was to have the other leg amputated. Another pal from Georgia was killed when he stepped on a land mine.

Searcy was not permitted to rearrange his guard duty schedule—which was commonly done—to attend Vietnamese language classes. His superior did not consider it a valid justification. But Searcy disregarded his gratuitous admonition not to learn the language at all. He befriended his regular cyclo driver, who took him one day to have dinner with his family as curious neighbors peered in the windows. When Searcy casually told his captain that he had dined with this man's people, and pointed out on a map the location of his house on the other side of the Saigon River, the officer was shocked. "Jesus Christ, Searcy, are you crazy? That place is controlled by the VC." With equanimity Searcy responded, "Well, they were nice people. Maybe they were VC, but they were very hospitable. I don't think it was so dangerous." He doesn't know whether his friend was VC and, in retrospect, he doesn't care.

Searcy was moved to educate himself about the background of the conflict, and in his spare time read Marvin E. Gettleman's *Vietnam: History, Documents, and Opinions on a Major World Conflict.* Published in 1965, the book would become a bible for the antiwar movement. "It was a very straightforward compilation of unedited documents—everything from letters to treaties to the text of the Geneva Accords. I think it contained Ho Chi Minh's [1945] constitution. All kinds of things that were eye-openers for me. By the time I left I had read a good deal about Vietnam. I had read nothing before I came here. I couldn't even have found Vietnam on a map." This, of course, is a refrain among Vietnam veterans.

When his tour ended in mid-1968, Searcy was convinced that the American effort was misguided. "When I got home, I was really angry and very bitter about the situation here. And I was sad because I had come to like the Vietnamese people and appreciated the scenic beauty of the country and its culture and its history. I really had great respect for Vietnam and its people. For anybody who felt that way, I don't think they could help but be sad and feel pained about what I was leaving behind. For example, the area of our compound, which had been attacked during the Tet Offensive, what was once a thriving, bustling residential area—with old men and their pipes and little kids running around playing in the street, chickens and ducks and pigs, palm

trees and coconut trees and banana trees, rice cultivation—when I
left was destroyed. There was not a house left standing, there was
not a tree left standing. The only things left were our compound,
which was surgically protected, and the motor pool. Those two
military units were completely intact and unscathed. Everything
else was just blackened rubble. A painful memory."

Searcy himself escaped Vietnam free of any personal guilt or
trauma. But while some of his bitterness hinged on the suffering
of American GIs, he never felt that it was "exclusively an American sacrifice." "To me," he says, "it was a loss of tragic proportions
on both sides, and more so for the Vietnamese." (Well over one
million Vietnamese, South and North, are estimated to have died
in the war, versus 58,000 American soldiers.) In 1971, after completing his military service in Germany, Searcy returned to the
University of Georgia (earning a B.A. in political science), joined
Vietnam Veterans Against the War, and became head of the Georgia chapter. In the South, the VVAW took a more conservative
approach than it did in, say, the northeast. There was no guerrilla
theater or the like, but rather speeches to churches, schools, and
community organizations like the Kiwanis Club and the Rotary
Club, voter registration drives, and only the occasional protest or
demonstration. Still, Searcy's father considered him unpatriotic,
and Searcy became *persona non grata* in his parents' house.

His activism ceased in 1973, when the Paris accords were
signed, U.S. military involvement largely ended, and the 591
POWs were returned. After a couple of years' icy silence, Hayes
Searcy called Chuck and told him that he was "just passing
through" Athens en route from Columbia, South Carolina, where
he managed a Coca-Cola bottling plant, to Alabama to visit relatives. Would Chuck like to meet for a cup of coffee? he asked.
They sat down together at a waffle shop. After some "awkward
small talk," Chuck's father, as he remembers, said: "Your mother
and I have been doing a lot of thinking about the war. We've

decided that it's a really bad policy and doesn't make any sense, and we really ought to stop it. We've decided that you're right. We'd like for you to come home for a visit sometime." From that moment until the elder Searcy's death in 1990, father and son remained close.

After the Vietnam War ended, Searcy started and for twelve years ran a weekly community newspaper with a friend in Athens, Georgia (the *Athens Observer,* still in operation), worked in the Small Business Administration in Washington, and served as an aide to Senator Wyche Fowler (D-Ga.). "Although Vietnam was not really on my agenda, it was something that I never could quite escape from and never really wanted to. Almost every day something would make me think about Vietnam or remind me of Vietnam." In 1992 Searcy was offered the job of deputy assistant secretary of defense for POW/MIA Affairs. Senators Jesse Helms and Strom Thurmond held up his appointment on the basis of Searcy's earlier antiwar activism. Meanwhile, Searcy had returned to Vietnam for a visit and approached Bobby Muller—president of Vietnam Veterans of America Foundation, which splintered from Vietnam Veterans of America over the latter organization's suspicions that Hanoi was still holding back on POW/MIAs—with the idea of going back to Vietnam to start a humanitarian aid operation. The idea carried, and, first testing the waters after Vietnam was reopened to Americans, Searcy returned in 1995.

Since coming to Hanoi Searcy has been dubbed a "one-man Marshall Plan." On a $400,000 annual budget for Vietnam, VVAF has opened clinics for providing braces and artificial limbs to children at the Olof Palme Children's Hospital, sponsored the expansion of Bach Mai Hospital (poetic justice, given that the building was badly damaged in the 1972 Christmas bombing), established a mobile medical outreach program, trained doctors and technicians, and set up professional exchanges between the United States and Vietnam. He bankrolled the Bach Mai Hospital

project by organizing a charity bicycle race—the Vietnam Challenge—from Hanoi to Ho Chi Minh City that netted $200,000.
VVAF also helped a group called Peace Trees carry out a tree-
planting project in Quang Tri province near the former Demilita-
rized Zone (DMZ) (which had been defoliated by Agent Orange
during the war), followed by the construction of a land mines education center where children will be taught how to recognize and
avoid unexploded ordnance. Next on his agenda are a program for
eradicating Japanese encephalitis—a scourge of children in rural
Vietnam that can kill, paralyze, or mentally impair them—and a
pilot project with the Ministry of Police to improve traffic safety.

Searcy does not see his considerable efforts as something primarily to be proud of. Rather, he characterizes his attitude as one
of gratitude for the opportunity to make amends to the Vietnamese people for what, he believes, must be regarded historically
as a colossal, tragically destructive misstep. "It's the kind of experience that so many of us [vets] have wanted, and I'm one of the
lucky ones who found a way to come back here and do something
that's beneficial for the people of Vietnam." The Vietnamese, he
says, have been extraordinarily forgiving in light of the egregious
circumstances. He gives Vietnam policymakers "the benefit of the
doubt" in conceding that the war may have been intended to benefit the Vietnamese, but still a "monumental policy mistake" and
a failure of leadership. "I don't think there was any deliberate mal-
ice toward Vietnam or the Vietnamese people, but I think there
was an awful lot of arrogance and deliberate avoidance of [Viet-
namese] history, culture, and politics and of trying to determine
who the Vietnamese were and what their national agenda was."

Moreover, he regards as indefensible the United States' punitive behavior (derisory humanitarian aid budgets, attempts to
deny Vietnam assistance from the International Monetary Fund
and the World Bank, the long-term communications blackout,
and protracted refusal to lift the trade embargo) subsequent to

1975. In his view, one of the serendipitous ironies of the POW/MIA quest—which he believes, with some justification, has been hijacked by cynical extremists and used as a pretext for the continued castigation of Hanoi—is that Vietnam's extraordinary level of cooperation has brought the two countries closer together, and perhaps broken the ice with respect to large-scale reconciliation. "They have done more than any country could be expected to." Younger military officers who worked on the Joint Task Force for a Full Accounting of MIAs, locating the remains of American soldiers in Vietnam, back up this point.

Searcy thinks it's about time the United States showed some compassion and appreciation. Indeed, in 2000 diplomatic and trade relations were substantially normalized. "I was involved personally, and the U.S. as a nation was largely responsible for the devastation [of Vietnam] which has resulted in such a slow recovery. And after the war, in a very punitive way, we tried to isolate Vietnam, cut off Vietnam, strangle the country. And we succeeded to some extent. They really went through some terrible times—worsened by the government's ineptitude, by its inability to deal with governance as opposed to waging a war. I mean, we didn't even allow medicines to be imported under the embargo. Only last year [1997] did the Vietnamese announce no reported cases of polio, and that should have been eradicated years ago. So the U.S., I think, has never provided the kind of accountability and responsibility that should be graciously offered under circumstances as tragic as this. And the Vietnamese don't want to blame us, they don't want any abject apology. They just want something."

A story from Searcy's antiwar salad days acts as his touchstone for reconciliation between Americans divided over the war. When he returned to the University of Georgia in 1971 after serving in Vietnam, Dean Rusk (secretary of state under Kennedy and Johnson, and an unwavering advocate of U.S. intervention in Southeast Asia) had left the government and become a professor at the University of Georgia Law School. Rusk stated in an article in the campus newspaper that he had no knowledge of any war crimes or atrocities committed by U.S. troops in Vietnam. Then active in the VVAW, and shocked by the recent My Lai revelations, Searcy wrote an angry letter to the editor suggesting that Rusk was not being honest. Rusk published a letter of his own, reiterating that he had never seen any reports of atrocities. Searcy, disinclined to continue the debate in print, then called Rusk's office and made an appointment for a fifteen-minute meeting.

The two met and got into a heated debate about the whole war effort, in which Searcy said that he found it incredible that a man of Rusk's intelligence, experience, and stature could have carried out such a wrong-headed policy. Rusk angrily responded that Searcy failed to understand the hostile intentions of the Soviet Union and China. Searcy returned that he did not condone those countries' actions but could influence only those of his own government. An hour of loud argument passed. They were at an impasse and shook "clammy hands." Searcy left the office and was chagrined to see an array of "ashen" and "embarrassed" law students—Rusk's backed-up appointments. They had heard the whole exchange.

About five years later, Searcy was running his weekly newspaper, the *Athens Observer.* A young community newspaper publisher from Alaska, with relatives in Georgia, called on him to learn how better to run his own enterprise. His name was Rich Rusk. After a few days and a few beers, Searcy asked him who his relatives in Georgia were. "My father teaches at the University of Georgia Law School, but I grew up in Washington," he said. *"Dean* Rusk?" asked Searcy. The young man said yes, and subsequently explained that he and his father had a bad falling-out over the Vietnam War, impelling Rich to move "as far away from Washington as I could get." By this time Searcy had mended fences with his own father, who had come to see the Vietnam War as futile, and the Rusks had enjoyed a partial rapprochement.

A few weeks later, Searcy ran into Dean Rusk at a dinner. They spoke politely but stiffly. Searcy allowed as how he'd met Rusk's son and liked him. Rusk responded that Rich had liked Searcy also, and added that he, Rusk Sr., thought Searcy's paper was very good. They shook hands and parted, but Searcy was left with a nagging sense of "inconclusiveness." The next day he called Dean Rusk and said he did not want to leave their old debate hanging. Rusk told Searcy to get a couple of sandwiches and come to his office for lunch. This time there were no students waiting. Searcy reiterated that the Vietnam War was misguided. Rusk calmly stated that the United States did the best that it could at the time. Though Rusk did not say so, Searcy sensed that his views on the war had moderated. The two "civilly" agreed to disagree. They became good friends and got together frequently in the ensuing years.

In December 1994, a couple of weeks before Searcy was due to relocate to Vietnam for VVAF, Rich Rusk called him to say that his father had passed away. Searcy attended Dean Rusk's funeral a week before boarding the plane to Hanoi. During that lunch conversation over twenty years earlier, when Dean Rusk said that he did what he thought was right at the time, Searcy felt he was genuine and gained new respect for the man. That was possible because the war was over. Both men, at least, were glad of that. Rusk also came to respect Searcy and his views—otherwise, the two would not have maintained contact and, indeed, become more than acquaintances. Perhaps for Rusk, Chuck Searcy was a stand-in for all the other GIs he helped send to war, and a kind of conduit to his own son and the corresponding generation. Whatever was in Rusk's own heart, from Searcy's point of view the relationship was a dream come true: a dialogue with the powers-that-be of the Vietnam era—one which thousands of antiwar activists could only have conducted in their bathroom mirrors.

The United States itself, in his opinion, has not enjoyed a comparable collective dialogue. "I think we would learn so much more about ourselves and so much more about the appropriate role for the U.S. to play in the world if we better understood how we got into Vietnam, the decisions that were made and the mistakes that ensued, and therefore how we might avoid similar mistakes in the future. But unfortunately, I think, broadly speaking, we have learned very little from Vietnam. We want to avoid a painful experience like that again, but we don't understand the real reasons why it occurred. It's very superficial. To some extent, it's a long-term institutional reaction—distance and avoidance, and not wishing to analyze or evaluate for any useful purpose what really happened there. We don't want to talk about it. I mean, in 1975, we basically turned our backs on Vietnam and a very dark curtain dropped over Vietnam as far as the U.S. was concerned. The only changes in our attitude after [the U.S. withdrew from Vietnam] were a hardening of the negative views based on the flight of the boat people, and the terrible conditions in the country at that time—which we of course blamed wholly on the unified government. It was partly true, but not entirely true—a lot of [the hardship] was due to the embargo we imposed. And then the POW/MIA issue was promoted to mythological proportions in the U.S., so the U.S. has just had an erroneous perception of Vietnam ever since."

Searcy sees his current duty as correcting that misperception. "I and most other Americans who are here, because of the unique nature of our history and the relationship between the U.S. and Vietnam, feel a certain level of responsibility to be ambassadors with a small 'a' and to convey the good aspects of the U.S. and its policies, and the fact that a lot of people didn't endorse or embrace the war policies. But whether we did or did not, a lot of people want to show the Vietnamese that we can move beyond that and establish a new and a better relationship. And at the same time, when we go back to the U.S.—I think anyone who has spent some time here feels that we have a mission to try to explain to Americans the reality of Vietnam today."

Searcy's wholesale rejection of the war and the VVAF imprimatur (Bobby Muller led the first group of Vietnam veterans to return in-country in 1981) makes it easy for him to get along with the Vietnamese. He is, in fact, not merely their friend but their advocate. "It's unfair the way Americans view the Vietnamese," he says. "We either put them out of our minds, or we think of them with anger and bitterness and blame. There's a lot to be angry about, but it shouldn't be directed toward the people of Vietnam."

When a Vietnamese woman harangued him about the way Agent Orange deformed her daughter's hand, his heart as well as his social sense moved him only to sanction her outrage and admit his country's transgression, and to hook her up with a surgeon who could help her daughter. In a bar, when a well-oiled younger woman angrily put him on the spot with the question, "What do you think of the terrible things your country did to my country?," Searcy was inclined simply to nod and hand her his business card to encourage a more sober conversation later. The next morning she called to apologize, and they talked more amicably about the Vietnam War. An ex-Marine friend of Searcy's, Joe Bangert, met an old woman in Quang Tri province, who, after confirming his nationality, catalogued her losses from the war: three sons killed, two brothers killed, her house destroyed twice, family separated, water buffalo and pigs killed. After ticking off these debits on her fingers, she asked, "What do you think about that?" He said that he couldn't go back and change anything but he was sorry, very sorry. She folded her hands, bowed, thanked him, and walked away.

Toward Searcy the Vietnamese have been, he says, "either warm or welcoming or disinterested" but rarely hostile. Other than drunken bar fights he has heard about, those three incidents are the only resentment-fueled Vietnamese-American confrontations that Searcy knows of. Even allowing for Searcy's benign, apologetic countenance, this seems a remarkable fact. At this stage, his views are familiar about town, so the social pressure is off. His barber on Hang Hanh, when about to apply the straight razor to Searcy's chin for a shave, one day said to him while brandishing the blade, "Are you afraid?" Then he teased, "I am VC!" The barber knows Searcy, knows he's a veteran, and has shown interest in his war experiences, laughing jocularly when Searcy admits to having been frightened at times during the war.

Searcy is a novel part of Hanoi's cityscape. People wave to him as he rides through town on his motor scooter, cab drivers zip automatically to his favorite restaurants, waiters know he is a vegetarian and bring him the right beer without having to ask. His Vietnamese friends continually set up the twice-divorced Searcy with fetching Vietnamese women in an undisguised campaign to marry him off. No magic yet—they never seem to be older than twenty-eight, and he runs out of conversational fodder quickly— but it's the thought that counts. His relationship to the Vietnamese is altogether cozy. From his standpoint, this is not at all craven but utterly consonant with his condemnatory view of the war. Yet Searcy still considers himself an American patriot, at least under his own definition: he does not proffer blind allegiance to just any U.S. policy, but rather feels a strong sense of responsibility to act as a thoughtful citizen to promote and support the best interests of the United States and to help his government to do the right thing.

In keeping with this attitude, Searcy gives a learned exposition of the revisionist view of the Vietnam War. It is misleading to cast the conflict as a mere civil war with a Cold War overlay, he says, in which one side was supported by the United States and the other by the Soviet Union and China. From the Vietnamese perspective, the United States (on grounds of containment) denied their country the independence they had earned by defeating the French at Dien Bien Phu in 1954. The north-south boundary and the DMZ were intended to be temporary, drawn only to allow for an orderly French withdrawal and overall demilitarization; the planned nationwide election would have inevitably resulted in a victory for Ho Chi Minh. Further, the United States had spurned his overtures of a *rapprochement* in favor of French colonial interests—here Searcy cites Ho's letters to Roosevelt and Truman—and forcibly delayed the national election for twenty years.

By Searcy's reckoning, the Vietnamese had little choice but to enlist the communist great powers to help them wrest what was rightfully theirs from the United States. The United States may have had valid geopolitical reasons for trying to entrench anticommunist democracy in Vietnam. But, continues Searcy, though Washington earnestly attempted to install a viable democratic government in South Vietnam, Diem's inability to inspire the confidence of the southern population probably—and Nguyen Cao Ky and Nguyen Van Thieu's failure to do so clearly—showed that the American experiment had failed. The U.S. should then have given up.

Still, Searcy's case does not completely cleanse the brutal North Vietnamese regime of blame, or negate the concerns of committed anticommunists in South Vietnam or critics of the current government. And to cite the failure to co-opt Ho Chi Minh in the forties and fifties as a reason not to intervene in the sixties, as Searcy and others sometimes seem to do, is like arguing that the British should have appeased Hitler because the Treaty of Versailles was ill-advised. Not even the brilliant arch-revisionist A. J. P. Taylor would make that claim. And in any case, given Ho Chi Minh's Maoist "land reform" terror in the 1950s, the notion that Uncle Ho was more an avuncular nationalist than a hard-line communist who could have been controlled had the United States seized the day in 1945 is hardly a slam-dunk.

Finally, Searcy may go too far in excusing Hanoi's "unapologetic" response to human rights critics as a genuine expression of the official view that Western standards are culturally unsuited to Vietnam. "The police are oriented toward stability and security," he explains rather palliatively, "and they're held responsible for any criminal problem in the neighborhood, so they have to keep tabs on people. I don't see it as at all malicious. The government may not be completely benign, but I really think that they take the interests of the people to heart."

Dean Rusk might view this stance as exceeding their agreement to disagree. There may be a more judicious balance to be struck between the renunciation of brutal neocolonialism and the endorsement of equally pitiless authoritarianism than Searcy might allow. But his critical, searching treatment of his own Vietnam experience has enabled him to live nobly by a qualified definition of patriotism. While his dedication to abnegating virtually all official American policies with respect to Vietnam is unsettling, it would be a mistake to tally up Chuck Searcy to political correctness.

AMERICA LOST

If Searcy remains a tentative patriot, Eric Herter, to his own sorrow, cannot say the same. There is fine irony there, because he's cut from the same cloth as many of "the best and the brightest." Christened Frederic P. Herter, Jr., he was raised in Boston. His grandfather was Christian Herter—a congressman, then governor of Massachusetts, and later secretary of state in the Eisenhower administration after John Foster Dulles's death. His father was a well-known Boston cardiologist, and served in Japan during the postwar occupation. During that period Herter's mother died, and at age three he went to live with his grandparents. His father returned to the United States and remarried. They moved to New York.

A tall, willowy man with brown eyes, ample iron-gray hair, and a trimmed beard, Herter moves elegantly and speaks in an offhand, professorial key befitting, perhaps, a cool diplomat. He went to St. Paul's School, then Harvard, graduating in 1966 with a degree in "government," which meant twentieth-century history. He disliked the homogeneous composition of St. Paul's— "little preppy boys, looking like Wall Street lawyers and government bureaucrats"—but he found Harvard energizing. "I got there in the early sixties, and Bob Dylan and Joan Baez and the Jim Kweskin Jug Band and leading edge of hippie craziness was happening there. It was wonderful. Leary was dosing people and it was legal. Now it would look kind of quaint, like something from *Laugh-In,* but there were parties in lofts with bicycles and umbrellas hanging from the ceiling. For somebody whose background was conventional until then, it was a real eye-opener. It was really fun. And I practically flunked out."

He did not think much about Vietnam. Like most students, he got into the "flower power" rising in Cambridge and was generally against war, though not an abject pacifist. But he had seen the war photographs of Larry Burrows in *Life* magazine and knew he wanted no part of Vietnam. (Burrows, a Briton, was killed with four other photographers in February 1971, covering South Vietnam's invasion of Laos in Operation Lam Son 719, when their helicopter was shot down by the NVA.) Like many young men on the East and West Coasts in the mid-sixties, Herter was a desultory proto-hippie, not a budding soldier. The last course he had to take to meet his major requirement was a dull one on the government bureaucracy, which Herter took to skipping in favor of a class on impressionist painting known as "Spots and Dots." "This guy would just weave word-magic while you sat in the dark and watched slides." When the final exam was imminent, he had read nothing. He took some speed, read what he could overnight, and wrote gag answers in his blue book. Herter failed the bureaucracy course, effectively delaying his graduation until the fall. Immediately thereafter he was drafted into the Army.

He tried unsuccessfully to finesse induction by diverting to the Peace Corps. He thought about Canada or jail (conscientious objector standards then were too stringent—"you had to have been a Quaker or a Mennonite"—to work for him), but his father and grandfather informed him that Herters did not shirk their duty. His uncle, a hero of the Battle of the Bulge, encouraged him to go to Vietnam and talked about honor and country and duty, and about the prospect of family shame. Herter felt no palpable sense of duty or patriotism, but he listened to the part about shame. He convinced himself, à la Camus, that even as a soldier he would always have an existential choice about whether or not to follow an order. "I bought that idea," he remembers, "and I said to myself, this is my ticket to a clean conscience. If you knew that you could say no, no matter what, it seemed to me that you'd come out morally okay. By the time I'd finished a year in Vietnam I couldn't believe that anymore."

After basic training Herter was sent to film school at Fort Monmouth, New Jersey, where he graduated first in his class. That level of achievement usually meant an instructorship, and exemption from Vietnam. The Army, however, was bringing out the rebel in Herter. He made one movie entitled *The Army Donut Factory* by filming upside-down a row of hungry GIs eating donut after donut, then running the film right side-up and backwards. The effect was to depict the soldiers regurgitating whole, intact donuts and neatly wrapping them in cellophane. Everybody thought it was funny except Herter's superior. No instructorship. Vietnam instead.

When Herter got to Saigon, he was a fish out of water. Herter, like Searcy, found the chicken wire over the transport vehicle windows inconsonant with a people who were supposed to be over the moon about getting American help. The Ivy Leaguer, inevitably a patrician liberal, also didn't like to hear blue-collar guys calling the Vietnamese "gooks," just as he'd have objected to their calling blacks "niggers." More substantially, he saw GIs bully Vietnamese like slaves, when they were supposed to be helping them. "All of a sudden these eighteen-year old American boys had Vietnamese servants," he recalls. Rather than allowing a young Vietnamese woman whom Herter had befriended a week off to have her baby, her GI employers summarily fired her.

Neither Herter's sheltered upbringing nor his refined sensibilities mixed well with military machismo. "I had no idea what to expect. I had never known anybody that was Asian. You know, one guy in the prep school that I went to was from China. The idea of a whole Asian country and everyone doing things differently—I didn't know what to expect, but I thought it was going to be massively different. On about my second or third day I walked into this club at Tan Son Nhat Airport in Saigon, where I was being processed with other people who had arrived at the same time. In this club was a twenty-year-old Vietnamese girl in an *ao dai* [the traditional Vietnamese dress for women: roomy flared pants and a matching top that binds tightly around the midriff, has a Chinese collar, slits at the waist, and hangs loosely down to the shins], singing French songs. She weighs eighty-five pounds, she's kind of like a bird, she's so tiny and slender and fragile. She's singing songs in French, and these big American sergeants are down in the front row slamming their beer bottles on the table, saying, 'Take it off, take it off, come on, enough of this shit, take it off!' She's trembling. And I'm seeing *Casablanca.* I'm seeing the Germans in that café."

At the same time, the Vietnamese now became human to him. Herter made some Vietnamese friends and rapidly developed a great affection for the people. Correspondingly, their dehumanization—hearing MPs talk graphically about killing them on the base perimeter, listening to one soldier speak salaciously about a Vietnamese woman who'd been shot dead and had given birth posthumously, seeing fellow Army photographers develop pho-

tographs of severed Vietcong arms and legs in the camp dark-
room—became increasingly hard for him to take. "You've read
Tim O'Brien, and it's true. All the Vietnamese were slopes and
gooks and dinks, and they weren't worth shit. And there was also
the stuff about death itself—'Joe just got greased'—you played it
all down because deep in your heart you were fucking terrified."
He didn't even want to see any helicopters come in from a medevac. And he decided that whatever was going on in Vietnam, the
Americans were not the good guys. After six weeks, Herter says,
"I was building a case for extricating myself because I felt like I
was going to be in trouble trying to explain this to my grandchil-
dren."

Though assigned relatively safe cameraman duty at the eighty-
square-mile Long Binh army base, he told a kindred superior that
he was disgusted and might just put on civilian clothes, go
AWOL, hitchhike to Tan Son Nhat, and explain his moral objections to the war to the powers that were, and go home. The
man—also skeptical of the U.S. effort—suggested that rather
than landing himself in Leavenworth, Herter should try to find
himself a humanitarian job in Saigon. This new benefactor would
cover for him. But Herter's quest was unavailing, as pacifistic
Buddhists couldn't give a serving GI work. In desperation, he
called on Ogden Williams, who was the pointman for the U.S.
Agency for International Development (USAID) in Saigon.
Williams was recruiting for advisers for USAID's end of the Chieu
Hoi program, which involved printing and distributing leaflets in
the effort to convince Vietcong to defect. And, as it happened, he
had known Herter's father at St. Paul's.

Herter expressed his reluctance to be part of a war effort he had
come to philosophically oppose. Williams smoothly argued that
in successfully marketing voluntary defection the Chieu Hoi program had taken 25,000 Vietcong out of the war—at least for the
standard one-year period of detention and debriefing, indoctrina-

tion, civilian employment, and exemption from conscription—who otherwise would have continued as Vietcong or, if captured, would have been jailed, killed, or forced immediately into South Vietnamese military service. Thus, explained Williams, the program was the only way any Vietnamese male, aged fifteen to forty-five, could get a break from combat. Torture or abuse, he assured Herter, was absolutely forbidden. "Without a lot of enthusiasm," remembers Herter, "I agreed."

Herter had tapped into the old boy network in spite of himself. In late 1967, Herter went "on loan" to a USAID advisory team to the multi-agency Civil Operations and Revolutionary Development Support (CORDS) mission in Ba Xuyen province in IV Corps, in the Mekong Delta south of Saigon and away from the heavy action, which at that time was up north. The job was designated for an Army major, but an exception was made for Herter whereby he was bureaucratically made a temporary civilian. The principal agency involved in CORDS was the CIA, and the Phoenix Program was part of the overall package. But while Mark Smith would soon be liquidating Vietcong with Fifth Special Forces under the auspices of CORDS, Eric Herter was trying to avoid anything remotely like that.

Herter's immediate boss was a Major Riddle of the Australian army who sported a swagger stick, a bigot who told Herter that the worst moment in Aussie history was when the government allowed Aborigines to attend universities and "to think they were human," the best moment when they were rounded up and driven off cliffs. The province senior adviser was an ex-USMC colonel named Nicholas George Washington Thorne—Herter invariably refers to him by all four names, framing the "George Washington" in off-key tones of casual disdain—who wore drip-dry suits and carried a little Beretta in a shammy holster. Also attached to a swagger stick, he exuded the insidious aristocratic air and Greenian cynicism of the ugly American. Though "a great raconteur and a cultured gentleman who played Bach and Mozart on his big Akai tape-recorder," Thorne was, to Herter, no better than the noncoms who littered their banter with "gook": a redneck in an ascot.

Among his frequent visitors was Robert Thompson, the Brit who had masterminded the neutralization of Malayan guerrillas, authored *Defeating Communist Insurgency* (highly recommended to all CORDS employees), and designed the United States' early pacification program in Vietnam. "Thompson would show up in Ba Xuyan province, Thorne would regale him with anecdotes. They'd drink good brandy out of nice glasses and smoke big cigars and tell great war stories. They were Kipling characters. And [Steve] Shepley [Thorne's assistant] had it written under the glass on his desk: 'East is East, West is West, and never the twain shall meet.' He was living the Kipling mythology." (Ogden Williams, Herter notes by-the-by, committed suicide. "I had the feeling that he was a humane man, and I had the feeling that he decided that he'd made a major mistake somehow in being involved in USAID in Vietnam. I think he was involved for a long time.")

Shepley showed Herter the ropes. Son of an American publisher, he wore tailored tiger-striped camouflage suits and blue-tinted French half-moon glasses. Herter likens his appearance to that of "a jungle fighter in drag," and speculates that he was "being bad in Vietnam, his parents' worst dream." On paper, then, this collection of men did not comprise the ideal custodians for young, frightened Asians.

Moreover, according to Herter, the program tended not to deliver what it promised. Those who admitted to having been Vietcong were rarely given civilian jobs. Instead, after the sixty-day detention period, they were organized into paramilitary units known as armed propaganda teams, or APTs, who would travel to contested villages with loudspeakers and extend bribes to Vietcong to defect. A particular incident sticks in Herter's memory.

On his first day, he was present when two APT members saw a young villager run and gave chase. As they converged on him, he turned around and pulled the cord on a Claymore directional mine that was strapped to his stomach. He cut himself in half and blew off his pursuers' hands and faces and tore open their torsos. Back at the Chieu Hoi center, the APT men's bodies were placed under yellow- and red-striped South Vietnam flags, blood soaking through them as their teenage wives lay crying on the top of the featureless, cloth-covered heaps. "Steve Shepley in his tiger suit, with proper deference, gently pulled one of the widows to her feet, drew a big wad of bills out of his pocket, handed her some U.S. dollars, and said, 'On behalf of the South Vietnamese government and the U.S. Army, I'd like to give you something for your husband.' That was my introduction to the Chieu Hoi program."

Yet, at the Chieu Hoi detention center in his province, a converted old farm, Herter never saw any Vietnamese mistreated by Americans or South Vietnamese. The detainees included both boys and girls. Their average age was eighteen, but some were as young as thirteen. Every morning Nicholas George Washington Thorne, Major Riddle, and the CORDS advisory team (two CIA officers, and an FBI man charged with training the local police), would brief Herter and his fellow Chieu Hoi advisers. "As much as I could at that time, I opposed what I saw going on, yet I didn't really see a great way out." So, to the extent that he could do so short of court-martial, he turned his back on the war, smoking marijuana, drinking a fair bit, developing an empathic friendship with his Vietnamese interpreter.

The Americans in Ba Xuyan province did not push the South Vietnamese toward armed engagement with the Vietcong. As Herter snidely puts it: "The South Vietnamese had good sources of intelligence—you know, everybody's related to everybody else. They'd know that the Vietcong were moving around to the northeast, so they'd go off in tanks and trucks and bandannas and machine-gun bandoliers to the southwest. They'd steal some chickens, cook them for dinner, maybe rape somebody, have a good day, and come back home. No contact. They were purposely avoiding each other." With impunity communists would sit and drink booze-spiked smoothies alongside Herter in the village near the Chieu Hoi center. "It was a *Catch-22* kind of non-war up until the Tet Offensive." That massive VC operation was a watershed in Herter's personal history as well as that of the war.

It was also, of course, a surprise. On the first night of Tet, the Buddhist new year, Herter put together a pantomime mocking both sides of the Vietnam War, to which he had archly invited Nicholas George Washington Thorne and all the other CORDS honchos. They all sat in folding wooden chairs and enjoyed the fun. At midnight, Herter was sitting in his room on the second floor of a two-story tavern/whorehouse requisitioned by the U.S. known as the Bungalow Bar, sipping drinks and loading tracer rounds into an old M-1 carbine, firing them into the air in celebration as firecrackers burst all around. Then he heard the more ominous sound of machine-guns. Before long the Bungalow Bar was taking fire in the windows.

The attack tapered off by morning, when Thorne held a meeting. "Thorne's roaring drunk," recalls Herter, "staggering around talking about 'little dink assholes with penis envy' and their little pop guns and how they think they're going to scare us. A very weird rant." Later in the day the CORDS team got intelligence reports that they would likely be overrun that night. Herter's reaction was to flirt giddily with the Vietnamese girl who put ice down his shirt. "Everybody's in this semi-delirious mood because we're gonna die. There's nobody to rescue us. People are on the phone to Saigon, and Saigon is saying everybody everywhere is fucked, don't expect any help." They hauled a crate of grenades to the second floor of the Bungalow Bar. At some interlude during Herter's game of slap-and-tickle with the Vietnamese girl, a Peace

Corps volunteer type performed a wedding ceremony. As far as she was concerned, Herter was her husband. They slept together platonically that night, and in time the relationship would grow sexual. Near the end of Herter's tour, she would become pregnant.

The next day the Chieu Hoi team burned its documents and evacuated the center, relocating to a secure air base ten miles away. Nothing happened, so they returned to town the next day. That night the Vietcong attacked in force. They overran the ARVN barracks, across the street from the Bungalow Bar, and took undeployed ARVN soldiers and their wives hostage as insurance against counterattack. Herter and other Chieu Hoi personnel were holed up yards away, on the verge of capture. He was elated to see two F-4s swoop in to liberate the area. His relief—indeed, his latent patriotic appreciation—turned to horror when the two planes bombed, napalmed, and strafed the area. More planes and helicopters followed. By the time the air attack was over, "thousands and thousands" of Vietnamese civilians were dead. Thenceforth he spent his days smoking pot. If anybody asked him about anything operational, he would simply answer, "It's all fucked, I'm waiting to go home."

At this point, due to a combination of sympathy for the Vietnamese and disgust with his compatriots, Herter felt more Vietnamese than American. This mind-set had been long in developing. "When I overheard the talk about arms and legs in the photo lab—I think from that point on I had checked out of the U.S. effort. I was against it, I was happy to see it get thwarted. I was not a communist, I was not explicitly on the other side, but I was against the U.S. I thought the U.S. was arrogant, and had no regard whatsoever for the Vietnamese, who I thought were admirable people in many ways—amazingly resilient in the face of disaster, amazingly humorous and amazingly willing to communicate with gigantic weird foreigners who'd come to trample all over their country and call them gooks. Humane people in one way or the other, and the U.S. was destroying things in a very unknowing and unseeing way. Essentially, the idea was that it doesn't matter who the Vietnamese are or what they think or how to speak their language—we have so much force that sooner or later they're going to do it our way."

De facto, then, Herter did back the communists in Vietnam. He came to view the entire U.S. involvement as "somewhere between misconceived and criminal, and way more on the side of criminal." He does not concede even that Washington meant well. "There were well-intentioned people involved in the war effort, and there were well-intentioned people who supported the war effort, but they were grotesquely misinformed primarily by the U.S. government and the U.S. military. I think the press actually was fairly heroic, and I give the press a certain amount of credit for creating the antiwar movement and building its strength until the war became politically untenable. Anything the U.S. was doing, like pediatric surgery by the Quakers—fixing children who were bleeding from shrapnel or bomb pellets or bits of a mine or whatever—was misbegotten. The kindness of the doctors was part of the American propaganda that showed how good we were and how right our cause was. My feeling was that even the doctors shouldn't be here. Nobody should be here. It's not just that it isn't our business, it's that we had absolutely no understanding at all of Vietnam or the Vietnamese people or what they're doing or what they think of us."

Herter's enduring belief was that the Vietnamese were a morally superior people, and might well forge a wonderful country without malevolent U.S. interference. He DEROSed, got his Good Conduct Medal and the other standard decorations, and was honorably discharged in October 1968, intending to return to Vietnam to retrieve his wife and baby. She lost the baby. When he heard this from a mutual friend, he decided not to return. He lost focus, and tried acid for the first time in the middle of a cornfield in Indiana. For a year Herter became a "zonked out hippie," addled with "drugs and despair," fearing and loathing across the country in his VW van, taking refuge in the occasional crash-pad: a cliché. Then the My Lai story broke.

For Herter it was a twisted inspiration, but a fleeting one. "There were antiwar people who made big blowups of the body-strewn pathway [at My Lai] and they read, 'And Babies: Lieutenant Calley's Answer.' I watched with, I've got to say, a kind of maniacal glee as the story moved from page thirty-eight of *The New York Times* to page one, to the color spread in *Life* magazine to the posters on the sides of the buses. Because now people were going to understand: this was a fucking atrocity, and it had to stop now. Then, when *The Ballad of Rusty Calley* came out, when he goes to Heaven and salutes the big commanding officer in the sky and says, 'I did my duty, sir,' and when Congress debated and decided it was okay, and when Calley and two other people were convicted of depriving twenty-two Oriental human beings of their human rights after over five hundred were killed—when all of that happened and Calley gets put in his bachelor officer's quarters with a bar and his girlfriend and his subscription to *Playboy* and his color TV and he gets his sentence overturned [in fact, commuted] by Nixon several years later, that's when I just gave up."

Calley was released on parole after serving three and a half years under house arrest. In Herter's view, if the American public's inclination to deny and rationalize was so strong as to exonerate Calley, nothing he could do or say could possibly drive home how wrong the war was. "I was burned out and washed up and ready to die. I didn't care about anything. I'd fried my brain on lots and lots of pot, acid, and amphetamines. I'd been to every rock concert standing next to the speakers, I'd been to every demonstration standing next to the speakers." À la Kerouac, Herter remembers, "I had a huge crash and breakdown in New York City, where I just barricaded myself in a third-floor apartment with no telephone, no doorbell, absolutely no way even the best-meaning friend could get to me, locked in with a record that played the sounds of waves breaking at 16 rpm all day to drown out the sound of traffic and people saying 'fuck you' to each other. I took a sledgehammer to all the partition walls. I thought it would be nice to have one big room. I ate TV dinners because I couldn't face going out in the street. I slept all the time." With cool understatement he concludes: "I was depressed."

Herter, adrift, moved back to Cambridge, Massachusetts, and started to work on a book on the value of the arts as a catalyst for community life. He also seized a small opportunity to air his angst publicly. Just before his income tax return was due in spring 1971, Herter hand-delivered an open letter to the Internal Revenue Service to the *Boston Globe.* Accompanied by a photograph Herter had taken of two dead Vietnamese boys—one face-down, the other spread-eagled on his back—the letter occupied a full page of the newspaper of April 16, 1971. In pertinent part, it read as follows:

Dear Sirs:

Enclosed (above) is a picture I took of two of the enemy shortly after the Tet offensive of 1968, while I was serving in the Army in Soc Trang, Republic of South Vietnam. The ropes with which the armored personnel carriers towed their bodies can still be seen, tied around the ankle of one, the neck of the other. If they were lucky, they were dead when they were captured.

They could be brothers. The older of the two was, maybe, 17 or 18; the younger, 14 at most. Neither got any older than they were the day I took their picture; they were and are the Viet Cong—the inhuman, faceless enemy we kill and kill and can't rid ourselves of.

They were VC, perhaps, because they and their family grew up in an area which had known no government other than the Viet Minh and the VC since the fall of the Japanese government of occupation at the end of the Second World War.

They were VC, perhaps, because their father was machine-gunned—for fun—by a passing helicopter gunship. Or their VC uncle was captured and tortured to death by the South Vietnamese National Police. Or their older sister went off and became a whore for the American GIs. Or their grandparents were burned to death by white phosphorous. Or their baby sister was blown to small bleeding bits by a random round of Harassment and Interdiction fire.

There are lots of reasons for becoming VC—many of them provided by our presence and our conduct of the war, rather than by Communist propaganda.

I doubt seriously that either of them really understood much about either Communism or the free-enterprise system. Most likely, they simply thought of us as invaders of their country, bombers and torturers of their people, corrupters of their culture, destroyers of their lands and cities. And they had the courage, at an age when American kids are in the 8th and 11th grades at school, to stand up and fight the invader. And be killed by him.

This was three years ago, and they and many others like them have been sprinkled with lime, then stacked with other bodies, then bulldozed into ditches and buried. These boys' parents never received what was left of them in an aluminum box with a flag on it. And I have done nothing about them until now, except print the picture of their bodies.

I have a lot of other pictures of Vietnam, both on film and in my head, which I have done nothing with, either. But I am sending you this one to explain, in some small way, why I am not paying a percentage of my income tax this year. I should have done this long ago, but I was fooled into thinking that we were putting an end to the destruction of Indochina. I can no longer think this, and I cannot, in good conscience, continue to support our war by contributing to the financing of it.

I am willing to accept the consequences of this refusal; my conscience is worth more to me than consequences. And this won't begin to clear it. I wish more Americans would care more strongly about what we, all of us, did to those two boys. And to millions—millions—of boys and girls and men and women and children—Vietnamese, Cambodian, Lao, Australian, Korean, Filipino, Thai, American.

It is hard to believe that we are all that numb, confused, indifferent, evil, whatever. It is hard to believe that a nation that had, and still has, such potential for the good of humanity is squandering its conscience, its blood, its prestige, its treasure, and its promise for the future in an action which has already cost millions of lives and billions of dollars. And which continues.

Continues without any real promise of termination, in spite of the fact that almost everyone—the President and the military included—knows that the war was misconceived; that it cannot be won without either decimating the entire Vietnamese population or risking massive Chinese intervention.

Continues, although most of us realize that it has been a national mistake and national tragedy of immeasurable consequence. Continues as though no American thinks it is in his power to stop it.

When the French people decided to stop the Algerian War, they stopped building bombs in their factories, they stopped flying the planes and sailing the ships that took those bombs to Algeria, they stopped burying the bodies of dead French soldiers sent back from Algeria. And the war stopped. A war cannot continue if nobody will participate in making it continue.

My refusal to pay a percentage of an income tax of 200-odd dollars is an absurd gesture in the face of what is going on in Southeast Asia. But I would like to be able to face my children years from now. And to face the parents of these two boys, or any of the many, many boys killed so far, and say that at some point I stopped going along.

According to my understanding of the United States Constitution, the power to declare war is in the hands of the legislative, and not the executive, branch of government. The wars in Vietnam, Cambodia and Laos have never been declared by Congress. Yet the tax monies of American citizens and corporations are the source of funds for the Indochina war. . . .

This letter represents—I am ashamed to say—my first act of civil disobedience. And I have still, in spite of my grave concern—horror, even—about the U.S.'s actions in Indochina, the greatest regard for the United States Constitution and the system of government which it defines.

I am sure I am not alone in looking forward to the day when we are, in fact as well as word, "dedicated to the proposition that all men are created equal," and when we act with more knowledge, justice and compassion towards all men in all nations than we have in our decade of war in Indochina.

Frederic P. Herter, Jr.
Cambridge

Within a day of the letter's publication, VVAW called Herter and asked him to come to work for the organization. The VVAW extricated him from his fugue state, and in fact, the work rejuvenated him. He arranged teach-ins in the Boston area and helped organize the veterans' march on Washington early that summer. In the fall of 1971, he put together a three-day symposium at Fanueil Hall on the air war in Southeast Asia that continued—in spite, says Herter, of Nixon's claim that the war was winding down. This was not, he stresses, a bunch of peacenik hippies preaching to the converted. The panelists included a B-52 navigator, air strike analysts, bomb-loaders, and reconnaissance pilots, as well as politicians like George McGovern, Ted Kennedy and Pete McCloskey, the Republican congressman from California who ran on an antiwar platform and gained the vote of one delegate at the Republican National Convention to deny Nixon his coveted unanimous nomination. "I thought the antiwar movement was actually one of America's finest hours," he reflects. "I am in many ways disaffiliated from America because of the Vietnam War still, 30 years later, but I am proud as I can be of the people who opposed the war. Some of them are among the finest people I have ever known anywhere, and many of them are veterans of the war."

After the symposium, Herter was hired as a press aide for McCloskey as he challenged Nixon in New Hampshire, and later worked for McGovern's 1972 campaign "in the very same burgled Democratic National Committee offices of Watergate fame." For all of that campaign's futility, Herter felt positive about his new activism. "When Nixon took forty-nine of the fifty states in November of seventy-two," he says wryly, "I liked to think that my letter had in a small way helped Massachusetts become the single state that had voted against Nixon."

In 1974 he went to Thailand as a Peace Corps volunteer. The idea was to recapture what he'd so admired in Southeast Asia, but instead it was the bad karma that he seemed to rediscover. While in Bangkok in mid-1975, Herter visited some fellow Peace Corps volunteers who had been hired by USAID to process Vietnamese refugees after the fall of Saigon. Steve Shepley turned out to be their boss. When he walked into the office and saw Herter, Shepley "retreated in shock." Herter told his friends what he knew about Shepley, whom they never saw again. In any case, laments Herter, Thailand "was a big disappointment. Thailand was sleazy and selling everything it had to the lowest bidder, and there was Vietnam dying." Back in the United States, the American accommodation of the Vietnam War was highly unsatisfying, even distasteful, to Herter. For instance, he detested *The Deer Hunter* because it demonized the Vietnamese; the film's compassion for GIs seemed beside the point. "I thought it was an atrocity. I saw it in Berkeley, California, where I lived in the seventies. There were these maniacal communist captors shrieking with glee as guys blew their heads off playing Russian roulette. I came out of the movie theater, with these Berkeley teenagers behind me, whose parents I'm sure were antiwar liberals as everybody in Berkeley was, saying 'Now I see why we lost the war.' And the whole thesis of the movie was basically that we lost the war because we were fighting against people who were cruel beyond our wildest imagination. They outcrueled us ten to one, and how could you possibly, if you're good Americans, combat people who were so evil and so maniacal. And it got an Academy Award."

Herter's favorite Vietnam movie conveys waste without gallantry. It is a crude, 16-millimeter loop styled as cinema verité called *Charlie Mopic.* Shot with a hand-held camera from the point of view of an Army cameraman, it chronicles a day in the life of an air-mobile platoon in which the cameraman's buddies are sequentially getting killed. At the end, Charlie Mopic films his own death by gunfire. "The reason it was so strong not just to me but to a lot of people," reflects Herter, "is that the conceit of having you see the action through the cameraman's eyes means you got killed." Herter, by military occupational specialty a cameraman, sees the movie as a notional autobiography.

His affection for *Charlie Mopic* reflects sympathy with the GI as well as the Vietnamese, despite his nonpatriotic protestations. But for PFC Eric Herter, the war was not really about the solidarity of men at arms; it was about sad, unnecessary death all the way around but disproportionately on the Vietnamese side. He returned to Vietnam in 1988 with a student group from Hawaii, in 1993 with the Vietnamese writer Le Ly Hayslip to do a video for her clinic in Da Nang, in 1994 for the East-West Center to do a research project on the effects of *doi moi,* the government's land allocation program. From that point he stayed in Vietnam as an Associated Press photographer, going freelance as of 1998.

Initially Herter was convinced that the country would be well-governed and even near-utopian. He admits to being badly mistaken—that the government is pervasively corrupt, and that post-1986 privatization has meant only the shifting of money from the state to the venal few rather than the people at large. So the Vietnam government "has a long way to go." He still loves Vietnam. Now a disarmingly youthful fifty-eight, he is married to a Vietnamese woman of about thirty, Tran Thi Hoa, and they have a daughter, born in late 1998. He has not yet sought out the woman who once bore his child, though he may yet do so. That reunion, he says, is "unfinished business. The woman was somehow a turning point in my life, and an important person in my life, and I have it in my heart that it's a good thing to say that to her, but I just haven't gotten myself together to go down there and do it."

Herter attributes his expatriation to both his affection for the Vietnamese and his disaffection with Americans. The two, of course, are inextricably linked. "I feel that the United States essentially avoided facing the enormity of what happened here. Still when most people hear something about it they just shut it off. When I first came back I was telling everybody everything I could—any details I could dredge up that would illustrate how bad I thought America was—and people would say, "Enough already, the war's over, get over it, I don't want to hear it. For six months I talked my head off, then I just shut up."

Nevertheless, Herter does not take kindly to anyone who presumes glibly to have Vietnam's number. In 1998, he was hired to take photographs for a piece by journalist Vincent Coppola that would appear in *Men's Journal.* The published article, "Midnight in Hanoi," portrays Hanoi as a repository for Yankee-trash out to glom the cachet of the clichéd Embittered Vet. A club owner who never served a day in Vietnam is celebrated for having dedicated his joint to "all veterans who'd been fucked over," none of whom the reader ever meets—though Chuck Searcy was supposedly "programmed" to kill gooks before his epiphany. (I think not.) The Vietnamese whom Coppola covered tended to be either hookers or corrupt cops, the venues bars like the campy Apocalypse Now—a rather typical meet-market for tourists. The concluding line suffices to convey the overall character of the piece: "Hanoi is a raw, inchoate place, where the apocalypse plays tag with revelation."

When Herter read the article, he was disgusted. He wrote a letter to the magazine, which the editors duly published:

As one of the photographers assigned to illustrate 'Midnight in Hanoi' and as a four-year resident of Vietnam, I strongly object to author Vince Coppola's take on Americans in contemporary Hanoi. Here's how my Vietnamese wife summed it up: "No heart." Coppola needn't have visited Vietnam to gather his material—the stereotypical characters he depicts have been seen in thousands of American movies and TV shows. No surprise, then, to find that when Coppola travels to a Vietnam he's never visited but already knows, he finds exactly what he's looking for. . . . It's of little interest to Coppola that the vast majority of Hanoians have never been to the Apocalypse Now bar, and that 99 percent of the Americans here haven't either. They're too busy holding down real jobs, and most Vietnamese are doing exactly the same thing—working, in the best American tradition, to make better lives for their families. . . . Most Americans still don't understand what happened in Vietnam because easy stereotypes block out who the Vietnamese are, what they do and think, and why they resisted us so fiercely.

Coppola's printed response was a puerile defense of his choice of subject matter, and obliquely accused Herter of "recounting the glories of this socialist paradise"—something he plainly does not do.

Born to the Establishment, Herter will never get there now and he's all right with that. His existential preoccupation is American vice, not Vietnamese virtue. He wears a wedding ring on the second toe of his right foot. He lives near the southern edge of Tay Lake, on the northwest edge of town. On the way to visit Herter, as I was wrestling with the erratic numbering of the houses on his street, two Vietnamese boys had asked me if I was looking for "the American." I said yes, and immediately they pointed to his home, which sits on the second floor above a garage. How had they known? Eric Herter is the only American for miles.

CHASING GHOSTS

There are probably no more than thirty Vietnam veterans living in Hanoi; a few are there for business reasons, but most fall into the "revisionist/reconciler" category exemplified by Searcy and Herter. In Ho Chi Minh City—whose port is still called "Saigon"—there are more like fifty to seventy resident expat vets. The city, though it no longer clamors with helicopters, gunfire, and air raids, resonates yet of things, for better or worse, American vintage 1969. Helicopter hulks haunt an unused corner of Tan Son Nhat Airport, close to derelict USAF hangers. U.S. military jeeps—models from 1968 to 1972, some beat up, some near-mint—still cruise the streets. Tucked into a corner of Saigon's central grid are war memorabilia merchants, specializing in paraphernalia they claim were taken off the bodies of GIs. Some of the stuff is probably authentic: knives, canteens, mess kits, rucksacks. The things they carried. There are bins full of old, dented Kodak Instamatic cameras that were so popular in the sixties and seventies. Some, perhaps, belonged to GIs. Others were merely imported during the war and sold, as they are now, on the street to whoever had the money to spend.

Certain items, especially small, easy-to-reproduce ones, are mainly bogus. One giveaway on dog tags is the obvious misspellings. The one that I buy, though, is the letter-perfect tag of one James Hardaway, Serial No. AF14821441, T-63. Blood type: B positive. Religion: Methodist. The name does not appear on The Wall, nor on any of the MIA or POW lists. Cigarette lighters—Zippos, naturally—are sold by both the stores and the street hawkers. Most are egregious fakes. The counterfeiters might put "USMC" next to the wrong insignia, or commemorate an event like My Lai that not even a war criminal would want engraved on his lighter. Occasionally, they get the hard details right, as in recalling "Ruby Tuesday" at "Khe Sanh" in "1967"—

the actual year of both the song and the siege—but they might also add the markings of a U.S. Army unit that was not involved.

It may seem curious that the Vietnamese are able to ply such a robust trade in mementos (real or ersatz) of their country's occupation, mainly to Americans who value them because they might have belonged to a dead countryman. The phenomenon bespeaks a kind of morbid repose: the war is over, and the best that is left is the commercial ethic that it brought to southern Vietnam. Indeed, Vietnam is not really communist. Although communist cells and structures were left intact to placate the Soviets during the bleak period of meager Soviet sponsorship in the eighties, the philosophy has not survived. While central control will take time to break down, Saigon's countless storefront distributors and shops now compete sufficiently to make prices low and turnover high. They are taxed lightly or heavily, depending on bribes to revenue authorities, but are not run by the government.

There is, of course, poverty, due to the economic inefficiency of ragged socialism and the corrupt government sector, curbs on development due to the war and subsequent restrictions on international aid, and the Asian economic crisis. Beggars, many of them cripples, cruise the sidewalks. One of the real pros is a lame, handless boy, blind in one eye, with a club foot. He is clearly no older than sixteen, but avers he was maimed by American bombs during the war. With his stumps he raises a card packet to his mouth and blows the cellophane loose, then extracts postcards with lips he has carefully smacked dry. For this neat trick he asks for and often gets a dollar, then bows and hobbles away. Street kids zero in on Americans and offer, along with postcards, cheap pirated knockoffs of two books—Graham Greene's *The Quiet American* and Bao Ninh's *The Sorrow of War*—for a buck apiece. The political astuteness implicit in this limited selection is admirable: a prophetic novel by one of the century's great world-weary colonialists about America's neo-colonial naiveté, and a primitive but full-blooded account of the suffering it visited on a primitive and full-blooded people.

Among the revelations of *The Sorrow of War* is the admonition of North Vietnamese party officials to NVA soldiers to "ignore the spirit of reconciliation, to beware of the 'bullets' coated with sugar, to ignore the warmth and passions among the remnants of this fallen, luxurious society of the South. And especially to guard against the idea of the South having fought valiantly or been meritorious in any way." Spiritually the Vietnamese still are not one people. Southerners are far friendlier than northerners toward Americans. Despite the fact that U.S. forces ravaged Vietnam south as well as north for a good ten years, rarely does an American encounter in Saigon the sullen stares that he will frequently draw in Hanoi. Hostesses shake a leg when Americans appear in the lobby. Several restaurants have adopted country-and-western motifs. In the huge dining rooms of the Rex Hotel, where military brass and the CIA blocked out entire floors, or the Caravelle, where journalists congregated on the roof and sipped drinks as they watched the war, Smith & Wollensky–caliber filets mignons go for five dollars a pop, complete with Chinese music and dancing even if there is only one other party in the place. More often than not, merchants are solicitous.

The cynical explanation is that they still want Yankee largesse, and did not prosper between 1975 and 1989 at the hands of the Soviets, who replaced the Americans as their Cold War sponsors, and whom the Vietnamese refer to as "Americans without money." The subtler reason is that southerners have no great affection for Hanoi, which sent carpetbaggers to take the good jobs below the DMZ and still favors northerners for university admission and civil service. Indeed, even Vietcong were suspect, and were not accorded especial esteem or priority by Hanoi. Most Saigon denizens do not count themselves as winners, and as a consequence may feel a dark bond with Americans: both came out on the short end. Perhaps the Vietnamese are so welcoming to Americans partly because they won, partly because they wish we had.

By comparison, the War Remnants Museum, until recently known as the American War Crimes Museum and renamed for the sake of the dawning period of reconciliation and normalization, offers a dissonantly one-sided view. In its presentation, there is no hint that the Vietcong and the NVA contributed their share of barbarity to the conflict. (Nowhere in the museum is the NVA's butchering of three thousand Vietnamese civilians in Hué during the Tet Offensive, for example, mentioned.) Photographs of presumed Agent Orange victims—deformed by cancer, amputation, or birth disorder—occupy entire rooms. Two jars preserve especially hideous malformed fetuses in formaldehyde. In one, two babies are joined at the belly into one monster, with a harelip; in the other, the head is grossly large and the face twisted into an inhuman snarl. Napalm created some of the more gruesome shots: missing eyes, half-melted faces.

Other enduring images record American atrocities. In perhaps the most vivid one, a tall, lanky American GI is dragging a head, some of which is missing, attached to the shreds of a neck, shoulder, and single arm. The rest of the body is gone, and it is such a bizarre assemblage that you have to examine the remnants hard to figure out what you're looking at. The soldier is looking down and could be grimacing, but the quote below identifies his expression as one of laughter. It's impossible to say, but he is carrying the dripping mangle with, if not mirth, undoubted nonchalance. In another photo six or seven soldiers are seated in the bush, elbows propped on their knees. Everyone is grinning. Before them are three or four carcasses, the necks mere stumps. According to the caption, the photo was taken as a "souvenir."

Outside the Museum are shot-up Huey helicopters, F-4 fighters, A-6 attack planes, and the Soviet T-54 tanks that took Loc Ninh and eventually Saigon. The War Remnants Museum and its counterparts elsewhere in Vietnam are probably the only places in the world in which an American can see for himself the captured fruits—tanks, planes, weapons—of an American defeat. To an American it is sobering and a little rattling. Yet the warmth of the southerners belies the crude moral spoils of the museum, which takes a shot at southerners too. At the end of the prescribed tour is an elaborate reconstruction of the "tiger cages" in which ARVN kept VC and NVA prisoners, and diagrams of the tortures employed by the South Vietnamese: hosing water spiked with lime through the nostrils into the stomach, then jumping on the distended stomach until the water gushes back out the mouth, now laced with blood; applying electric shocks to the genitals and nipples; subjecting prisoners to confinement so extreme and extended that it led to permanent paralysis.

Plainly the legacy of brutality is not the Americans' alone, but they are the government's scapegoats. In the violent, surreal Vietnamese movie *Cyclo,* made in 1995 subject to government censorship, a Saigon pimp peddles his virginal girlfriend to a kinky businessman who pays him in dollars. She does not enjoy the trick. Poisoned by guilt, the pimp takes out a switchblade and slowly and systematically lacerates the john to death, burns his cache of American greenbacks, then torches his apartment. The cyclo driver whom the pimp has recruited to do a hit gets drunk and passes out instead. He returns to an honest job, for which he is paid in dong.

The War Remnants Museum furnishes only the official point of view. On balance, though, contemporary Ho Chi Minh City sends the message that all the players shared in the ignominy of the Vietnam War. This mildly exculpatory dispensation may be why some American veterans have found returning to Saigon a cathartic means of putting the ghosts of war to rest.

One of them is Greg Kleven. Now, at about five-foot-ten with rheumy blue eyes, thick wiry brown hair, and a red triangular face, he looks kind and gentle. He shakes a little, and smokes to calm himself. But in Oakland in 1965, he saw Jack Webb as the tough Marine sergeant in *The D.I.* and decided that was going to be him. "I wanted that kind of challenge. I wanted to put myself in that position and see how I would react, if I could stand up to this kind of thing. I didn't know anything about Vietnam. I wasn't at all political. I just knew what I didn't want, which was to go on to a university or to continue working as I had all through high school. Joining the military was a way out." Taking the anticommunist mission at face value, Kleven joined the Marine Corps at seventeen, despite the fact that he could have avoided service in Vietnam because his brother Mike was already there with the Air Force.

In November 1966, he shipped out with three-thousand other Marines on a navy transport vessel. Among the last Marines to go to Vietnam by sea, they arrived in Cam Ranh Bay on Christmas Day. Like Glenn Holthaus, Kleven ended up in Force Recon, operating behind the lines in central Vietnam and Laos in 1966–67, always in free-fire zones. He pulled twenty-five three- to four-day patrols, more than a third of which resulted in fire-fights. "Every patrol was a brand-new war," he observes. But he was surprised that upon arriving in-country, he saw a people going about daily life and not engaging in war. During his ten months in-country, Kleven got the distinct impression that most Vietnamese people did not want war, that the Americans and not the North Vietnamese were the prime antagonists. One medic he respected for his humanity deserted, some believe defected. On several occasions, ARVN soldiers and U.S. Marines knowingly fired on each other.

As he neared the end of his thirteen-month tour, Kleven began to question the propriety of the war. "I did evolve into a mental state where my heart wasn't in it. In the beginning I was definitely gung-ho, and I was very proud to be in the Marine Corps. I thought that I was going to contribute in some positive way to keeping America great, to having America as a leader in the world, which I thought was part of my responsibility as a citizen. Twelve years of Catholic school, twelve years of 'thou shalt not kill,' and now it's okay, go over there and start shooting—reconciling those kinds of things in my mind got more and more difficult. In the beginning I could just shove it aside. Later on, I couldn't. It wouldn't go away. The contradiction was just too great. I wasn't comfortable at the end at all. And I wasn't alone. One guy busted up his knees just to get out of going on patrol anymore."

Whatever his misgivings, however, Kleven never shirked his duty. On his twenty-fifth patrol, his unit was establishing a harbor site near Da Nang when it was ambushed by a numerically superior NVA force. He was knocked to the ground by a hand grenade blast and took shrapnel in his chest. Then he was shot three times in the back. Still he gained a firing position and killed two enemy soldiers attempting to penetrate his squad's defensive perimeter. Two fellow squad members were killed. For his courage under fire, and for his wounds, Kleven won a Bronze Star with a combat "V" (his CO had recommended a Silver Star) and a Purple Heart. The citation for valor reads as follows:

> His aggressive fighting spirit and calm presence of mind in the face of extreme personal danger were an inspiration to all who observed him and contributed significantly to the accomplishment of his unit's mission. Lance Corporal Kleven's courage, bold determination and unfaltering devotion to duty were in keeping with the highest tradition of the Marine Corps and of the United States Naval Service.

During his nine months in the hospital recuperating, he decided that the war was wrong: that the United States did not have legitimate interests in Vietnam, and that neither Vietnamese nor Americans should die for a marginal contribution to the containment of communism. "Up until I got shot, I had always thought: if I can just get out of here, if I can just finish this year, I'll be okay, I can chalk it up as a great experience and go on with my life. But when I got shot, that was it. I remember after they brought me back to the battalion aid station, the company gunny [gunnery sergeant] came down to meet me. I remember him telling me, 'Don't worry, we'll get you patched up and you'll be back running patrols in a couple of weeks.' I just looked at him and said, 'Gunny, I'm never going back out there again—never. I'm not ever going out on patrol again.'"

When his father drove him home for Thanksgiving, he looked out the window and thought, "Nobody even cares, nobody even knows, what's going on in Vietnam at this minute. So there was this feeling of betrayal. Then I started to see how vets got shit on. The antiwar people were blaming *us*. We were just the stupid ones who went. There were lots of times when I'd just say, fuck it, and buy a bottle. I was never bitter toward vets or the military, but I was toward America because I thought that [the people] didn't know and didn't care." After his medical discharge, Kleven got his college degree in the administration of justice. While adamantly against the war, he was uncomfortable with the near-treasonous talk of some antiwar groups (including the first incarnation of Vietnam Veterans Against the War) and not ready to write off his participation in the war as completely unjustifiable.

So Kleven did not speak up or join any groups, but, he says, "inside I was constantly thinking about Vietnam. But I could function. I was pretending that I was happy, that I didn't have any problems. In reality, I did. I couldn't get Vietnam off my mind." The VFW and American Legion stateside were hostile to Vietnam vets, and Kleven did not join. Instead he internalized his pain and conflict. "I could, on the surface, appear to be the average guy. I was pretending, basically, that I was happy and that I didn't have any troubles. In the early eighties, people started to write about

Vietnam. I used to look in the bookstores and the libraries. I would just devour anything I could find about the war. None of this seemed to answer these questions, or this conflict, that I had inside. So I just kept looking and looking and looking. I went to all the movies that were out. Most were trying to imitate Vietnam, and there was no way you can capture the feeling, the essence of being in the war, on film. So *Platoon* and *Full Metal Jacket*—I laughed at them. I didn't think that they came close to depicting what it was like. Whereas *Apocalypse Now* did, because it was fucking crazy. But I never was able to find anything out there that satisfied me."

Kleven married in 1972 and had two healthy sons, but his third child, a daughter, suffered from Trisomy 18 (three chromosomes instead of two in her eighteenth pair) and died at six months in 1981. Doctors suspected that the disease, which inhibited the formation of the heart, resulted from his exposure to Agent Orange. "It was just another reminder, another slap. It made me very, very bitter." Kleven could not find vocational satisfaction. Vietnam continued to gnaw at him, and his daughter's death brought the problem to the surface. He hopped from probation officer to carpet layer to freight dispatcher to postal worker. He started drinking more heavily, then fell into outright binges. But he read a book, *Soldier,* by Lieutenant Colonel Anthony Herbert, who wrote that he had been forced out of the Army because he opposed what he believed was criminal behavior on the part of American soldiers. The book opened Kleven's eyes. "He was a career military guy, loved the Army, but turned when he came to Vietnam. He saw that on paper, what they said they were doing wasn't true. A lot of the things that I read in his book opened my mind. I thought, if this colonel can complain, if he can criticize and say he didn't think it was right, then so can I."

In 1987, Kleven learned that visas to Vietnam could be obtained (illegally for Americans) through Mexico. He returned in January 1988. No doubt about it: this one's chasing ghosts. "I knew my real return to Vietnam was when we would hit Da Nang. I had never been to Saigon during the war, I had no idea what this city was all about. I still didn't feel like this was Vietnam. [Approaching Da Nang] it reminded me of the times we would be inserted in a patrol. There's this feeling as you're going in: you're on your way down, you can't stop. Are you ready? Have you done everything possible to get your shit together? It was that same kind of feeling: Am I doing the right thing? Can I survive when we touch down? It was very difficult. My mind was a thousand miles a minute, going back and forth to the time during the war. It was hairy."

Subsequently, in 1989, he started a newsletter called Vietnam Echoes through Vietnam Veterans of America's Chapter 34 in Akron, Ohio. "It was an attempt," he says, "to reach out and raise some new issues. I didn't want to talk POW/MIA, I didn't want to rehash war stories. I wanted to talk about consequences, about what we're doing today as vets. What is our place in society? I could imagine that eventually the Vietnam vet will have to take the place of the World War II vet as the senior vet in the country, and that when we did that we would have a chance to influence the younger generation just as the World War II vet influenced us. VVA's slogan was 'Never again.' We could teach our children to at least question the government when it says it's time to go to Somalia, it's time to go to Panama, it's time to go to Grenada, it's time to go to Beirut."

Over the next three years—then in technical violation of federal law—he arranged return trips for some sixty to seventy troubled veterans. "I wanted to let vets know that going back to Vietnam was a possibility, and that for me it was what finally allowed me to put an end to the war." For most it was salutary; for some, returning to the scene just amplified old problems. For Kleven himself, the whole process showed him that Vietnam had survived and would thus allow him to "conclude the story." "It was a relief," he says, "that no matter how hard we tried we didn't blow this country off the face of the earth." He met other vets who had experienced what he had, and thought what he'd thought. Kleven thus "no longer feels strange."

After these epiphanies, Kleven felt compelled to come to Vietnam permanently in 1991. His wife refused, and they divorced. "When I went to war, I wanted to come home a hero, to say I was part of something that was good, needed, necessary. But everything was turned upside down. What I thought was real wasn't real. Leadership that I thought was honest and fair wasn't, so all of my beliefs in the American system were shattered. There wasn't a connection between the ideal and my experience of the war and of going back into society. I realized that I was tricked and used, then wasn't even rewarded. I did my job. I killed, I did what I was supposed to do. Then when I went home, there was nothing."

He is now married to a Vietnamese woman in her early forties—some applause may be due him for staying, against the trend, in his own age group—and teaches English for a living. He was one of the first Americans permitted to teach English in Vietnam, and one of the first to write stories in the *Saigon Times*. Kleven no longer considers himself an American patriot in the "America right or wrong" sense, though he certainly embraces most of what might be considered American values. Before packing his bags for Saigon he actively protested against the Gulf War, helping to block the Bay Bridge in San Francisco. "Kuwait isn't a democracy," he refrains, "it's a fucking gas station." Searcy and Herter would probably share that sentiment.

Denis Gray, left, in the ROTC
at Yale just prior to his service
in Vietnam and, right, with two
Cambodian stringers in 1975
while covering the Cambodian
war for the Associated Press.
Courtesy Denis Gray.

5
VALOR IGNORED

Mark Smith is in Bangkok because he won't give up a fight he considers noble as well as effective but for which he does not feel duly recognized. Holthaus, Taylor, and Richter have conceded the futility of Vietnam and tried to salvage some value from their sacrifice. For Searcy, Herter, and Kleven, the American effort in Indochina was not noble; it was past futile all the way to unjust, and requires on-site expiation. Other veterans are motivated, in varying degrees, by the positive features of their service in Vietnam. Invariably, these are cultural or personal—not military.

WAR'S SERENDIPITY
Perhaps the rarest species among expat veterans, in his largely

serendipitous relationship to Vietnam, is Mike Byrne. He grew up in Chester, then Upper Darby, Pennsylvania to working-class parents with little money, graduating from high school in 1967. He did not think much about the war one way or the other, and joined the Air Force (after the Army turned him down due to poor vision) in order to get an education. He became a sheet-metal specialist, was sent to Vietnam in early 1970, and was assigned to Tan Son Nhat to repair damaged airplanes and helicopters. Although "only support" in a rear area, the base was frequently attacked by sappers and Byrne saw dead and wounded GIs choppered in every day. The memory "took years before it went away." About half a dozen times he was dropped by plane into the field, where his crew was protected inside a wide perimeter by Marines in foxholes while they repaired disabled aircraft, which the crew then had to fly back to Tan Son Nhat. His unit received several citations for valor.

During his first few months in Saigon, Byrne drank and womanized as most soldiers did. He came to like and trust local Vietnamese. Here's one reason why: he was walking through town stone drunk, and a Saigon hooker diverted him from a building that promptly blew up. It was two GIs fragging an officer; she probably heard about it in pillow-talk. And there were good times, wild-west style. This was the drill: go to a bar, find a girl, get the address of the whorehouse; trail her out to the street, watch her get on the back of a motorcycle taxi, then get on the back of one yourself and follow her; enter a house that is candle-lit only, and proceed to a room with a bed on each side; ignore the couple screwing in one bed; go to the other bed and have sex. One night Byrne went to a brothel, took his girl to one side of the room, with business in progress on the other. A gunfight broke out in the street below and all four parties hit the deck. Byrne lit a cigarette, illuminating the face of the other GI, who was none too pleased about the *coitus interruptus*. He turned out to be an Air

Force buddy Byrne had roomed with before shipping out to Vietnam and hadn't seen since. They finished what they came for and had a drink. Warm, stirring, cinematic-quality moments.

He didn't plan to fall in love with a Vietnamese girl, Mai, who, like Byrne, had been raised a Catholic. She and her family were also vehemently anticommunist, and remain so. Still, while walking with Mike she was arrested as a prostitute. In fact, she was nothing of the sort, but the pretext was used by the Saigon police at the Americans' behest to neutralize female VC spying. Byrne got her out of jail in a few hours with the help of his commanding officer. Mike and Mai married, and he re-upped for a second tour to allow her to have her papers processed and say goodbye to her family. They warmly received and accepted him—a factor that made him fonder still of the Vietnamese. When he returned home with his wife, he came face to face with the antiwar movement and the indifferent attitude of the public to Vietnam veterans. He began to study the history of the Vietnam conflict, and concluded, as many did, that if Washington had constructively engaged Ho Chi Minh back in the forties and fifties we might have been able to keep him out of the international communist orbit. But he also thought that having rendered anticommunist Vietnamese dependent on us, we owed them our help.

During the seventies and eighties, while building a successful career as an electrical components salesman with Westinghouse and Rumsey Electric and later as an electrical contractor, Byrne was active in programs sponsoring and housing Vietnamese refugees, and helped to get three of Mai's relatives and their children out of the country and settled in the United States. Three of her brothers escaped the post-1975 regime on their own, but Mai's mother, brother, and sister were among the "boat people" lost at sea in the late seventies. In the early nineties, one momentous lawsuit and subsequent bonding problems forced his business into bankruptcy. He landed on his feet, but at about the same time Hanoi invited Viet Khieus—Vietnamese emigrants, most of them southern political refugees—back to the country. Mai, the oldest of twelve children, became keen to return long-term to rejoin what remained of her family. She came back for a few months in 1991, and tracked down relatives who had been dispersed from Saigon through "resettlement" in agricultural camps. Mike was willing to take a shot. They came to Saigon in 1992.

Whereas many of his friends had brought home nightmares, Mike Byrne brought home the love of his life. "There are times when you think about the Vietnam War and say, 'Man, what the hell was that all about? Jesus, what happened there?' But I can't tell you how fortunate I was in meeting Mai. People came over here and died, turned into drug addicts, ended up handicapped, Agent Orange. Not me." The war had an enduringly happy aspect for him, and the legacy only got better. Mai routed him back to a new, increasingly liberal Vietnam. He and Mai were unable to have kids, but have now adopted three Vietnamese children. He's fifty-plus but he has all his hair and has avoided paunch, and figures he can pull off the fatherhood thing. He is also learning Vietnamese. These outward signals of "going native" give Byrne street-cred with his Vietnamese neighbors—some of them former VC. They also have relaxed the Vietnamese authorities, who a few years ago thought "every American who got off a plane was CIA" and monitored Byrne through civilians who played friendly, then reported back to headquarters. No more, says Byrne.

While making it in Vietnam as a small businessman can be tough because the Vietnamese are looking for big money from foreigners and usually require bribes, a change in the law allows him to do licensed business cheaply because his wife is a Viet Khieu. Thus, he built a miniature golf arcade in a big, popular Saigon park. (As we approached the site in his jeep, he mused that three decades ago that stretch of road was part of his vast airbase, where it took him twenty minutes to drive from his quarters to his unit's sheet-metal warehouse.) Though he ran into political problems with the Saigon operation, Byrne started another miniature golf course at a resort in nearby Vung Tau. They can live for $20,000 a year in Vietnam, and reside in a large, ostentatiously outfitted house in a Saigon suburb, Ba Diem, that cost him about $40,000 (with additions). He drives a mint 1972 Army jeep that set him back $3,000. If he runs just one mini-golf facility at only 35 percent capacity, he'll make $60,000 annually. Yet he admits, "I couldn't spend $1,000 a month here if I tried."

It is Mai, not Mike, who unrelentingly recalls that many of those who opposed communism were as committed as the NVA and the VC, continues to denigrate the communists, and wistfully laments the demise of South Vietnam.

Mike is committed to staying in Vietnam to enable his son Michael to understand his own culture, learn the Vietnamese language, and get to know his Vietnamese relatives. So far, this plan requires no psychic or material hardships. For Mike Byrne and his family, life is grand. Close your eyes and it's suburban America, right down to Mai's idiomatic English and Welcome Wagon warmth. Mike is a refreshingly uncomplicated guy, but also observant and sensitive to where he is. Nobody won the war, he says, since after 1975 the government mistreated most of the population. Friendly ex-Vietcong neighbors confirm this observation. He admires the industriousness and resolve of the Vietnamese people, and their capacity to persevere. He tosses off the idea, with a hint of irony, that Vietnam "could have become another Japan" absent the war. He has been to the War Remnants Museum. Yes, it's totally biased, but each side is entitled to a chance to tell its side of the story. His is the voice of repose.

The same goes for Colonel André Sauvageot, USA (ret.), who had a much longer, stranger trip in Vietnam. By title, Sauvageot is chief representative for General Electric International, Inc., in Hanoi. About five-foot-eight, slight, nervous as a cat but warm and genial, he literally wears his attitude on his lapel, which displays a pin consisting of the famous GE logo flanked by the American and Vietnamese flags. With a cell phone in his pocket and miniature earphones clipped to his collar, the guy looks dead set on bringing Vietnam into the twenty-first century.

But there's a twitch in his personality. When his Vietnamese assistant, an efficient, Poindexterish young man, tells him that he has anticipated and fixed a scheduling conflict, Sauvageot embraces him as though he were a long-lost son and sings fulsome, near-tearful praises in his ear in fluent Vietnamese which he then translates into English for my benefit. When asked whether he ever took the life of a Vietnamese *mano a mano,* he hyperventilates, sniffles, and begins to cry. Between hacks of grief and relief, he testifies as to how thankful he is that on account of his rank he never had to "put a Vietnamese in the sights of a rifle or a carbine" and pull the trigger. "I was lucky, because I was a captain, an adviser, that it was not my job. I couldn't have, I just couldn't have." How could he kill anyone as beautiful as his assistant? he asks rhetorically. At the same time, he confesses, "I could not live with myself knowing that I had become a professional army officer and then not carried out the mission that we were entrusted to carry out." This uneasy mixture of sentiment and obligation made for an unusual military career.

After enlisting in 1956 to avoid the peacetime draft, he spent twenty-seven years in the Army and the better parts of eight years in Vietnam, from 1964 to 1973, starting his career as a private and retiring as a colonel. Upon completing basic training, Sauvageot liked the idea of getting $55 per month extra pay for parachuting out of airplanes, so he enrolled in jump school and wound up in the 82nd Airborne Division. Then he went to Officers Candidate School, receiving his commission as a second lieutenant in early 1959. A stint in Germany and Ranger School followed. Then Vietnam started to heat up. "The Kennedy administration was increasing the number of military advisers to the South Vietnamese. This is where my interest in Vietnam began— not so much an interest in the country per se, but in the fact that it had become a point of concern for America's strategic interests. Because I was at that time, remember, an Army captain, infantry branch, Ranger-qualified, airborne-qualified—in other words, totally a combat arms officer. My philosophy at the time—and I think it's still correct—is that any time that the United States begins to have a military involvement when one is on active duty as a combat arms officer, then one should volunteer for that involvement. You're not there for retirement pay or PX privileges. You're there to practice a profession, and that means going to war when there's a war."

But, he adds, "whether the war is wise is another question. But I took it as axiomatic [that it was wise because] the Soviet Union combined with China represented a viable strategic threat to the survival of the United States. There was no doubt in my mind at that time. And in retrospect, there's still no doubt in my mind that that was absolutely correct." This attitude, when unpacked, is not as gung-ho as it seems at first blush. While he believed then and still does now that it was right, in the context of the Cold War, to try to teach the South Vietnamese to survive against the communists on their own, sending GIs to do the job wholesale he felt was wrong. He volunteered to go to Vietnam only to advise. Even that he quickly found problematic in practice. "We reported to Military Assistance Command and General Westmoreland gave us a briefing. He told us all about how he had a policy that everybody had to work a minimum of sixty hours a week so that we could win the war." Such McNamaran notions of victory-by-prospectus did not particularly impress Sauvageot. "You know, right when you hear something like that, it just comes across as bullshit."

When Sauvageot found that no posts with ARVN Ranger battalions were available, he opted to become a district adviser to a South Vietnamese army captain in a little village near My Tho, which was about sixty kilometers south of Saigon. This meant that he would patrol with smaller platoon-sized units, which he thought would allow him to become familiar with the country and the local people. That he did, and he quickly learned the language and came to admire and respect the Vietnamese people. Thus, despite his bias against wholesale military involvement, even as the U.S. mission crept and then leaped, John Paul Vann and others known (rightly or wrongly) for their deeper understanding of the Vietnamese were able to convince Sauvageot to stay until the end.

In short order he learned that "many things were different from what was said in Washington in [government] papers like 'Aggression from the North'—it wasn't really like that, it was much more complex. I developed a respect for Vietnamese on both sides of the war. Very early on I became even more wedded to the idea that we should never go beyond the level of advisers, that basically the Vietnamese should settle their affairs more on their own without so much foreign involvement." Within the limits of his rank and influence, Sauvageot did what he could to bring these views to bear on U.S. policy, to make the war less rather than more violent—usually to no avail.

After his first tour as a district adviser, he migrated into less conventional assignments, substantially on account of his facility with the Vietnamese language. First he worked with a South Vietnamese survey cadre to determine rural Vietnamese attitudes about the Saigon government, next became a political officer at the National Training Center. Then, from 1969 to 1971, Sauvageot was William Colby's liaison and coordination officer at the South Vietnamese prime minister's office while Colby was director of Civil Operations and Revolutionary Development Support (CORDS), through which the Phoenix Program was conducted. His final assignment in Vietnam was as interpreter for the United States' delegation to the four-party joint military commission that met for sixty days after the Paris accords were signed. Along the way, he co-authored a study commissioned by Robert Komer, deputy director of CORDS, recommending better ways to thwart the communists (including the creation of a "night army"), but MACV sat on it. Thus, although he distinguished himself as an officer (winning numerous decorations, including an Air Medal with a "V," a Purple Heart, and Bronze Stars), Sauvageot concluded that "the United States was culturally and intellectually unable to do it right."

Because of his assiduous coordination of duty and conviction, during the war he felt no personal guilt vis-à-vis the Vietnamese for his own role in the Vietnam War at the time, nor does he now, though he deeply regrets the tragic humanitarian consequences of the enterprise. Leaving aside the few known atrocities like the My Lai massacre, he does not believe the United States waged a gratuitously brutal war from a military point of view. But falling in love with the Vietnamese people complicated Sauvageot's worldview and, inevitably, his conception of his mission. He forbade troops under his command to call Vietnamese disparaging names like "gooks," "dinks," and "slopes." He married a Vietnamese woman in Saigon in 1970. Today he weeps when he talks about America's having created "new widows" and "new orphans" among the Vietnamese.

Having worked closely with the CIA and with Colby—in fact, a Freedom of Information Act (FOIA) request for his service record turned up nothing, probably, according to the Army officer processing the request, because he was a "spook"— Sauvageot became a member of the Pentagon's Army Staff after the war. With barely contained passion Sauvageot declares that during his time in Washington, Hanoi "as a matter of indisputable fact" militarily stopped the Chinese-supported Pol Pot and Khmer

Rouge—putting an end not only to the Khmer Rouge's vicious cross-border raids into Vietnam, but also to the killing fields, the torture chambers, and the worst genocide since the Holocaust. (He elides the fact that Hanoi strategically supported the pre-genocidal Khmer Rouge in their fight for control of Cambodia against the pro-American general Lon Nol.) Sauvageot strongly counseled the Carter administration to support, or at least not interfere with, Vietnam's 1978 invasion of Cambodia. But Jimmy Carter rejected his argument that no country defending its people and territory should be condemned because Hanoi's action drew on Soviet support, engraving, says Sauvageot, a "dark, dark, dark footnote in American history."

Sauvageot's last military position was as Vietnamese interpreter for Richard Armitage when he was assistant secretary of defense for National Security Affairs under Reagan—translating, for example, testimony given before Congress by an exiled Hanoi doctor known as "The Mortician," formerly employed by the NVA, concerning POW remains. Sauvageot retired from the Army in 1984, but never lost his regard for the Vietnamese as a heroic people and gradually worked his way back to Southeast Asia. He did stints as an executive with the Northrop Corporation, as a political adviser (to Armitage) on East Asian issues in the Pentagon, as a specially appointed assistant to the U.S. ambassador in Bangkok charged with political analysis of Vietnam, and as a U.S. embassy contract employee responsible for facilitating the voluntary repatriation of Vietnamese living in Hong Kong, Malaysia, Thailand, and the Philippines.

In 1992 he returned to Vietnam with GE. His hope was and remains to help reconcile the United States and Vietnam through mutual economic advantage and thereby improve U.S.-Vietnam bilateral relations. Though his job is ostensibly commercial, he isn't shy about his politics. A photograph memorializing his participation in the official opening of the War Remnants Museum in

Ho Chi Minh City hangs near medals donated by stateside GIs with their testimonials of regret for helping to prosecute an imprudent war, and a framed reprint of Robert S. McNamara's laundered *mea culpa* from his memoir *In Retrospect*. While McNamara's statement seems cynically aggrandizing, Sauvageot's high-minded conciliatoriness is not. He might agree with Chuck Searcy that Ho Chi Minh's most important priority was Vietnamese independence rather than strengthening the global communist monolith. But whereas Searcy deploys the argument to impugn American shortsightedness, Sauvageot considers it mere historical speculation with the benefit of hindsight. If for Searcy the American war was a sin for which he is trying to atone, for Sauvageot it was an honorable mistake that he is trying to ameliorate.

Lands of Opportunity

Denis Gray was born Zdenek Mecir in 1944 during an American bombing raid on Pilsen, Czechoslovakia, where his father was recruited by the CIA. The family escaped (hairily) to West Germany in 1951, and his father became a case officer for the Agency, spending time in different parts of the world over a twelve-year period. He decided not to make spying a career and eventually became a vice president of IBM. Thus, Gray's family's story was a classic "land of opportunity" saga with a Cold War twist, and the obligation he owed the United States was planted in him from an early age.

"America done good for us," he quips. More seriously he notes: "Some of my father's friends who escaped Czechoslovakia decided to go to England, for example, and one or two to France. Those who went to England never quite became British, were never quite fully accepted, never quite made it to their potential, whereas my father, through hard work, was able to become a vice president of IBM even though to this day he has a horrible foreign accent. They gave him an opportunity. It sounds like one of those nineteenth-century Yankee tales, the proverbial guy-makes-good-because-of-freedom-and-equality story. In my family's case it just happened to be true." This history has made him a lifelong American patriot.

Given his background, Gray was anticommunist and generally favored the war effort. "It was more a psychological gut feeling than an analytical one at the time," he recalls. He certainly did not entertain going to Canada, but neither did he want to be a "grunt" in Vietnam. At Yale he enrolled in ROTC, then moved on to George Washington University for a masters in international relations. He entered the service in 1968, when war protests were raging. While many of his friends strung out their college deferments, he considered this to impose an unfair burden on working-class men and especially blacks. "I don't think I was ever anti-Vietnam until I went to Vietnam. I didn't necessarily believe in it, I wasn't all that political at the time. I wasn't involved in campus politics. I didn't turn a blind eye to it, but I felt resigned about going into the military, because at that time the draft was on. My classmates at Yale either went or they just wanted to study forever. That I decided was not fair. The kids from the ghetto were getting called up and sent to Vietnam, while most of my classmates at Yale—not all of them, some of them were killed in Vietnam, actually—said to hell with it, I'm not going to do it, I'm going to study for a Ph.D. or go to law school or go to medical school, ride it out."

He was assigned to the 500th Military Intelligence Group and was sent to Japan, where he spent two years and fell in love with Asia. Once in service, he felt a pent-up surge of patriotism. "I guess my parents had inculcated it in me because they felt gratitude, as well they should, to the United States, to the government, and to the U.S. military, too." Gray re-upped for a year, and to his surprise was forthwith sent to Vietnam, with the 525th Military Intelligence Battalion, for a one-year tour from mid-1970 to mid-1971. Gray did a good job as battalion "S-1" in charge of personnel and administration (winning the "standard" Bronze Star for merit), but came to believe, as he does still, that we should not have been in Vietnam when the regime we supported was so erratic and venal.

By then he considered it a foregone conclusion that once the Americans withdrew, ARVN would lose the war. "It was not a dangerous assignment, but a very disillusioning one. We already had instructions to pull out. We knew we wouldn't win the war before '73, and we knew that ARVN would be left fighting the war and that they would lose. The first day I got there was sort of a horrible introduction to Vietnam. I'd literally just got off the plane, and had to be helicoptered some place. The helicopter was diverted, and we picked up a Vietnamese peasant woman in the Mekong River delta. She had just been shot by a GI right through the throat. She was bleeding all over. This wasn't even an operational thing; he just got pissed off at her and shot her. That was Day One in Vietnam. That was the time of fragging, people defying their officers, smoking marijuana in their faces. So at that point I was very disillusioned with the war and the American effort. ARVN and the elite in [South] Vietnam were not behind the war, basically. They were out for their self-interest. There were certainly genuine anticommunists there who believed that communism was wrong, but I think they were a small group. So I realized that no matter how many resources we put in there, no matter how much we bribed and persuaded them, kicked them in the ass, it just wouldn't work. In the meantime, while we were trying to make the push, we were literally destroying a country and a culture and a society that didn't really want to fight in the first place. Frankly, I was hoping the experience would be over as soon as possible."

He also developed the view that the U.S. prosecution of the war was criminal in some ways—for example, the bombing of Cambodia. On the other hand, what he saw of Vietnam that wasn't war-related he found beautiful and beguiling. Ellsworth Bunker, a Yale man, Skull and Bones, was U.S. ambassador to South Vietnam during Gray's tour, and invited all the Yale men stationed in Saigon to meet the reporters who were covering the war. Gray was impressed with what he saw, and wrangled a job with the Associated Press after he left the Army. Following summary stints covering New York state politics in Albany and West German affairs in Bonn, he was sent to cover the serial falls of Saigon, Phnom Penh, and Laos in 1973 and then on to Bangkok to become bureau chief in 1975. He has never looked back. He married a Thai woman and with her had a daughter, now college-age.

Gray was attracted by the pulse of Asia, and, he admits, by its very instability. He has covered many wars, and put himself at far graver risk as a journalist than he was subjected to as a soldier. And it was the events that he witnessed as a reporter in Cambodia, not as a soldier in Vietnam, that clinched his condemnation of American involvement in the Indochina wars. "South Vietnam was its own enemy. The Americans did come in as allies. Cambodia was much more *used,* a much more cynical exercise. For Vietnam, you can make a case that some stratum was genuine about fighting. For Cambodia you cannot make that case. It was drawn into the war, used, and finally discarded." Prudently, however, Gray adds that he does not buy William Shawcross's argument that American bombing was primarily responsible for working the Khmer Rouge into a collective frenzy and fertilizing the killing fields.

He cannot say that he likes war itself. Twelve of those he has hired for AP have been killed or wounded, mostly by the Khmer Rouge, and he chokes up when he thinks about them. He believes, ruefully, that the figure represents a company record that he would just as soon not pad. It is more broadly the change in Asia and its striking sensuality and perpetual surprise—what he calls its "visual explosions"—that he is passionate about chronicling. Vietnam was part of that, but not the most positive part. And Asia is ever-changing. "Some people say, well, you've been in Asia for so long, aren't you repeating stories that you've written? But the Bangkok of 1976 and the Bangkok of 1998 is a totally different universe. In every one of those twenty-some years, I would have written a very different story. I'm not bored." The "pure greed" of the Thai economic boom and the squalor of the sex trade are lamentable, perhaps, but not dull.

Like other expat vets, Gray is keen on Southeast Asia's fundamental divergence from the West. But where they see it sardonically as a refuge from a post-Vietnam America they barely recognize, Gray embraces Asia earnestly and affirmatively—as an alternative world that pleasingly complements the United States. While the Air America alumni, for example, have simply iterated their own homegrown provincialism on Thailand and fortuitously found the two compatible, Gray's very urbanity makes him able to appreciate both worlds without decisively or chauvinistically rating one over the other. Although he acknowledges that American noncombatants have shortchanged Vietnam veterans in failing to recognize their adherence to duty in an unpopular war, his personal premium on dynamic observation seems to be an antidote to his participation in a consensually futile conflict that has insulated him from the resentment that other veterans feel.

To oversimplify, he looks on the bright side of Vietnam. "During the Gulf War I was with one of the Marine divisions, in one of the [media] pools. We were out on the desert for three weeks with nothing to do before the war started, so I had a lot of chances to talk to the old sergeants and colonels and even the generals who'd been in Vietnam. Although they never got into any heavy stuff and weren't tested, and as much as I was disillusioned with the Army in the waning days of Vietnam, I was extremely impressed with what a great unit those Marines were. They were really good soldiers, and they had learned their lessons from Vietnam. I heard none of the racial slurs that went around in Vietnam, they were very professional. There's a book to be written about the military between 1973 and 1991, the Gulf War, on what the military did to reform itself."

And Gray is too smart to write Vietnam off as some immoral spasm in the American narrative. "It was not just a mistake. The forces that propelled us into Vietnam were part of a historical impetus rising from our victory in World War II and the way in which America saw its position in the world, the Korean War, the spread of communism. I don't think you can see this as a criminal war and everything before it as different. It was part of the sweep of history, and has to be seen in the larger context of what went before it. But I do hope that most historians will look on Vietnam as a war that America should not have been involved in, even though the forces for us to go in were pretty strong and for many people very compelling."

∞○○∞

Another Bangkok-based vet, Bill Maddox, is only slightly easier on the war as history. Born in Macon, Georgia, son of a phone company engineer and World War II veteran, Maddox got caught in the draft in 1966 between junior college at Middle Georgia College and a four-year program at Georgia State. It may have been hard luck except that he took to the Army, possibly due to the preparation that junior ROTC gave him in high school. "Because it was mandatory, at that time it was the largest junior ROTC program in the country," he remembers. "We had to wear our little Eisenhower jacket uniforms three days a week to school. I did not have a great gung-ho attitude. But I wasn't going to go to Canada, and I certainly wasn't going to go to jail. You did your duty, but I didn't even know where Vietnam was at that time."

The Army is a regimented organization and he's a regimented person. He's about five-foot-nine and wiry, with freckles, blue eyes, thinning red hair, and a gray mustache, no fat, and his bearing is still cheerfully military: no wasted movement, an agenda even for leisure. He eats liver and onions at Jool's, fish and chips at the British Club, sausages at Bei Otto, fried okra and greens at Bourbon Street—no variation. He runs ten miles at a jaunt, four times a week, and never has a single bite to eat beforehand. The photographs in his albums all bear carefully crafted typewritten captions. It's no surprise, then, that Maddox scored high on Army aptitude tests, and his lieutenant recommended Officers Candidate School. He became a helicopter pilot and helicopter maintenance expert with the First Cavalry Division—the unit that defined Vietnam-style air-mobile infantry operations—logging 750 combat flying hours in Vietnam between August 1969 and August 1970.

He earned a Bronze Star for flying Hueys in and out of (often hot) landing zones and keeping them in the air. That decoration would have meant "a little more" with the "V" device, but without it, he found, "in most cases it meant, 'I was there and I didn't get court-martialed and I came home.'" He did win an Air Medal with a "V" for piloting his helicopter in the van of the U.S. Army's invasion of Cambodia on May 1, 1970. But, with the same tang of cynical wistfulness, he comments: "There were a lot of medals passed out that day, probably far too many. Until you get to the Silver Star and, for aviators, the Distinguished Flying Cross, the medals don't mean a great deal. I don't mean to trivialize them, they do mean something, but I think there was probably a proliferation of medals in Vietnam and they probably got carried away." And yeah, he adds, the Cambodia invasion was a clusterfuck.

He knew and thought little about Vietnam before the Army, and once in-country did not form what he would consider mature opinions about the war. Thirty years have ripened his views. "More than a military action, it was a political action I think. It was prosecuted by the politicians and not the military. I think that the military leadership may have participated in [the politics] a little too willingly, but that's strictly a personal opinion. I have no firsthand knowledge on that." He decided firmly, though, that men should not be sent potentially to give their lives unless the government has a clear objective in waging the war in question—which it did not with respect to Vietnam. "The senior leadership of the Army is still primarily Vietnam veterans that were in my grade or lower in Vietnam. I think they do think it was wrong to put people in harm's way without a plan. If you're going to fight a war, fight a war. If you're not, don't send people over there as cannon fodder. The first time you began to see a visible effect [of this lesson] was in the Gulf War. Vietnam was a television war, but the Gulf War was *really* a television war. When Powell and Schwartzkopf got up and gave those briefings, they—Powell in particular—made it very clear that he wanted specific goals laid out before committing American troops. Powell was a company commander in Vietnam, and I think that's a direct fallout of that experience."

But Maddox is careful to distinguish the absence of a military plan from strategic wrong-headedness. "That doesn't mean I think the war was wrong, because I don't. I don't know what the purpose of the war was, and I don't know if anyone does even to this day. As 'containment' I think it may have been right and it may have succeeded. I think that it bought time for other places like Thailand and Malaysia where communism was taking a foothold. But if the purpose of the war was to save South Vietnam, that was a poor purpose to start with and we didn't succeed in it. I'm not sure anybody could have because I don't think they wanted to be saved." In any case, he feels that U.S. soldiers generally did all that was asked of them. And the war had its cultural pluses. Because the Vietnam War was the first one brought to the

U.S. viewing public every night on the news, it showed people that American soldiers sometimes wind up not like John Wayne, with the glory and the girl (notwithstanding *Sands of Iwo Jima*), but rather dead or crippled.

Maddox was sensitive to loud noises for a couple of years—startled by construction sounds and heavy traffic—but does not suffer from any type of post-traumatic stress. Though he's seen the horror of war, he does not dwell on Vietnam. Some do, he admits. One of his best friends in the First Cav, a fellow helicopter pilot from Brooklyn, was traumatized by a single incident from the war. He was assigned to go and recover a downed Huey, in which the pilot and co-pilot were killed. ARVN troops were supposed to remove the bodies, but had not done so. Bill's friend looked in the cockpit and found two charred American bodies, both of them decapitated. He has never gotten over it. After two beers, says Maddox, that's all the guy ever talks about. The man now has a severe drinking problem. For Maddox's part, he admits he will never forget the smell of burned flesh and remembers finding a severed arm in a cold landing zone. But he makes the point that all wars install those permanent, harrowing images in the psyches of combatants.

Maddox is an unusually surefooted man, both intellectually and practically, with an aggressive outlook on life and a balanced appreciation for the past. He did not feel ostracized when he returned to the United States from Vietnam, but to a degree he was insulated from the antiwar movement because he stayed in the Army. While he did venture onto the campus to earn a B.A. in psychology, he attended North Texas State in Denton—a conservative school in a demographically pro-war state with a number of military personnel matriculating—and caught little flower-power flak. Maddox ended up staying in the Army for twenty-five years. He was stationed in Thailand in 1980–84, then in the Pentagon and Korea for three years each, and spent his last two years on active duty back in Bangkok. He retired in 1992, as a lieutenant colonel.

With his expertise in military logistics, he stayed in Thailand not because of any especially negative feeling toward the United States, but because he had a positive Army experience in Asia, his American wife was posted at the U.S. consulate in Bangkok, and he was offered a lucrative business opportunity—selling Humvees and other logistical ordnance to the Thai military—in civilian life. But there remain aspects of post-Vietnam America that bother Bill Maddox. He believes that Vietnam veterans are generally underappreciated, and effectively blamed for a losing effort that was really the fault of politicians and, to an extent, the media. "I don't dwell on that," he says. "I do feel kind of shortchanged sometimes, and I won't say it doesn't bother me because it does." Like many expat vets—and vets, period—he had no time for Bill Clinton. Upon his retirement from the Army, Maddox was entitled to a certificate of appreciation signed by the president for his twenty-five years of service. Clinton had just been elected to his first term. Maddox declined the certificate. "I didn't want it if it was signed by him," he growls.

Maddox is not the sort to let a few bad vibes drive him into permanent exile. And while he harbors a prurient affection for Bangkok—he snickers that "Thailand is the only country in the world that includes pussy in its gross national product"—there is an aspect of the typical expat veteran's existence that he sees as self-demeaning. He notes that Thai wives of American ex-GIs, for example, are often unsophisticated "trophies." Their standard reading material might consist of comic books containing lurid romances sold at Thai newsstands. This fact alone is a disincentive to such vets to bringing their Thai wives back to the States, where they would find it lonely and difficult to adjust and the vets themselves might well find their wives embarrassing. The novelty of the Orient has worn off for Bill Maddox. He joined the Army and saw the world. He and his wife will retire quietly to the Florida panhandle.

THE MAKING OF THREE CYNICS

L. C. Linder joined the Marine Corps in emulation of his older brother Tom, who was serving in an artillery unit in Vietnam when L. C. shipped out. Having waived the second brother's privilege of avoiding combat duty, Linder did his thirteen-month tour around Hué in 1969 and 1970, first serving briefly in an infantry unit, Zulu company, in charge of guarding the perimeter of the Marines' base at Marble Mountain, and then as a helicopter doorgunner on a Boeing CH-46, which the Marines used as the Army used the Huey. He was not hurt but earned several Air Medals and saw enough heavy action to educate him about the horrors of war. Stuck in his mind: a huge mortar attack on Marble Mountain, in which he "alternated between cursing and praying" and truly thought he would die; the enemy soldier firing at him whom he shot from his helicopter and saw die; and a GI whose legs and arm had been blown off, who stayed conscious as Linder and his crew medevacked him and who kept asking whether he was going to die. The medic on the ground said quietly to Linder, "Unfortunately, he probably will."

Linder had nightmares for a few years after the war. And he drifted. He rejoined the Marines to become a pilot, only to be dropped from the aviator program because of poor depth perception. He owned a restaurant in Columbia, South Carolina, his birthplace. It failed. Linder scuba dived on oil exploration projects, coordinated defense communications initiatives, helped develop an expert system computer program, worked as a private investigator, and with another vet marketed early antivirus software known as Victor Charlie (mnemonically referring to "virus catcher" as well as "Vietcong"). Along the way he also spent a couple of years in Saudi Arabia with Vinell Corporation (sometimes a CIA contractor) as a technical analyst and instructor training the Saudi Arabian National Guard. He did not take to the puritanical Muslim world, and vacationed in Thailand. By 1990 he was spending parts of the year there, and eagerly jumped on the opportunity to come there permanently to head an old Marine pal's helicopter maintenance business in Southeast Asia.

A few years back he walked into the New Cowboy Bar, a few hundred meters down Soi 22 Sukhumvit from Washington Square. He ordered a beer. A couple of other expats were sitting down. With characteristic warmth and cheer, L.C. asked aloud whether anyone knew when or where the VFW met in Bangkok, as he was a lifetime member (courtesy of his brother). An older man piped up and said he too was an active VFW member, and queried what war L.C. was in. When L.C. answered, "Vietnam," the man blurted that the guys who fought in Vietnam were a bunch of losers, and not real veterans. L.C. responded testily, "Well, it seems to me that the men who died in Vietnam are just as dead as those who died in World War II and Korea, and their families are just as bereaved." Barely in control of his temper, he left his money on the bar and walked out.

L.C. Linder is single—he has never married—but he has a steady Thai girlfriend in her thirties. He likes younger Thai women, and has dated them when opportunities have arisen since he first came to Thailand in the Vietnam era. He has all his hair, none of it gray; he looks far younger than his fifty-plus years; his manner is reassuringly relaxed. Raised a conservative, patriotic southerner, he believed in the war when he joined the Marines, but once in Vietnam started to believe that the war was wrong— that most Vietnamese didn't care who governed them as long as they could eat, that most Americans didn't feel especially kindly toward the Vietnamese, that "we were doing more harm than good. I saw the damage we did in flying around the country, huge areas defoliated and destroyed. The A Shau Valley, a nasty place, looked like a lunar landscape from B-52 strikes. We'd support battles in one area and a week later [be doing] the same thing. No front lines, no gains. Territory is gained and held by making the local population of that territory on your side. The Marines had a program called the Combined Action Group. They would take a company of Marines and marry it up with a company of Popular Forces, and get down to the platoon and the squad level, living and working with the local people, so they weren't gooks or Charlie or whatever. They *did* win the hearts and minds. But overall, we had a flawed strategy."

He also saw two atrocities, both committed by marines from the Republic of Korea, who were renowned for their toughness, cruelty, and vigilance, and for making Cam Ranh Bay, which they were in charge of guarding, the safest place in Vietnam. "A village was burned and civilians killed," he remembers. "It certainly registered with me, and I'd already heard about the My Lai thing. That was our only insertion into that particular area, just that one time, we saw it and left. Me and the crew might have talked about it, but nothing was ever said to anybody else. What are you going to do? After a while people just got the word: don't mess with them." On a different occasion, Linder and his helicopter crew had to extract two ROK marines from a hot landing zone and return them to their fire base. One of them was wounded, and they had captured the female Vietcong who had shot him. As the helicopter lifted off, one of the Korean soldiers drew a K-bar knife, popped the buttons off her blouse with the point, and began to trace circles with it around the girl's breasts as she screamed. The pilot and Linder saw what was going on and warned the Koreans that they were not to harm her. The Korean soldiers relented. But as Linder's chopper departed, he saw a mob of Korean soldiers trundle their prisoner off. As to her fate, Linder assumes the worst. "I shudder to think what happened to her *before* she died. It's one of those things that stays with you."

Further study has convinced Linder that the political objective of containment might have been attainable without war had we understood that Ho Chi Minh was more a nationalist than a communist. (Linder cites *Why Vietnam? A Prelude to America's Albatross* by Archimedes Patti, former head of the Office of Strategic Services' French Indochina mission during World War II and one of the early Vietnam War skeptics.) Economics won the Cold War by exposing the "dictatorial scam" of communism, he continues, so he does not think Southeast Asia would be any different today had we never intervened in Indochina. More technically, he feels that the emphasis on body counts over territory, and the "limited escalation" policy, reflected a flawed military strategy that derogated American lives. So too did persistent support for a corrupt, unenthusiastic ally. He was shocked when an ARVN sergeant major tried to make him purchase a black-market refrigerator; when ARVN was responsible for securing the camp perimeter on Marble Mountain, Marines would set up their own perimeter patrol inside the ARVN ring because they did not trust the South Vietnamese soldiers.

One of Linder's recollections seems to encapsulate the constants of all the postmortems. "A unit had been partially overrun. [Reinforcements] tried to get to them at night, but couldn't do anything at night. At first light the attack was over, so we went in to start hauling the dead and wounded out. It looked something like Custer's Last Stand. There were just an enormous number of enemy bodies still out there, all around. Some of them that had made it into the perimeter, they just had stacked up like cordwood. We flew the casualties out, then started flying American dead out, then flying their dead out. We just had big bundles of them. That was one of the big things—our kill ratio was a lot higher, but it was proven that there was no way we would ever win a war of attrition. The strategy of the war was wrong from day one. When I left, I just felt we were doing a lot of damage over there."

In 1975, Linder was a communications officer on the *U.S.S. Mt. Whitney*, and got a play-by-play from real-time radio traffic between the Pentagon and Saigon when the city fell. "The guys in the embassy would say, 'We've just barricaded the stairway,' 'we're on the roof now,' 'the last helicopter's here.' You could have heard a pin drop. Then you'd say, like, what was it all for?" For all his pensiveness, Linder has made the most, psychically, of having served in the Vietnam War. "It was handled improperly, but I don't hold it against my government. I'm definitely an American, I love my country." While he does view it as "the adventure of a lifetime" that exposed him to a world—Southeast Asia—that he would never have seen otherwise, he says, "I could have come home in a body bag. I don't break down and weep but I do get misty-eyed at memorial ceremonies. It was a waste."

∞∞

Like Linder, Jeff McLaury worked in the United States after the war and retired—at least tentatively—to Southeast Asia, having spent 1996–99 in Saigon and 2000 in Thailand. Unlike Byrne, Sauvageot, Gray, and Maddox, his shrugging off of his Vietnam service is not retrospective; it began during his first tour in Vietnam. He is an American story and looks the part: a brawny, six-foot-tall Coloradan, with ruddy sun-drenched skin, blue eyes, and a ready, matey smile. Once he starts to talk, he pauses only to light cigarettes.

McLaury came by military service naturally, his father having won a Silver Star and a Purple Heart serving in Germany in the Second World War. After being recruited for football by Columbia and attending for a few months, he decided he was "too dumb" for the Ivy League and switched to the Naval Academy. Upon graduating from the Academy in 1963, he elected to serve in the Army. The reason he gives reveals a fairly mature brand of patriotism for a twenty-two-year-old man: the Cuban Missile Crisis was a wake-up call in terms of mobilization, revealing disarray in our ground forces' preparedness. McLaury was airborne trained,

169

and as a second lieutenant commanded the top platoon at Fort Benning, beating out two West Pointers in the brigade.

Then he was a star, and ready to rock and roll, but not "too dumb" to perceive the salient problems with the Vietnam War. McLaury read books about Vietnam even then. While he certainly believed in containing communism, he also thought that in light of the South Vietnam government's instability U.S. intervention was a bad idea. "We were backing a side, getting involved in a situation where nobody knew who was in charge—though I could see the bigger picture, too. I had big misgivings. I didn't want to come to Vietnam. I didn't graduate determined to make the military my career. I intended to spend my four years in and get out into civilian life anyway."

In 1967, after training for Vietnam in the Panama Canal Zone, he was assigned to the 25th Infantry Division, which had relieved the First Infantry Division (the Big Red One) at Cu Chi, in the Iron Triangle. "I'd been through this intensive training, so I got off the plane at Tan Son Nhat expecting attacks from the Vietnam out on the tarmac. But the first thing I heard was the Air Force Band playing 'I Left My Heart in San Francisco.' While you're processing at the replacement depot, all the guys that are going home are giving you the finger and saying, 'Hey, have a good year, baby.' They're getting on the same plane to go home. You started counting days the minute you got in-country. Then they loaded us on deuce-and-a-halfs for the run up to Cu Chi. I was the only officer. An enlisted man gave M-14s to all the men in the truck, and I said, 'Wait a minute, where's the fucking magazine?' This was when I knew how fucked up Vietnam was going to be. He said, 'No, we don't give out live ammo anymore.' I said, 'Well, why not?' He said, 'Well, we had too many accidents, so we just give everybody guns and hope that the Vietcong think they're loaded. But it's too dangerous. You guys might shoot each other.'"

He saw some combat as junior officer for brigade operations,

and may have been the only American officer to have reconnoi-
tered the Cu Chi tunnels. But he served his tour mainly at headquarters, opting not to seek a rifle company command and in fact
declining one when offered because he "didn't want to fucking
die. I didn't believe in the way the war was being fought, and
everything I saw only made me more discouraged. The one-year
tour made absolutely no sense. [Same with] the effort to make the
war comfortable—to get the ice-cream in for the general. So much
was done for show and not substance."

McLaury's decision to turn down a company command was
based on his doubts about the U.S. political strategy and overall
military approach. "The episode took place in an informal atmosphere. The incumbent wanted to turn his command over to me,
and informally convinced the executive officer that I was the man.
It was considered an honor to get command so there was no direct
order for me to refuse. I would not have refused orders to assume
command. Further, I had made the decision in advance—I would
not seek company command. Nevertheless, it was still difficult to
turn down the hero who wanted me to take care of his men. I
think it is important that he didn't say, 'take my company so you
can kill more of the enemy.' Rather, he said, 'take my company
and keep my men alive.' I said no, another man said yes, and many
of the men did die in a single engagement within weeks. There
was an air assault, and he stepped on an antipersonnel mine. His
foot was still attached when I saw him, but it was pretty fucked
up. All his troops had gathered around him, and blew an antitank
mine. I met him at the evac pad, and this was the first time I'd
really seen gore. They were bringing in stretchers with just body
parts. There was one black guy, eyes still wide open, and only a
couple of pockmarks on his body, nothing on his face, but everything else [i.e., all four limbs] gone."

However absurd he felt American war-fighting in Vietnam
was, he still feels guilty. "Could I have made a difference? I'll

never know, but if I could turn back the clock I think I would take the command. The fact that I viewed our approach to the conflict as misguided and misdirected had a great bearing on my choice to decline command of a rifle company. I think I would have volunteered in World War II because the issues were probably more clearly defined. But for all I know, I would have considered our approach to World War II lacking, too. Therefore, had I seen the situation as simply a choice between furthering my career by accepting command or improving my chances of survival by declining, I honestly have no idea what I would have done."

McLaury was never hurt in Vietnam. He did see several atrocities—minor ones by ARVN, one major massacre by Korean troops—but none committed by Americans. Tactically as well as strategically, he felt that the Americans fought a stupid war—for example, by following set patterns and thus violating an obvious convention of guerrilla warfare. He refused an order to patrol the Oriental River in Popular Forces landing craft, with helicopter cover, over a course of several days in order to secure the western flank—not for an operation, but to protect a discretionary brass meeting with the MACV commander, General Creighton Abrams. McLaury believed that the repetitive screening activity would get him killed merely to indulge the vanity of some ranking officers who liked the idea of meeting close to harm's way. "It was just bullshit. What they wanted was to give a nice show to General Abrams. They could say, 'Well, we've got Captain McLaury, who's a Naval Academy graduate, with a seaborne force screening our flank,' and it would sound good. I knew if I died, it would only be for a dog-and-pony show. Any air-mobile operation was telegraphed to the Vietcong two or three days in advance. I would not lose my life to accomplish nothing more than create a colorful anecdote for the evening briefing. This is no way for a soldier to think, but I was prepared to accept a court-martial and disgrace."

The Special Forces unit in charge of the boats agreed with

McLaury's assessment and initially refused to release the craft. Brigade insisted, and someone else ran the patrol without incident. McLaury was threatened with a court-martial but it was never brought. When later requested to conduct a similar patrol for operational reasons, McLaury agreed provided he could mix up the timing so as to keep the Vietcong off-balance. He was sidelined as "a pain in the ass." Two other GIs did it instead, and they were shot dead. Despite all this, though, McLaury won two Bronze Stars (for merit, not valor, he makes sure to say), several Air Medals, and the Air Force Commendation Medal for coordinating ground operations and tactical air support at division level. Of the latter he is somewhat proud: at least he helped the Army get something right in Vietnam.

On his second tour, McLaury was a transportation officer, first at Long Binh, where he was in charge of logistical air operations between Vietnam and the Pentagon. It was a powerful job in that he had authority to prioritize soldiers' DEROS dates depending on what ordnance requirements were, and a dangerous one insofar as he had to contend with the infamous NCO "Khaki Mafia." During the latter part of the tour, he controlled all of the in-country logistical transportation assets in central Vietnam, with an airport, seaport, and train line at his exclusive disposal. Despite the relative safety of his assignment, he saw enough to add to his skepticism about the war. Several times the Vietcong had been successful in blowing up trains, and once managed to sabotage one right near the town that served as brigade headquarters. Korean forces were in charge of security. At the scene of the explosion, McLaury spoke to their commanding officer, who was bowing in mortification, and impressed upon him that this must not happen any more. The Korean, plainly ashamed, bowed some more to the tall American and vowed that no more trains would be blown up. McLaury dismissed the ROK officer, and began consulting the Vietnamese railroad people as to how to repair the track. A few minutes later, he heard the pop-pop-pop of .50 caliber machine guns. He climbed on top of the locomotive and saw that the Korean troops had pulled their gun-mounted jeeps up to the edge of a nearby village and were stolidly, with goggles on, firing pure tracer rounds into it. In no time at all the village was in flames.

McLaury resigned his commission in November 1969, got divorced from his American wife, and returned to Vietnam for three years in 1971—two as a freight forwarder for SEALAND (the world's largest container ship company, which handled resupply cargo for the Army), and one with the charter airline Transamerica that sold tickets to GIs for home leave. He transferred Transamerica ops to Hong Kong in 1974 when things got too hot in Saigon, but kept an apartment in Saigon and came back once a month to look in on his Vietnamese girlfriend. McLaury had no intention of marrying this woman, but lived with her and felt some responsibility toward her, so he filled out papers stating his intention to marry her in order to facilitate her eventual evacuation.

It came in spring 1975 as Saigon fell. McLaury agreed to go back to Saigon when the NVA had ringed the city and was poised to take the capital—ostensibly to negotiate a Transamerica contract to charter Americans and Vietnamese friendlies out, proximately to get her out. He decided the charter flight was imprudent in light of aerial photographs furnished to him by CIA officers, who by then were running the evacuation. But he found his girlfriend and took her to Tan Son Nhat. Their Flying Tiger plane, full of 120 Vietnamese illegals whose escape McLaury had finessed on the fly, was the first to depart Saigon after April 21, 1975. Without a flight plan they flew through the Philippines' airspace and were ordered to land. As Manila had made it clear that it would not accept evacuees, McLaury told the pilot to ignore the request. The Filipino authorities threatened to scramble interceptors, but they never materialized. They made it to Guam, where they were interned for a day, and then moved on safely to Honolulu. McLaury sent his girlfriend to Denver and went back to Hong Kong with Transamerica. She married another American, they bought two restaurants, and they live happily in the United States.

He put the war experience behind him, married a Chinese woman, left Hong Kong in 1977, and, as he is an animal lover, ran pet boarding kennels for ten years in Denver. They had no children because he feared birth defects due to his exposure to Agent Orange. He sold the kennel business, which gave him independent means, and tried golf and retirement stateside. It didn't take. He craved Asia and with his wife returned to Hong Kong for a visit in 1994. Again he caught the Asian bug, but his Asian wife did not. After a few months back in the States, they divorced. McLaury went to Vietnam in 1996, once again in the freight-forwarding business, selling golf simulators on the side and hoping that Vietnam would win Most Favored Nation status from the United States.

Both nostalgia for the exciting days of the war and the lure of benign Asian decadence (beer, broads, and bribery) brought him back. "In 1975 Saigon was a pretty bustling place. It didn't have all these tall buildings, but walk out of a tall building and across the street you can be in a tin shack. The city has the same flavor, the same look that it did in 1975, which is an unusual thing in this world. I was out of Hong Kong for four years, I went back, I didn't recognize the place. Other places—Singapore I don't recognize, Bangkok I don't recognize. But Saigon? Virtually the same place. There are the same buildings I used to go to, the same bars I used to go to. It's like reliving my youth. Money couldn't buy it. I've talked to other veterans and people who worked as civilians during the war, and [the feeling] is not uncommon." His friends have accused him of indulging a midlife crisis. "Maybe I am. I don't care. I'm having fun. It seems as if the minute I stepped off the plane in Saigon the years from 1975 to 1996 never happened, or at best I had been in a state of limbo. Memories of 1967 to 1975 were vivid and real. The later years were bland and vague in my mind. It was like coming out of hibernation and being reborn. I was thirty-five years old again in every regard."

McLaury still thinks that the U.S. stand in Southeast Asia did stall the spread of communism in the region, and he believes that although ARVN leadership was poor the line soldiers fought valiantly and sacrificed enormously. "In terms of containment, the war had some meaning. In fact, in hindsight I'm not so sure that maybe Vietnam didn't serve a very real purpose in that it did stop the movement of communism in Asia for a time and led to difficulties between Russia and China. A case could be made that in the big picture the war was successful." Like many vets, he believes the Pentagon blew any chance of military victory by failing to exploit naval power after Tet, when he felt the VC were thoroughly depleted and the north could have been blockaded without producing a confrontation with Russia or China.

A political conservative, he decries the pampered whininess of contemporary American culture—the need to blame someone for everything—and has come to dislike living in the United States for that reason, too. He feels that Americans have failed to come to grips with Vietnam, and resents the assumption that as a Vietnam vet he must be emotionally unstable. The post-Vietnam generation, he says, is "soft." Ergonomically, America now, transformed by the Vietnam War, does not suit a man whose patriotism springs from America in 1963. "My decision to live in Vietnam has nothing to do with unresolved conflicts or guilt. The decision was to reject the politically correct nonsense that permeates American society. The obsession with minority rights, the victim mentality, the lack of personal responsibility, the whole touchy-feely attitude gives me a dim view of the future of America. I choose not to be a part of it. I find the Asian approach to life much more suited to my views and those of the America I grew up in. I think the biggest effect the Vietnam War had on my life is what it spawned in terms of leadership in America."

Bill Clinton, says McLaury, "was a pathological liar, a cheat, and a fraud. That 43 percent of the country would vote for a man I wouldn't invite into my home shows how far out of touch I am with America. If I am a patriot, how can I throw up my hands and walk away? Let me clarify. I am loyal to what I think America stood for. However, I believe the principles which made America great have led to extremes that are beyond repair. The radicals of the sixties have won their war. I see no way of changing course when 70 percent of the population supported a whore [as president]. I say this with apologies to whores who normally live by a code of conduct and show respect to family and friends."

McLaury, in his dissolute negativism and his abandonment of a traditional life in favor of golf, girls, and the nineteenth hole, has resigned himself to a kind of cheerful self-loathing. He is supremely cynical and a little inconsistent—admitting, for example, that the Vietnam War was misguided and not worth dying for, but castigating contemporary U.S. leaders for their unwillingness to take a stand as we did in Vietnam. The war did seem to damage Jeff McLaury's existential spirit. Nevertheless, he is both candid and astute about his motivations, and seems compelled to judge himself, when appropriate, harshly. It's an admirable trait, but must make him toss and turn upon occasion. In a sense, he was caught: he came of age as a young Army officer fighting for a country he believed in but in a war that he thought was poorly executed. Then he came home to find a society transformed by that war in a way that the war, problematic as it was, still didn't justify. Maybe, therefore, it's not so surprising that those years after 1975 seemed like a bleary dream to him: McLaury, as a critic of the war who still defended its motivation, couldn't find a "middle ground" on which he could stand.

Les Strouse, left, in April 1963
and Mac Thompson, right, with
the U.S. Agency for International Development in Laos
before retiring to Bangkok.
*Courtesy Les Strouse and Mac
Thompson.*

6

VALOR DEFENDED

Southeast Asian vets run the gamut of retrospective Vietnam thinking—from "it was a horrible mistake" to "the politicians didn't let the soldiers fight for a just cause"—and the vast majority accordingly report mixed wartime experiences. But not all of them do. Some stayed in Southeast Asia not just because they are unappreciated at home, and not just owing to bonds formed with locals, but because the war was the best time of their lives.

Alan Dawson is a good example. He is about five-foot-eight, medium build, with red hair and blue eyes. He's sun-reddened and befreckled. His hair is slicked back and extra-shoulder-length. He wears gold-rimmed glasses, has yellow teeth that he clicks with enthusiasm, and talks in a slightly hoarse but confident timbre. Dawson looks like a superannuated hippie, compulsively moves the conversation along with "That's cool," and issues the departing salutation, "Peace, man," complete with the sixties-era two-fingered gesture, with less irony than one would have expected. But Alan Dawson's views belie this appearance: he's expressly nonpacifist; he defends the Phoenix Program—the CIA's pacification campaign, which involved the assassination of suspected Vietcong—as legitimate (if sometimes excessive) guerrilla warfare; and he believes Vietnam was well-intentioned but poorly executed by a "big, stumbling giant."

He was a journalist before, during, and after the Army. Though born in Ontario, he moved to Oregon in 1965 to write for the *Eugene Register*. As a legal U.S. resident of draftable age, he was eligible for military service. Seeing Vietnam as a journalistic opportunity and an adventure, Dawson declined a generous offer from his local draft board to return to Canada and was inducted into the U.S. Army in 1967. He wound up as an army reporter with the First Signal Brigade, and served in Vietnam for a year and a day. Dawson traveled all over South Vietnam, "doing hometown radio interviews and writing little stories for hometown newspapers: 'Private Jimmy Jones is having the time of his life in Vietnam and really likes it and says hello to Mom and Dad.'" In the middle of his tour, though ordered not to go to the besieged Khe Sanh by his commanding officer, he hitched a ride there on a C-123 transport plane to interview six members of his unit who were establishing long-range communications for the embattled Marines. Within minutes after Dawson arrived, all six men were killed by a rocket strike. He filed a poignant story about their heroism. Several major newspapers picked up the piece, which enhanced his CO's status and career. Instead of being disciplined he won a Bronze Star—for "typing faster than anyone else," he hastens to add, and not a Bronze Star with a combat "V" for valor.

He was discharged as a buck sergeant and stayed in Vietnam as a civilian journalist, mainly with United Press International. As UPI's Saigon Bureau Chief from 1973 to 1975, he covered the NVA's occupation of Saigon. While he never fired his M-16 in the Army, he did fire the gun he carried in the field as a civilian. He doesn't know whether he hit anyone. "I certainly hope so." Later he wrote *55 Days: The Fall of South Vietnam,* an estimable book that was translated into Thai and became a bestseller in Bangkok. When the North Vietnamese kicked him out of Vietnam, he landed in Bangkok and became UPI's Bangkok Bureau Chief. After Vietnam, Cambodia was still up for grabs. He stayed at UPI until 1980, whereupon he joined the *Bangkok Post.* Why so long in Asia?

In 1980, Dawson had spent more than a third of his life in Asia. His father was dead, his mother self-sufficient. He had no siblings. He loved his job in Bangkok. There was no reason to go home. The baths of chicken blood and taunts of "baby-killer" that many of his fellow soldiers got as they arrived home at Travis Air Force Base disgusted him. He was bearish on a post-Vietnam America that seemed to distill that disdainful dispensation toward veterans into a social norm. Now he has thirty-year-old twin boys by his first wife, an ethnic Chinese woman from Vietnam, who are grown up and out on their own. The three children by his Thai wife are all under fifteen. The five of them live quietly in suburban Bangkok. After years of decompressing in Patpong bars most nights, Dawson now drinks hardly at all. He is wistful about the wild-west Bangkok of old, when fresh milk and NFL football were hard to come by, though he does cherish the anarchical residue that still hangs over Asian life but can't be found in the States: "I can bargain with the tax man; try doing that with the IRS."

Yet by virtue of his military service Dawson is a U.S. citizen and proud of it. He is fond of quoting Michael Herr from *Dispatches:* "Vietnam was what we had instead of happy childhoods." And Alan Dawson is a happy man. He unapologetically extols

Vietnam as the most compelling experience of his life, and has no qualms about saying that he loved being there in 1967 and 1968. "I wouldn't have enjoyed Korea, getting frostbite. But Vietnam had a strange combination of things that just came together. They had a hell of a war. I don't feel even slightly politically incorrect to say that I enjoyed that war—to include the part where I personally got shot at, without result, as Winston Churchill once said. I enjoyed the excitement, the adrenaline, I enjoyed the male companionship, the bonding. I enjoyed being around American troops and the Vietnamese. Naturally there are days that you don't like in a war. That goes without saying. Mine was when five of my very best personal friends died in a helicopter crash over Laos during the invasion that went so terribly wrong. But on the whole, I found it exhilarating. That was what kept me there, more or less, for nine years. It's kind of like, you get to the Arctic, and you've been there for three months, you might as well stay all night." Since the fall of Saigon, he says only half in jest, "it's been all downhill. I covered the fall of Saigon when I was thirty-three years old, and you'll hardly ever get a bigger story than that in your life."

Dawson shares "the general feeling in Southeast Asia that the American effort in Vietnam gave the rest of this area, including Thailand, the time they badly needed to get their act together and become what they became in the late seventies and eighties: rapidly developing and expanding countries, bringing up the middle class. The Americans came in against the communists, who had good momentum, and the Vietnam War stopped the communist advance. They had to pay so much attention to Vietnam that they couldn't expand their war into Burma, Malaysia, Indonesia, the Philippines, and so on." He notes that Lee Kuan Yew, the former prime minister of Singapore whose father-knows-best moralism has given enlightened illiberalism a degree of legitimacy, publicly espoused precisely that view and carried several other Asian leaders with him. Two architects of Washington's Vietnam policy, Walt Rostow and the late McGeorge Bundy, echoed this assessment, and now Michael Lind, in *Vietnam: The Necessary War*, has advanced a similar argument. However else Dawson may explain his staying power in Southeast Asia, it has something to do with his observation that "the prevailing view in the United States is just about the opposite." He is not alone.

AMIABLE THROWBACKS

Mac (for "MacAlan") Thompson is moderate everything—height, build, and demeanor—and his slightly protruding ears underline a naturally genial nature. He smiles a lot, and has an earnest yet jaunty approach to life that makes for a qualified sense of adventure. In 1963, Thompson joined the Army as an engineer out of Reserve Officer Training Corps at Oregon State University. His father had served in World War II. Wars happen and young men fight in them, he was raised to believe. It was part of life. He served a year in Korat, Thailand, from February 1964 to February 1965, helping to construct the Air Force base there as the Vietnam War build-up began. He was more pragmatic than actively political, and did not have any strong feeling then that we should not get involved in Vietnam. He was, however, neither ignorant nor unperceptive. Thompson had taken due notice of Thich Quang Duc, in June 1963 the first of several Buddhist priests to set himself on fire in protest of South Vietnamese president Ngo Dinh Diem's policies. He had written an essay in ROTC maintaining that the United States should not back Diem in Vietnam because he was a corrupt and unreliable ally who seemed to derogate the Buddhist faith of his own people. This feeling, however, was not so strong that he would have shirked his duty as a soldier, and in the event he assumed an active role in the Indochina war effort as a civilian.

Thompson was discharged from the Army in late 1965, having

done the two things his father believed a man should do in his life: "graduate from college and get out of the Army." Thompson retained some knowledge of and appreciation for Asia and, after ten months of beer drinking and skydiving in Oregon, he spent most of the next nine years in Laos. In 1966, the "secret war" there had already begun. Thompson started in International Volunteer Services, working in forward-area rural development programs. Four or five IVS people were killed. Subsequently he came on board USAID, helping to run the Lao refugee program. He carried a pistol and kept an AK-47 in his hootch. USAID and the CIA worked hand-in-hand in Laos. With Air America pilots he arranged rice drops for Hmong anticommunist rebels where CIA officers told him the rice should go. More broadly, his job was to make sure that people displaced due to a guerrilla war, generally anticommunist, got food, fuel, shelter, tools, medicine, and education. Numerous members of each government organization were killed.

The Lao rebels that the United States supported, unlike the Khmer Rouge in Cambodia (where Thompson served on temporary duty in April 1974), did not target civilians on a wholesale basis. That war, he concludes, was reasonably chivalrous, and not in any way an embarrassment to have fought. Thus, Thompson considers himself to have contributed to the humanitarian and support side of U.S. war efforts in Indochina, and believes that contribution was positive. He is not prone to hindsight, and tends to have a low-key existential view about the war. What he will say is that he is not certain that things would have turned out any worse in Southeast Asia had the United States not intervened militarily. He also suspects things might have worked out with less loss of life had the U.S. elected to support Ho Chi Minh after the Second World War, or (more speculatively) had John F. Kennedy not been assassinated and Johnson not been "bulldozed" by McNamara and company into escalation.

On the other hand, he notes cheerily, if there had been no war he never would have come to Asia and would not have had such an interesting life. After the war, in 1975, he went back to Thailand to coordinate the refugee relief program, then worked for several years for AID in Africa. He retired to Thailand, and lives about sixty kilometers north of Bangkok with a Thai girlfriend he's been with for seven years and her three children. His adopted son, a Thai now over thirty, lives in Thompson's house in Alexandria, Virginia. Thompson does not, however, feel alienated from the United States on account of his involvement in the war. Rather, he spends his retirement in Thailand because he knows that most of the people he knew during his career in government service either have stayed there also or pass through frequently. Thus, he says, he has more close American friends in Thailand than he does in the United States.

"Who ever visits Portland, Oregon?" he asks as a lead-in for rattling off his heavy social calendar in Thailand. "Last Saturday at the Lone Staar, my buddy from Battambang was in town, enroute to Kansas for Christmas. Another former USAID friend from the Vientiane [Laos' capital city] days, pre-'75, was in town from Mexico City. He's headed back to Florida for Christmas, just diverted a tad for a Singha beer and a visit. Sunday morning, back to the Lone Staar for a late breakfast. One of the visitors was a former State Department boss from my 'refugee' days; he's in from D.C. Another guy, also former USAID/Laos, and his wife were in from South Africa. A third guy, also a former refugee colleague, is in from Seattle. Then, of course, there was the afternoon party at Jeff Johnson's [ex-Air America]. Made it a full weekend, including a bunch who've never been to Portland. Detox now for a couple of days, then back to the Lone Staar on the afternoon of the twenty-fourth for Christmas dinner. A lot of people fly over Portland, but not many ever come through there."

Indeed, two of Thompson's closest friends from the Laos days—"Pop" Buell of USAID and CIA man Jerry Daniels—

retired and died in Bangkok. Yet, though obviously a committed expat, Thompson would never consider renouncing his U.S. citizenship. He stays in Thailand more for the American connections than the Thai ones. He nurtures those friendships diligently. He also monitors and contributes to a veterans' Thailand-Laos-Cambodia (TLC) news and discussion group on the Internet, and reads all of the postmortems on the war in Laos, sometimes pointing out inaccuracies to the authors. In a similar vein, he thinks CNN's now-discredited documentary on the "Tailwind" operation—alleging that Americans used sarin nerve gas on friendlies and defectors, shown and roundly jeered at the Lone Staar—was ludicrous, and distributed published refutations via e-mail to a substantial network of expats in Thailand.

As a career expat, Thompson's taste for his native country runs nostalgically to its bluff, muscular transitional years on either side of the Second World War—vintage Roadside America, when billboards were folk-art and advertising offered nonsubliminal wit. Each of his e-mails ends with a Burma-Shave poem enshrining the connection between romantic conquest and a chin as soft as a baby's butt. These bespeak a man with a sense of history. A quirky sense perhaps, but an acute one nonetheless.

Thompson's semipublic electronic countenance suggests that from the Depression until Pearl Harbor, we were a penitent, downtrodden people, and responded to prim, dour proclamations: *Be a modern/Paul Revere/Spread the news/From ear to ear* (Burma-Shave 1935); *He had the ring/He had the flat/But she felt his chin/And that was that* (Burma-Shave 1934); *Bachelor's quarters/Down on the rug/Whiskers to blame/No one to hug* (Burma-Shave 1935); *He's the boy/The gals forgot/His line was smooth/His chin was not* (Burma-Shave 1940). After VE-Day consumers got a little risqué ambiguity—*She raised Cain/When he raised Stubble/Guess what smoothed away/Their trouble?* (Burma-Shave 1945)—that came perilously close to what today would be called an endorsement of date rape:

Many a wolf/Is never let in/Because of the hair/On his chinny-chin-chin (Burma-Shave 1945). As the public's adrenaline cycled down, Burma-Shave dialed back the sex-o-meter a little: *A man who passes/On hills and curves/Is not a man/Of iron nerves—/He's crazy* (Burma-Shave 1948); *If you think/She likes your bristles/Walk bare-footed/Through some thistles* (Burma-Shave 1948). Finally, the prophetic James Dean allusion: *Cautious rider/To her reckless dear/Let's have less bull/And lots more steer* (Burma-Shave 1951).

If you don't find these at least a little charming, maybe Green-peace is the answer. The rhymes are from a time in the United States when unselfconscious tackiness, as long as it had some snap, was cool. That time is now in Bangkok. Though he only looks at them, Thompson says, with his droll penchant for technical phrasing, that "at least 70 percent of Thai women are at least Grade C or above," whereas "in Washington, D.C., only 30 percent are Grade C or above." And he likes being able to inspect Bangkok's choice females without getting slapped or sued. His friends too embrace this kind of benevolent Rat Packism, perhaps none more resolutely than the Air America boys. In Thailand now there are at least ten American veterans who worked for Air America. While technically civilians when Air America employ-ees, these men participated in guerrilla combat in an anticommu-nist U.S. proxy war designed, in part, to distract North Vietnam from the main event. About ninety Air America people were killed in the Indochina wars.

Unlike most Thailand-based vets, the Air America boys are close-knit and stay in regular touch with one another. They party frequently and share their hangovers. Their reminiscences are sprinkled with dry logistical references to places in Laos ("Lima Site 272," "Lima Site 118 Alternate") loaded enough with memo-ries of adventure to conjure instant private magic. At Air America reunions, they wear badges stenciled with their old code names (e.g., "Yellow Hat"). They tend to have the same views on most subjects. Ask any one of them about the 1991 film *Air America* with Mel Gibson, and you'll get the same stock answer: *It's a piece of shit.* Expatriate ex-Air America men were given the script and invited to a press conference in Bangkok prior to the film's release; the studio had hoped to get their endorsement, but instead got an angry scene.

The unanimous consensus is that the film's portrayal of the pilots as careless, unprofessional thrillseekers and, worse, drug runners, is a lie. The smarmily judgmental label "mercenary" frosts them because they made far less than people commonly believe—a helicopter pilot on average $3,000 per month (based on 70 hours of flying time, plus $50 for each takeoff and each landing), a "ground-pounder" at best half that much. They do not deny, but in fact celebrate, their individualism, their stoicism, and their self-sufficiency. These guys are adventurers, and also patriots, from the old school. They were not in it only, or even mainly, for the money.

Locally the best known of the bunch is Israel Freedman, known as Izzy, who lives in a studio apartment on a secluded and thus charming side street in downtown Bangkok, next to a Catholic school and a couple of blocks from his bar on Patpong. He is bald, mustached, and a tad heavy, tanned and firm of grip. Born and raised in Willimantic, Connecticut, he did poorly in high school and wound up going to The Citadel, undeterred by family concerns that a Jewish boy with a conspicuously Semitic appearance would be eaten alive by South Carolina's "lords of discipline."

He survived and joined the Air Force, where he learned to fly. He spent six months in Da Nang in 1963, when he embraced Vietnam as "just a big adventure" during which he "wanted to be a hero." There were only twelve thousand Americans in-country then. He flew C-123 Provider and DC-3 transport planes during those early days, sometimes delivering ARVN paratroopers. Generally Freedman saw little action, but someone coined the nickname "Superjew." It stuck, and helped secure his legend. In 1964, he was assigned to Thailand to perform rescue operations as the U.S. air war got under way. In March 1965, he made the first USAF helicopter rescue of a downed U.S. pilot in Laos, on then-unfamiliar terrain, for which he was awarded an Air Medal with a "V." Freedman came to believe in the war, but more out of a sense of national duty and a committed opposition to communism than a close political analysis. In 1967, still in Thailand, he made captain. When the USAF told him he'd have to sit out the heavy action in Ubon Ratchathani he resigned his commission.

Back in Connecticut, living with his mother, he answered an anonymous advertisement in a newspaper seeking pilots with three hundred hours of light aircraft experience. The source turned out to be Air America. He was asked to come to Washington, expenses paid, for an interview with a man named H. H. Dawson. Freedman got a haircut, flew down to D.C., and went to an address on K Street, which he subsequently learned was a CIA office. He signed a nondisclosure form and joined Air America. Originally created by the CIA to support the French at Dien Bien Phu in 1954, Air America had only two clients: USAID and the CIA. Under its charter Air America was not permitted to bid on jobs for any other organizations, though its personnel have never been eligible for government benefits—a source of resentment for some.

Freedman spent a year in Saigon for Air America, then went to Udorn Thani, on the Thai-Lao border. As a Sikorsky H-34 helicopter pilot, Freedman provided logistical (food, fuel) and tactical (weapons and troops) resupply—"soft rice" versus "hard rice"—and rescue mainly for the Hmong highlanders, in the covert war run by the CIA and supported by USAID in Laos. From 1968 to 1975, he flew over seven thousand hours, took a great deal of fire, and was shot down once. "Superjew" indeed.

Jim Agnew was one of Freedman's mechanics. He is small and

quiet but not quite diffident, and a winning, unabashed smile hints at a sense of adventure and degree of confidence that contrasts sharply with his soft voice. After three years in the Army as a helicopter mechanic from 1959 to 1962, serving mainly in Germany, he went to school to get a Federal Aviation Administration license. In 1966, he answered an innocent-looking ad as Freedman did two years later, only this one was for helicopter mechanics in Vietnam. He knew that a successful application would land him in a combat zone, but he wanted an adventure and was undeterred. He also believed that the war effort, as a fight against communism, was right. When Agnew discovered that the ad was for Air America, and that it was a CIA company, he felt even more excited. At headquarters in Taiwan, he was diverted to Udorn, where he remained based for almost five years.

During his last year with Air America, 1971–72, Agnew was head helicopter mechanic in Laos and was stationed at the main CIA base. In Laos he met Jeff Johnson, who himself came to be there by familiar channels. After attending Norwich University, a military school in Vermont, and being trained there as a civil engineer, Johnson entered the Army as a lieutenant in the Corps of Engineers. After a year's delay of duty, during which he and his college roommate drove out to San Francisco in the roommate's 1967 Austin-Healy and built houses on Twin Peaks "before the queers got there," Johnson was sent to Korea for military service. For fourteen months he built airfields and roads in one of the Army's most strategically important forward areas, in a period when the North Koreans' seizure of the *U.S.S. Pueblo* knocked Vietnam off the front page for two weeks. The roommate, a close friend, was killed in Vietnam.

Following Korea, Johnson went to Vietnam as a civilian contractor for Pacific Architects & Engineering, building and maintaining roads, buildings, and landing zones for the 101st Airborne Division near the DMZ and around Saigon, and later in the delta region south of Saigon (IV Corps). Having spent a hairy year and a half hopping from site to site in Caribou planes, in summer 1971 he answered an ad for an "Air Asia" ground engineer and heard from his parents that a government security man had been asking questions about him in Worcester, Mass. The outfit turned out to be Air America. Johnson's first assignment was to build a runway on the Plain of Jars, which changed hands several times during the Lao war and became the index of which side was winning. The only nonflyer in Air America to get hazardous-duty pay, Johnson spent about three years living in Laos side-by-side with a CIA case officer, and constructed about fifty runways for Air America planes, which, unlike the Thailand-based helicopters, were based in Laos itself. A few of the runways, however, were in Cambodia.

One of the pilots who had to land his planes on "the horrible airstrips that Jeff built" was Les Strouse. Raised in Doylestown, Pennsylvania, a hard-line patriot, and enamored of flying from an early age, he was a pilot in the Air Force from 1954 to 1964, for part of the time in the Air Commandos—the USAF's version of Special Forces. In 1964 he left the Air Force and joined Air America, spending six months in Laos and then four and a half years in Saigon, where he flew five different types of aircraft. (Air America was frequently used for resupply to line units in Vietnam due to the ability of its small planes to land on short, remote airstrips.) During the Tet offensive, only Air America personnel were at Tan Son Nhat Air Force Base in Saigon ("Everyone else was downtown," says Strouse ruefully) and Strouse ran ammunition to units that desperately needed it. He left Saigon in October 1968. After "goofing off" stateside, losing his seniority at now-unionized Air America, attending to his divorce, and freelancing in Cambodia, he went to Laos for Continental Air Services, Inc. (the other company that worked Laos for the CIA) in 1970. He flew C-46s (mainly USAID rice drops for Mac Thompson) and took heavy ground fire frequently, as did most pilots in Laos.

Although Air America largely pulled out after the Paris Peace Accords in 1973, CASI and Strouse continued to operate in Laos until June 1975, when the Pathet Lao took over for good. Before that, he loved his life. "I wouldn't trade the eleven years I spent over here for eleven years in the Air Force to collect the retirement pay. I loved the flying, naturally. And the countries. Laos is one of the most scenic countries in the world, especially from the air, fantastic. Vietnam is a beautiful country. The people. The Laos were probably the most laid-back of the whole bunch. People say 'lazy'—well, not necessarily. They just don't do any more than they have to. *Efficient.* We worked hard and we partied hard, and Laos was the place to do it. When it was over, I had a real letdown. I said, 'What am I going to do now?'"

A common refrain. As the war in Laos wound down in 1973, Freedman spent substantial portions of time in Vietnam for Air America (that is, the Agency), and helped evacuate Da Nang, Hué (where he was ordered to blow up Voice of America), and Saigon in 1975. He flew the first rescue chopper out to the USAF C-5A Galaxy that famously crashed with Vietnamese orphans aboard. He left Vietnam on the *U.S.S. Hancock,* spent a day interned in the Philippines at Subic Bay, and landed in Hong Kong. After twelve years, the Indochina wars had ended for Izzy Freedman and his fellow Americans.

Air America folded in 1975. At thirty-eight, with the American job market flooded with younger ex-service aviators, Freedman stood little chance of finding work as a commercial pilot. He stayed in Asia because that was where the work was. Based in Bangkok, he flew helicopters on oil exploration projects, first for Bristow Helicopters in Indonesia and Nigeria, then for Mobil Oil back in Indonesia, until 1986. Agnew also made for Indonesia to fix helicopters (sometimes Izzy's) involved in oil-rig construction until the same year, when he became technical representative for Bell Helicopters (manufacturer of the Vietnam-era workhorse

UH-1 "Huey") for South and Southeast Asia, based in Bangkok. Johnson went to work for Bechtel and other engineering firms on the Alaska Pipeline and in Saudi Arabia, but he gravitated back to Bangkok to run his own engineering firm.

Having acquired a preference for tropical heat, Strouse relocated in Florida. Except for a stint in Panama providing security for the Shah of Iran when he was exiled on Contadora Island, he drifted in and out of property maintenance and real estate jobs. He helped Lao refugees resettle in the United States, at one point housing thirteen of them. Restless and unhappy out of airplanes, he left in 1980 to fly a Twin-Otter for Chevron in Sudan. There he saw more action: when the Sudanese People's Liberation Army attacked Chevron's base camp in south-central Sudan in February 1984, killing three people and wounding more, Strouse ran medical evacuees into Nairobi all night. Chevron pared back its expat personnel, leaving only Strouse and a small crew to run once-a-week payroll and supply flights. For part of his remaining time there, Mac Thompson, who was posted in Khartoum with USAID from 1987 to 1989, kept him company, as did Bangkok-based ex-CIA man Jack Shirley, whom Strouse recruited for Chevron in 1984 to shore up security. From Sudan in 1989, Strouse went to Thailand to fly for Bangkok Airways, mainly as chief pilot and director of flight operations, until the end of 1995, when he retired.

Now in their fifties and sixties, the Air America boys did not run scared. Izzy Freedman was shot down but kept on flying. Jeff Johnson was pinned in a bunker during a seven-hour mortar siege on the Plain of Jars; fifteen Hmong were killed and he very nearly perished, but he never thought about leaving Laos. Les Strouse had three engine failures in Vietnam, and took nineteen rounds in his fuselage in his first nineteen days in Laos. And there is a pervasive "last guy out" theme in Strouse's life: he was the last man to fly a Western civilian airplane out of Cambodia in 1975, the last man to fly a Western civilian airplane out of Laos a couple of months later, and the last Westerner to fly out of Sudan for Chevron after the Sudanese People's Liberation Army began their attacks on government interests in the late eighties. Though balding, his chest still precedes his gut. He still flares his broad shoulders, wears Western-style shirts, and smokes Marlboros defiantly. Strouse and his pals may be the closest thing to cowboys that Americans have left, anywhere. Ironic that their pasture is so far from home. I ask why.

For starters, Southeast Asia is the place they have come to know, and (not least) a place in which they are regarded as heroes. They trade on it a little. Izzy Freedman's exploits are famous. He got into the bar business in the eighties by accident, when a Thai friend asked him for a loan. He still manages the Crown Royal—though on Patpong, not a girly bar but a cocktail bar, and a nice one at that. His name is still a draw, as American tourists seek out the place they have heard about that's run by "the Air America guy." Les Strouse's young Thai wife, a customer-service representative for an American packaging manufacturer, tells her neighbors proudly that Les worked for the CIA. This presumptive adulation is comforting, and to an extent sustaining.

The motivations run deeper, though. Each man feels a bond with Asians, and this bond was made stronger by the American *failure* in Vietnam, Laos, and Cambodia. Freedman believes that the Hmong truly wanted to resist communism and that it was appropriate for the CIA to recruit them, arm them, and instruct them. Agnew adds that the Lao war, for most of the time, was a well-orchestrated low-intensity guerrilla war that helped a genuinely anticommunist people resist the North Vietnamese and effectively diverted Hanoi's resources from South Vietnam. Both men feel that the war in Laos should have remained a guerrilla war of harassment and evasion, as it had begun under CIA station chief Bill Lair's original concept, instead of being turned by subsequent careerists into a more conventional and confrontational war. Freedman chimes in that the Vietnam War could have been won in 1972 had air power been fully exploited.

Jeff Johnson is even more sanguine about what might have been: we could have won it if we had applied ourselves. While he understands the political compulsion to pull out of Vietnam, abandoning Laos is harder for him to take—to some extent because he ascribes very traditional American frontier motivations to the Hmong. "You know, it pissed me off when we pulled out of Laos because Laos was cheap for us, for the United States to support that thing. The Hmong genuinely hated the Vietnamese because they would come in their villages and take their women when they were out farming and just destroy the village. I think that would make anyone angry. That was one of the major reasons the Hmong were fighting: you can't come into my home and take my women. Oh, they were great fighters, superb."

Strouse believes the United States helped the Laos, though he concedes the tacit circularity of that position: if we hadn't been involved they might not have needed our help. Still, it was right in principle—viz., anticommunism—for us to intervene. He has come to love Thailand for its weather, women, and wide-openness. And he does not like post-Vietnam America partly on account of Americans' utter lack of appreciation for those who fought in Vietnam and Laos. "This is not what America was about. I'm not a great flag-waving patriot, but I am a patriot. Hey, you've got GIs over there, you're supposed to support them. You're not supposed to be out there demonstrating, you're not supposed to spit on them when they come back, call them baby killers and all that shit. And nobody wanted to talk about it, nobody was interested. I had two neighbors in Florida, old guys in their seventies—they were interested. My old grandpa was the only one in the family that was interested. My grandpa was a baseball nut, but if I went over to his place with a six-pack of beer he'd turn off the game and say, 'What are you doing over there?' And this was not being polite, because Grandpa wasn't polite. It was because he was interested."

Agnew states outright that the American populace has neglected Vietnam veterans. He cites a poignant example: his brother, who served as a mechanic and door gunner with the First Cavalry Division at Cu Chi, is riddled with cancer he believes was caused by Agent Orange—but he gets no compensation from the government. Adds Johnson: "I don't think anybody cares. You go back and ask the average person in America where Vietnam is, and they don't know where it is. And Laos. 'Laos? What's that?' When I first went back to America I learned my lesson. I don't talk about the war or things that are happening in Asia. Oh, I'll talk about it at an Air America reunion or with people that I know who have been in Southeast Asia. But my sister, my brother-in-law, my daughter—they don't know and they don't care. 'Who wants to listen to that?' So I don't want to talk about it with them either."

Short and now roly-poly, Johnson likes to relive his war days from a barstool in his house. Conversation with him is sprinkled with "cute stories" about Laos and Vietnam, which he tells in an endearing Worcester, Mass., accent: "cute *starries.*" "There's an old Siamese king site, a contested site right on the border between Thailand and Cambodia. There was an Agency case officer there, and I had to build a runway there. There was a lot of rock, so I brought some explosives—I built a lot of runways with explosives—so anyway I go to this case officer. He says, 'I gotta show you my toilet.' He's got this shithouse built over a cliff, sitting on a cliff, and Cambodia's right down below it. 'So I can go in my shithouse, and I can be sittin' in Thailand and shittin' in Cambodia.' It was cute. There were a lot of cute experiences like that."

It bothers Johnson that nobody in the States seems too interested in those recollections. But in Thailand, thanks to a ready expat community full of veterans with the common bond of having contributed to a frustrated war effort, he gets to be a raconteur, to celebrate a cherished time of derring-do and brotherhood in his life. "Our group here were all involved," says Strouse sardonically, "so we sit here and we tell the same lies to one another year in and year out. It's a mutual admiration society."

Agnew believes, proudly, that they were all part of something bigger and not altogether futile. USAID (Thompson, et al.) was helping the Laos immensely by building roads, schools, and other infrastructure. Those efforts, it's true, stopped cold when the Paris accords were signed. But Agnew, as both an eyewitness and a player, testifies that the U.S. presence in Southeast Asia brought technological expertise to the area, "taking kids out of the farms and training them," and thus improved life, particularly in Thailand. He continues to make a genuine humanitarian contribution to Asia. He teaches Thais, Cambodians, Laotians, Vietnamese, Burmese, Bangladeshis, Nepalese, and Sri Lankans how to repair and maintain helicopters that his company manufactures. Those helicopters help find oil; they rescue fire victims in Indonesia and flood victims in Bangladesh; they improve lives; they save them. Asia, then, still needs and appreciates Yanks.

The contemporary United States, on the other hand, depresses the hell out of Air America vets. They are unanimous in their distaste for President Clinton's draft dodging then and his dissembling in 1998 and for the soft, wet, navel-gazing America that they see as having evolved since the Vietnam War. Johnson, a self-described right-wing conservative, hoped against hope that Clinton would be convicted once impeached. Strouse and Agnew lament the American people's disengagement from the rest of the world and their self-centeredness, and, attuned to intimate clandestine involvement in strategic wars, dislike what they viewed as Washington's "gunboat diplomacy" under Clinton. Freedman rues the softness reflected in amnesty for draft evaders. Les Strouse ("Les thinks everything's shitty," notes Agnew) openly and angrily disdains the confessional, self-regarding character of post-Vietnam Americans and their un-American need for mommying, whether from the government or from Oprah Winfrey. These expats all believed, more or less, in the domino theory during the Cold War.

In Thailand, more so even than in Texas, you're on your own. That fits the Air America alumni, who get no government pension, who received no medals, who officially merit only a plaque at CIA headquarters in Langley commemorating the ninety Americans in the outfit who lost their lives in the Indochina wars. (On May 30, 1987, in the McDermott Library at the University of Texas at Dallas, a plaque was also dedicated in honor of the 242 total Air America personnel, American and foreign, killed between 1948 and 1975.) And the Thai people are friendly enough, but tolerant and unintrusive especially when bribed— also consonant with the Air America worldview.

Thailand is cheap to boot. As a consulting engineer Jeff Johnson has become rich enough not to have to work in Thailand and owns houses on Cape Cod and in Florida, though he keeps busy designing "clean facilities" for use in the manufacture of computer components. He lives in Nonthaburi, a few miles from Bangkok, with his Thai wife, their thirteen-year-old daughter, and a baby boy in a luxurious three-story house. After retiring from Bangkok Airways, Les Strouse tried consulting but didn't like it. He lives in rural Panthumthani (about fifty miles northeast of Bangkok) on savings and investments, which he can do easily in Thailand but could not swing in the United States. Freedman, recovering from cancer, has built a house in Pattaya, a honky-tonk beach resort about sixty miles southeast of Bangkok that was colonized by GIs on leave during the Vietnam War. Jim Agnew has also bought a second home in Pattaya, which is, away from the crassness downtown, a golfer's heaven.

The Air America group resents the social marginalization of Vietnam veterans in the United States. They live well not by grabbing for meal tickets but by working (or having worked) hard for a living. Stretching retirement pay doesn't come into this comparison, since Air America personnel were civilians and independent contractors who weren't eligible for government extras. The expats, perhaps more than stateside vets, are fearless throwbacks: they flaunt their neocolonial superiority; they value the unabashed male chauvinism of Asian society; they take working hard and playing hard not as an artificial cliché but as a creed.

There is plenty to envy about expat vets in Thailand. Their particular brand of posterity is in some ways enviable. It would be comforting to have lived a life full enough to permit the dismissal of the pesky, neurotic nuances of millennial America. *Many a wolf/Is never let in/Because of the hair/On his chinny-chin-chin.* Burma-Shave, 1945. To the Air America types—well, shit, it's just kinda funny, like one of Jeff Johnson's "cute *starries.*" Alan Cooper, a former F-4 ground crew chief who served quietly at Phu Cat Air Force Base during the Vietnamization period, grew fond of Asia, and relocated from Oregon to Thailand in 1994, wryly concedes that his favorite watering hole "is the Lone Staar, not a five-star." But nobody there or at the Crown Royal is going to tell veterans of the Indochina wars that their stories aren't cute.

Despite the odd symptom of laziness and inertia that could just as well attend middle age in the States, despite the fact that most expat vets are married to Thai women much younger than they are, most of the Thailand-based expat vets live in ways that are quite respectable by American standards. The vast majority still work—as newspapermen, airline or helicopter pilots, manufacturers representatives, consulting engineers, and the like—or did until retirement age. The fact that they have still chosen Thailand over the States, then, does not reflect any inability on their part to cope with the practical rigors of American life. Rather, it evidences their disenchantment with what they perceive as an overload of political correctness and an excessive sense of entitlement

in post-Vietnam Americans, and, more darkly, a lack of appreciation for their experiences in Vietnam. Such a selection of expat
vets does epitomize the qualities of many a stateside counterpart:
the bitterness, the defiance, the acquiescence to frustration, the
jauntiness, the conceit of being both a lost breed and a breed
apart. Common to all of these traits is a sense of being out of step
with mainstream America and the acceptance, unfazed rather than
tortured, of that incongruity.

PEACE WITH HONOR

Those Vietnamese who boldly commemorate the effort of the
South Vietnamese have a comparable form of dissonance to con-
front. On a standard day-long bus tour to the Cao Dai Temple and
the Cu Chi Tunnels in Tay Ninh province, northwest of Ho Chi
Minh City, the guide, a slender, handsome man with dark skin,
speaking excellent English, sticks cheerfully to his patriotic script
for most of the tour, pointing out bomb craters from B-52 raids
and hammering home the great loss the Vietnamese people experienced in war. But his sheepish attitude toward the Cao Dai religion—a wacky, eclectic faith that counts Sun Yat-sen, Victor
Hugo, and Louis Pasteur among its deities, underwritten by the
French to stave off anticolonial movements—is an initial clue to
his savvy.

He betrays some skepticism about the new Vietnam when the
bus stops near the tunnels, on the official pretext of beholding a
grand Buddhist temple, so that tourists can avail themselves of a
firing range. Using one of three combat weapons—an M-16, an
AK-47, and a compact shotgun used by U.S. "tunnel rats"—they
get to fire live rounds at target silhouettes. The attendants simply
hand the weapons to the patrons; the range of motion is unre-
stricted. The commercial cynicism of this venture—war as carny
sideshow—is almost as unsettling as the realization that such an
enterprise could not operate for more than about fifteen minutes

in the United States without producing multiple casualties. (Suppose a Littleton or Jonesboro community group had sponsored a trip to Vietnam and the wrong teenagers had signed up.) The guide blushes, pointing toward the firing range without looking in its direction. "Please relax at the temple, or"—he lowers his tone in chagrined resignation—"you can pay 50,000 dong (more than $4.00) a bullet to shoot these guns."

On the way home, with half the tourists (mainly Europeans and Australians, none of them too interested in the nuances of the war) falling asleep, the guide turns lugubriously to his own story. He was born in 1947 in Hanoi, but his parents moved the family to the south after the Vietminh's victory over the French at Dien Bien Phu in 1954. After completing high school he began studying at a Catholic seminary for the priesthood. The war forced him to abandon his studies, and he soon became a translator/interpreter for the 101st Airborne Division of the U.S. Army. Though he conceded the heroism of the VC guerrillas who worked the Cu Chi tunnels, he pointed out that they committed atrocities against ARVN (e.g., hanging their internal organs on trees), just as ARVN committed atrocities against them (e.g., decapitating soldiers, mounting the heads on roadside posts and placing cigarettes in their mouths). "That's war," he shrugs. He also underlines the bravery of American "tunnel rats" and seems to snicker to himself at the preposterously propagandistic film shown before the tunnel tour (featuring the female "Hero American Killer"). While the War Remnants Museum highlights the My Lai massacre, he asserts that the North Vietnamese Army killed 20,000 Vietnamese, mostly civilians, in 1966 in the Central Provinces, and 6,000 in Hué in 1968 during the month that they controlled the city.

After Saigon fell, he was taken into custody and moved to a re-education camp, but was released after a week because, though paid the wage of an ARVN sergeant, he technically had remained a civilian. The conditions at the camps were horrendous, and many South Vietnamese internees died of malaria; many others (Major Smith's Montagnard friend Claude Clement, for example) were held for periods of years. On account of his activity during the war, he could find no work other than as a farmer for the next seventeen years. Only in 1992 did the government relax its scrutiny sufficiently for him to find a better paying job as a tour guide.

When he had earned enough money to leave Vietnam, he considered going to the United States to join his two sisters. They had made successful lives there, one of them as an executive with Motorola. But his father prevailed on him to stay so as to help build a better Vietnam "for Vietnam's children." By the time he was ready to conclude his remarks, the guide had become emotional. He exhorted us "travelers" that in America we get only the American side of the Vietnam War, while in Vietnam we usually hear only the North Vietnamese communist version. We should understand, he said, that there is also a South Vietnamese side of the story. It remains more difficult for southerners to get jobs and to acquire power in government. As a southerner, he is not altogether happy or satisfied, but he has decided to stick with his own country. Measured against the high degree of intolerance and authoritarianism in Vietnamese government, his impassioned semipublic comment seems a conspicuous and brave display of candor.

oOoo

The guide was one embodiment of peace with honor, and he has an American counterpart: a Vietnam vet superego, an archetypal Soldier of the War Nobody Won, a man who—given the checkered history of the war, given the suppression of its heroes, given how difficult these things have made it for any vet to walk tall—

has for himself made the right stuff out of the Vietnam War, crystallizing in a single personality both the honor and the humility suited to the reality. Among the vets I encountered, perhaps the one who came closest is the former U.S. ambassador to Vietnam, Douglas (Pete) Peterson.

He is about five-foot-ten, with steely blue eyes, a generous head of gray hair, and a military bearing. He sits up straight and looks you in the eye, though he is not harsh or severe. His story is well known. The ninth of ten children, Peterson was born and raised in Omaha, and as a teenager moved to Missouri and then Iowa. He enlisted in the Air Force in 1957 to serve his country at a time when communist imperialism was a looming threat. He "bought in" to the Cold War containment argument when he went to Vietnam as an Air Force pilot. "I was not into a questioning mode at that time," he says succinctly. "I was into what a seasoned fighter pilot did at that time, and that was to engage the enemy and do so as professionally as I possibly could." In 1966, after sixty-six missions, Captain Peterson's F-4 Phantom was shot down by anti-aircraft fire. He ejected, was captured by North Vietnamese militia, and was held for six and a half years at the infamous "Hanoi Hilton" (officially, Hoa Lo Prison) and five other camps in and around the city. Throughout his captivity he remained convinced that the American effort was an appropriate instrument for containing communist aggression.

Unaware of the widening rift in the United States over the war, he stayed committed to "continuing the war" while a POW. "We didn't know who the president was. We didn't know that a man had walked on the moon. We didn't know the details as to anything going on in the streets of America and clearly there was a lot happening back there. In fact, the Vietnamese would bring quotes back saying that this occurred in such and such a place in an anti-war demonstration and we discounted it totally as propaganda. We were still engaged in combat here, which sometimes is not recognized. We were resisting and attempting, to whatever degree we could, to be a burden on the system and to use up resources that might otherwise be used elsewhere. Our combat involved that and also survival. It was a full-time job, and looked upon as continuing the service that we had all signed up for."

He was tortured continually, still bears rope-burn scars on the backs of his elbows, and sometimes experiences numbness in his right hand due to nerve damage from the tight manacles he was made to wear. His convictions about the propriety of the U.S. intervention did not change for quite a while after his release in 1973. During his remaining eight years in the Air Force, he advanced remarkably for someone who might have been expected to rest on his status as what Major Smith would call "one of 591 designated heroes," and perhaps to have been hobbled by brutal long-term imprisonment. Peterson's last assignment before his retirement in 1981 was commander of the air support group at Seymour Johnson Air Force Base.

In civilian life, Peterson ran a successful construction company, taught administrative psychology at Florida State University, and later started and ran a computer retail and services business. "I was trying to get my own life back in order. I was essentially a Rip Van Winkle, trying to capture the essence of freedom and focus on the future. I was determined, having left here, that I wasn't going to live the life of a former POW. The rest of my life was going to be independent of that to the degree that I could make it so, to be measured on the basis of what I could do in the present as opposed to what I did in the past. So I was very, very sensitive to that. In the meantime, the policies of the country—the Nixon-Kissinger statements that POWs were all home—were refreshing and very comforting because none of us wanted to be home if there was the possibility of someone else being left behind. It was very believable, and a lot of us—myself included—said, 'Okay, that's behind us, let's go on and do something else.' It was only later that I started having doubts about the accuracy of some of those statements."

Beginning in 1991, he served three terms as a U.S. representative from Florida. Among his priorities were to ensure that all POWs and MIAs were in fact accounted for, and to advance bilateral relations between the United States and Vietnam. The president appointed Peterson to a cooperative effort to track down soldiers missing in action with the Russians, and he became chairman of the Vietnam Search Group. "It was during that time that I recognized the inaccuracies in our interpretation of the relationship between Vietnam, China, and Russia. It was very, very wrong. We did not have the accurate picture of that during the war. Therefore we made, I'm certain, in our policy as a country, a mistake or two or three or four or many, in the course of the war. I'd say that the whole conflict was potentially avoidable had we recognized the big picture. That's not something I'm ready to say with total conviction, but based on knowledge that I have, we probably could have engaged in a dialogue that would have been a peaceful one but opted not to at the very first."

In 1991 he made his first trip back to Vietnam since his days as a POW. He found a country whose middle-aged generation had, for obvious reasons, been decimated. "Only a small percentage of the people I saw had had any involvement with the war. Most were born after we'd left. And I said to myself, 'why should we disallow them the better life that they want, why should we disallow them the well-being of Vietnam?'" Peterson teamed up with senators John McCain and John Kerry to enhance the bilateral relationship, getting the communications blackout lifted, IMF and World Bank restrictions eased, and the trade embargo relaxed. Yet, determined as he was not to let Vietnam dominate his life, he did not seek the post of ambassador to Vietnam.

President Clinton and the National Security Council engaged in "something of a recruitment," and Peterson had to think long and hard about whether to reward their efforts. "It was not an instant decision. I had to evaluate whether coming back here would be recognized [by the Vietnamese] as a plus or a minus. I can say that Vietnam has been part of my life since 1954, because I can remember just as I was ready to enter the Air Force Eisenhower and others making speeches relative to the justification for assisting the French in their last days and doing what we did after the fall of Dien Bien Phu. So I was aware of Vietnam for the first time just coming out of high school, and it has been a piece of me whether I've wanted it to be or not. I've laughed about Vietnam becoming a disease I'd take antibiotics for all my life and not been successful in relieving. I think people do get attached to this country."

In deciding to take the challenge of the ambassadorship, however, Peterson mentally conditioned himself to be "fiercely focused on the future." While he naturally harbored some resentment toward individual Vietnamese tormentors, he was willfully determined not to allow anger or vengeance to tyrannize his attitude toward the Vietnamese people in general. "After the war," he explains, "I had two choices. I could go home angry, disenchanted, depressed. If I followed that path, I would always be walking backward. Or I could get on with my life. I woke up one morning and realized I had no control over yesterday. But I had full control over and responsibility for tomorrow. My choice was obvious."

His views are accordingly those of a man who does not deny his past but is reconciled to it. You will hear no complaints from him about any maltreatment during his long stay in Hanoi decades ago, notwithstanding the torture he endured. He drives by what remains of the Hanoi Hilton with stolid bemusement, and is unprovoked by the rumor that one of his former torturers there is now a local real estate agent. "I went back to the place where I was shot down and met my captors, and had tea with them in their residence. That question [of mutual guilt] came up. Simultaneously we both said, 'No.'" This stoicism earned him street-cred with the Vietnamese, who seek no apologies from him, either.

Peterson made a conscious decision not to add to his knowledge of the war while in Vietnam. When asked whether he has visited the Revolutionary Museum—Hanoi's version of the War Remnants Museum—he shrugs his shoulders, as if he's never heard of the place, and phlegmatically answers no. He manifests little interest in patronizing that museum or any place like it that conjures up disagreeable reminders of past relations between Vietnam and the United States. "I've done very little since I've returned here to add any bit of knowledge of the war. I am allowing other people to deal with the past." His psychological mission, it seems, is to show the Vietnamese that the United States is too big to be petty. If the Vietnamese are not warmongers broadly or narrowly construed—and Peterson reads them as "quite gentle"—then the United States should not be, either. He is an unabashed reconciler, but one with resilience and honor.

7

OUR OWN BURIED LIVES

The Vietnam War, like all wars, left existential scars on those who executed it. Stan Karber, a native of Fort Smith, Arkansas, is a former Green Beret (in-country 1970–71) who now lives outside Ho Chi Minh City, is married to a younger Vietnamese woman, and represents an American company that manufactures rice dryers and post-harvest rice-processing equipment. About the war effort he was pragmatically cynical (though not yet politically hostile) even while he was part of it. He was girded by the fact that Special Forces comprised professional soldiers, but discouraged in the knowledge that the young Cambodians (some only thirteen) they trained to face the Khmer Rouge were "cannon fodder." By the time the NVA rolled into Saigon in 1975, he thought that "the South Vietnamese were finally getting their comeuppance." There had never been any doubt in his mind that the NVA were a superior fighting force. A recovering alcoholic, two-time divorcé, and middle-management nomad, he returned to Vietnam to visit in 1994 and "smoked a little dope and got laid on the beach," then came back permanently in 1995. He can't quite put his finger on what the war has meant to him, but he interprets its personal moment as well as anyone. "No doubt the Vietnam conflict has weighed my life down, but I don't feel as if it is all negative. It's hard to describe how I have looked at life since that time. I will say this: *nothing has ever seemed very important to me since the conflict.*"

Bill Maddox is a little clearer. "I went out to investigate a helicopter crash one time, about two days after the crash," he remembers. "We were walking around and saw a guy's arm that they had missed. The thing I remember most is the smell of burning flesh." He continues hesitantly. "It's one of life's experiences. You can't say it didn't have an effect because everybody was so young. I mean, I was twenty-two years old when I got to a company in Vietnam, and I was one of the five oldest people in the company. It has a profound effect on shaping the rest of your life. I'm certain that some of the ways I am today are because of my experiences in Vietnam. There's no doubt in my mind. I'm a little pessimistic, a little cynical, a little more serious perhaps. A lot of people like to say it robbed me of my youth. I don't know about that, but certainly you came back a different person. You came back a harder and more cynical person. That's not always good."

Veterans who opposed the war were no less vulnerable. Herter, Searcy, and Kleven felt the burden of national guilt as well as their countrymen's suspicion and dismissal. Keith Mishne—a sandal-wearing former "hippie soldier" who served during the depressive Vietnamization period of the war, found life in America stressful, and now spends most of his time in Vietnam—suffered daily headaches over the dissonance between his duty as an intelligence officer and his antiwar beliefs. When he applied for work and interviewers saw that he was an interrogator, some would ask pruriently, "What did you do to those guys?"—hoping to hear about water torture and the like. Beyond that, people didn't much care. "There was nobody really to turn to when I got back. They gave us as much as they could benefit-wise, as they did for the guys from World War II. Except it was a different scene. Everybody was for World War II, everyone wanted to win."

The war also left unique wounds of public chastisement. Glenn Holthaus was jeered when he got home, and later was shunned by neighbors who merely assumed from his combat pedigree that he was crazed. The whole process made him feel demonized, and inadequate as a civilian. "I was an E-6 [petty officer third class]," he recalls, "just married, my wife had a kid, and I was going across to Colorado from the Great Lakes marine barracks. Out, discharged, I got halfway across Iowa, with a brand new '69 El Camino, a brand new kid and an old lady, no money, no job skills other than fucking killing people. That ain't too required out there on the way to Colorado. I said, what the fuck am I doing? Turned around and reenlisted. You could reenlist at the same rank within twenty-four hours at the same place. They sent me right back to Camp Lejeune." The military cocoon did not save Holthaus from psychological damage altogether, but it allowed him to work continuously after Vietnam. But even after he'd finished his twenty, a cold-turkey return to "The World" might well have jangled him into dysfunction.

EXPLAINING EXPATRIATION

In the early sixties, few Americans translated their awareness of the Cold War into the need to get their hands dirty. President John F. Kennedy's signature moment of triumph, when Soviet ships acquiesced to the United States Navy's blockade of Cuba and Moscow withdrew its missiles, had occurred in October 1962. McCarthyism, Sputnik, and John Foster Dulles's po-faced policy of "massive retaliation" had receded. The Treasury had just run a gaudy surplus, and Congress had goosed the good times with a tax cut. The American stand in Korea had vindicated the Truman

Doctrine, or so it seemed, leaving only skirmishes for national liberation to be summarily mopped up with a few "military advisers." America's military heroes, people seemed to believe, would move upward into space to demonstrate technology too formidable to be used in anger, not across terrain to grind up soldiers armed with rifles and field artillery.

It was a dangerous world, but seductively so. JFK's magisterial rhetoric and cocksure smile gave Americans the impression that global geopolitics had been omnisciently arranged by the United States after World War II, and was therefore firmly controllable by Washington. There was still psychic room for James Dean and Jimmy Hoffa—guys whose foes were at home, whose landscape was proudly and provincially the United States, whose preoccupations were cars and trucks and the adaptation of Eisenhower's interstate to their whims. The young American men who would be asked to fight for the South Vietnamese were scarcely aware that short, tan, communist guerrillas derisively labeled "Vietcong" by South Vietnamese generals and their American advisers were on the verge of subverting Camelot from half a world away. Those men, for the most part, did not go to college. They did not forage the *New York Times* and the *Washington Post* for news analyses and wire-service squibs on Vietnam that spoke of Agent Orange, "strategic hamlets," the Ho Chi Minh Trail, or the watershed Battle of Ap Bac in January 1963, which convinced U.S. military planners that ARVN was not up to the job of resisting the North Vietnamese communists.

Images like that of an elderly Buddhist priest, Thich Quang Duc, silently assuming the lotus position and having monks pour gasoline on his robes and set him on fire in the middle of Saigon in June 1963 only made Vietnam seem more alien. Casual observers did not understand that South Vietnam was experiencing, as Frances FitzGerald aptly put it in *Fire in the Lake,* "a civil war inside a revolution." To most prospective American grunts, if they thought about these matters at all, ARVN troops were likely just green soldiers who needed a swift kick in the ass, Buddhists "inscrutable Orientals" whose passive resistance could not seriously affect determined militarists who had American support. But Johnson and his advisers, like Kennedy, believed in the domino theory. The CIA candidly apprised him of ARVN's inadequacy. On the pretext of one negligible and one fictitious North Vietnamese incursion on the *U.S.S. Maddox* as the ship gathered intelligence off the coast of North Vietnam, President Johnson cleared the way to send in U.S. troops wholesale by pushing the Gulf of Tonkin Resolution through Congress in August 1964. The U.S. buildup, then, was insidious. Nobody saw the Vietnam War coming.

Once it was underway, there was little teamwork between American citizens and Vietnam-era soldiers, hence little wider empathy for them. This only reinforced the veterans' outsider status. Because Lyndon Johnson's "guns and butter" economy did not require conspicuous practical sacrifices at home, such as rationing or the mobilization of "Rosie-the-Riveters," civilians had no emotional connection to the war unless they had family participating in it. The war was something they could see on television, and if it got too upsetting they could turn it off. When it was in the newspaper they could just turn to the sports section. Drastic differences of opinion among liberal and conservative Americans about whether the United States should be in Vietnam deepened cleavages between young and old and between intellectual élites and Middle America, and came to pervade political dialogue on virtually all issues—domestic as well as international. Whereas near-unanimous support for American intervention in World War II after Pearl Harbor gave the public a sense of ownership of the war, divided support twenty-five years later made the Vietnam War a historical tar baby.

On top of the domestic disconnect, whereas the two big wars

mobilized an entire world, most other countries rolled their eyes
at the American effort. Great Britain, our stalwart cousin, offered
no help. France—Vietnam's colonizer, prime mover of Washington's post–World War II policy in Vietnam, and a potential benefactor of an American/South Vietnamese victory—became
essentially neutral. Positive interest was regional: Australia and
Thailand contributed soldiers because they had geopolitical wor-
ries; the South Koreans were keen to pay off a large debt from the
previous decade and wanted to ensure that hands-on American
protection would continue.

Such a roundly unpopular war was hard to interpret as a salutary historical epiphany. By the time it was all over, in the mid-
1970s, the United States was a shadow of its former self, riven by
the war. The failure of LBJ's "Great Society" was a *fait accompli,*
and industrial decline was taking hold in places like the steel
town depicted in *The Deer Hunter.* The country seemed hollow at
the core. Patriotism had reached low ebb, no longer the social
norm. Many of those who served in Vietnam felt ambushed, then
discarded. Still, for some stateside veterans America was manage-
able enough, and has remained so.

In an appendix to *We Were Soldiers Once . . . and Young,* General
Harold Moore and journalist Joseph Galloway's aching account of
the Battle of the Ia Drang Valley, are the names of dozens of survivors. The stateside alumni of Ia Drang have had each other, by
way of associations, reunions, even book deals. Moore and Galloway admit: "[W]e rebuilt our lives, found jobs or professions,
married, raised families, and waited patiently for America to come
to its senses. As the years passed we searched each other out and
found that the half-remembered pride of service was shared by
those who had shared everything else with us. With them, and only
with them, could we talk about what really happened over there—
what we had seen, what we had done, what we had survived."

Veterans groups and unit associations in the United States

reinforce the profound and unique camaraderie developed among men who are in combat together. That bond may be the dividend paid to men who have risked their lives for their country and, more poignantly, for their friends. Those who have not been in combat covet that intimacy: they want to have lived through hell to talk about it with their buddies, and to walk down the street knowing that they have been subjected to the ultimate test and passed it; yet few of the spared are eager to get shot at. Thus, sociologically, combat veterans are entitled to a sense of superiority, and stateside they marshal it through solidarity not with the public at large but with insular groups of fellow veterans.

Expat veterans do not. They are loners who forfeit their dividends of valor. It is easier for them to do so because American society has deprived Vietnam War veterans of the prestige of battle. Generals can talk all they want about how the actions in the Ia Drang Valley in late 1965 demonstrated the same heroism and sacrifice that occurred at Gettysburg or on the Hindenburg Line or at Omaha Beach, but it carries little weight against the national assessment that the Vietnam War was an immoral one best forgotten. In *Father Soldier Son* Nathaniel Tripp describes a Veterans' Day parade in Vermont—intended to rededicate a rebuilt railroad bridge renamed "Memorial Bridge"—that occurred long after the Vietnam Memorial opened and Vietnam vets had supposedly been belatedly embraced.

> Chip [an army buddy] and I wanted to march in it, but none of the other vets in our group did, and none of the other groups, the VFW and the American Legion, wanted to have anything to do with us. So we marched alone, the two of us, down Main Street, down Eastern Avenue, down Railroad Street to the bridge, leadership and fatherhood out on a limb. It was very cold and windy that day, unusually cold even for northern Vermont, and the only compensation at the time was that we got to stand next to the cheerleaders and the wind kept blowing their skirts up in the air during the endless dedication speeches, which neglected to mention Vietnam.

Tripp did not go into exile, but he does live in the remote reaches of New England, far from the madding crowd. He recalls that in-country "[w]hat we didn't know, and could not even dream of, was how bad it could be should we survive, and experience this whole process in reverse going home, without the comfort of the men whom we had grown to love. There would be no parades, no ceremonies, none of the psychological devices that society had evolved over eons to re-assimilate men returning from war." Some indigenous Vietnam veterans like Tripp could go it alone, some could continue to revel among themselves in their success in spite of ostracization. But the siege mentality became tiring and exhausted many veterans into grim co-optation.

"Now, as I write, a quarter century later, gray-haired and forty pounds heavier," notes Tripp, "my fellow veterans are drifting into the VFW and American Legion halls that they once scorned, and that had in turn heaped scorn upon them. Now they sit drinking beer and picking at the scabs on old wounds, forgetting how the wounds got there, reinventing the war and themselves, because the truth is too terrible to face." That "terrible truth" is not the hell of combat but rather the solecism, the absurd injustice, that Vietnam veterans have been stigmatized on account of their *sacrifice*. A biased media, a sonorous intelligentsia, and a suggestible academy have perpetuated Vietnam's status as a black hole of U.S. history, and its veterans as unwanted reminders of the Vietnam era. From the expats' point of view, veterans lose little from living elsewhere.

Although not all expat veterans would admit or perhaps even recognize that their estrangement from the American mainstream drove them back to an area with which they had a poignant connection, albeit in some cases a dark one, that is surely the reality. Mark Smith, though he periodically returns to the United States for visits, has made his home in Bangkok and at this point is more committed morally to the people of Southeast Asia than to Americans. He is not uncomfortable even with the Vietnamese. "The

Chinese tried to conquer them, the French tried to enslave them, and the Japanese tried to starve them. Hell, we just tried to kill them." On a visit to Vietnam with Bob Taylor a few years ago, Smith cracked morbidly to a government functionary, "You know, I killed a lot of you people once upon a time." They all chuckled. Among the "One Hundred Soldierly Thoughts" privately solicited from Smith (but never promulgated) by a friend in the Pentagon is the following: "No man who refused to serve his country in war should be elected or appointed over men and women being sent to fight." He wrote that after the election of Bill Clinton. Jeff McLaury would echo the sentiment. Today's America is anathema to both men.

Alan Dawson remains a dedicated Vietnam contrarian. He wears his Tailwind vindication T-shirt, defiantly lettered with "SOG" on the front and "CNN—99% fact-free" on the back. He states—accurately and bitterly—that there were more Canadians who fought for the United States armed forces in Vietnam than there were American draft dodgers who skipped to Canada. "I feel pretty good about that, I feel *real* good about that. I had to take the place of some asshole from California or Nebraska or Florida who didn't have the guts and then later came whining, 'I wanna come home.' Well, fuck him." Dawson published *The Official Vietnam War Trivia Book* in 1987 and in the dedication wrote, only half in jest: "This book . . . is not for those who refused to go. It is not for those who cheered against us and now want to be on our team because it's the in-thing to support Vietnam-era veterans. They made their own beds. Now they can lie in them and die." From twelve thousand miles away, he had his finger on the pulse of much of Reagan America's sop to Vietnam veterans.

Later in the book, which is generally snide but has a stridently serious streak, Dawson introduces the "Anti-War" section with I'm-not-kidding passion: "Many people in the anti-war movement were not anti-war at all. In particular, people like what's-her-name the actress, her husband Tom thingmy and so on were less anti-war than William Westmoreland. They were *pro*-war. What they opposed was a U.S. victory or a stalemate in Vietnam. What they supported was a victory by Hanoi, by violent means, and the deaths and humiliation of the entire U.S. force in Vietnam. . . . I don't want any of those 'anti-war' people on my team these days, now that it's cool to be seen in the company of a Vietnam vet." On the subject of Jane Fonda, he added, "She wanted me dead. I take that very, very seriously. I mean, [in effect] she sat at the anti-aircraft gun and said 'I wish I had some of the bastards in my sights now.' She wasn't any more anti-war than Lyndon Johnson was. She was hiding behind the anti-war people." It's easier for him to avoid any reminder of her if he's in Thailand.

And he admits that the cool reception that veterans got in the United States queered him on coming home. "I really was confused, sad, upset about the treatment that veterans were getting because of the war, and I was really just as happy not to have to take part personally in whatever was happening—people spitting on veterans. I spent two days back in the States, and we were met by a demonstration at Travis Air Force Base. Nobody got close enough to spit on me, I had no idea whether they would have spit on me, but I thought it was really, to use an Asian expression, low-class to go out and show that kind of contempt for the troops. If you had that kind of feeling about the war that the antiwar people did, then surely you had to recognize that the troops were the victims of the government. I was quite distressed over all that and I was very happy that I didn't have to take part in it."

Bob Taylor says, "after Nam I swore I would never wake up and take the day for granted again." Stateside he concluded that the Veterans Administration—heavy on prescription drugs and light on serious counseling—dealt insensitively and unimaginatively with the uniquely alienating aspects of psychological problems related to an unsuccessful war. He helped himself through Christianity, and that ultimately brought him back to Southeast Asia. Taylor is fond of reciting the unattributed aphorism: "Life has a special flavor that the Protected will never know." Thanks to Vietnam, he is among the unprotected and for that perhaps he feels closer to Southeast Asians.

The federal government's dismissal of his brother's contention that Agent Orange gave him cancer sticks in Jim Agnew's craw. The fact that nobody likes to talk about the Indochina wars in the United States dampens Jeff Johnson's social sense. Beyond that, it saddens him. Izzy Freedman would have liked quiet credit for his "hero days" with Air America, while the American-made movie lampoons the outfit as a bunch of bumbling drug runners. He is still a hero in Thailand, but might be less than that in the United States. Les Strouse took in Lao refugees after his return to the United States in the late seventies and early eighties—housing as many as thirteen at one time—but none of his Florida neighbors seemed to appreciate why. When an old Air America buddy asked him to fly for Chevron in Sudan, he jumped at the chance and has never looked west since.

Disaffected combat veterans—Holthaus, and Kleven, for instance—are generally too tough and stoic to tally up their expatriate status to the American public's or the U.S. government's effective disinheritance. But it is a fact that but for their intimate participation in an unpopular war they would not have ended up at such a long distance—physically and emotionally—from contemporary American society. Holthaus says he will probably never return from Thailand to the United States again. Kleven was so drawn to Vietnam that he sacrificed his marriage to it and has no intention of returning stateside to live. These American military heroes will probably die far closer to the scene of their wartime exploits than to the United States.

Charity-minded veterans in Thailand like Holthaus, Richter, and Taylor are not chasing Vietnam ghosts in any specific, deliberate way. But they would rather help people in Southeast Asia than Americans. These men suspect that Asians apprehend their having served in Vietnam as something honorable, and their conversion to good works therefore as farsighted and beyond the call of duty. And they know that had they stayed in the United States, a transition to charity might have been read as the refuge of a guilty conscience. In Thailand, soldiering in Vietnam and helping those in need connect positively. In the United States, they do not.

The reconcilers and revisionists, like Searcy and Herter, were of course more sympathetic than the others were with antiwar sentiments of the people at home. But not even Vietnam apologists are happy that the protest of a policy evolved into the semipermanent eschewal of the GIs required to carry it out. While their own war experiences centered on handling perceived conflicts between soldierly duty and personal morality, they do not judge other soldiers who apprehended no ethical inconsistencies in performing their military duties, and do not believe that noncombatant Americans should collectively judge them somehow unworthy. To them this injustice was incidental—though an injustice nonetheless—to the greater wrong of ignoring the hardship inflicted on the Vietnamese themselves. Yet the one mistake led to the other: if the war was the fault of the soldiers, then nonparticipating Americans bore no responsibility for their deeds.

This rueful group of veterans *did* feel a sense of national (though not personal) responsibility. In each case returning to Vietnam constituted direct action on that feeling, and such action ultimately may have been necessitated by the nation's insistence on scapegoating soldiers and the extended official refusal to admit any wholesale error of judgment. Had Washington after the war made such an admission even implicitly by, for example, following through on reparations, pushing a policy of reconciliation, or lifting the trade embargo before 1994, some or all of these Hanoi-based vets might have stayed home.

Bill Maddox, philosophically and psychologically resolved though he is about the Vietnam War, wishes he'd had a chance to shine in a U.S. victory. His expertise was military logistics, and he calls the Gulf War, appropriately, "The Logistics War." On the subject of meritocracy in the Army, he reflects that at its core the Army system is based on merit because requirements of technical professional qualifications are stringently applied, but that other things being equal luck is also a factor. It was a matter of bad luck that despite what he considered superior qualifications, he was assigned to JUSMAG-Thailand during the Gulf War and had to watch the action on CNN from Bangkok. He missed his parade again, and that may be one reason he was in no hurry to get home.

Mac Thompson cites mainly positive reasons for staying in Thailand after retiring from a USAID career dominated by service in Laos, the United States' forgotten Indochina flashpoint. Yet Thompson is the most active member in an informal network of expat veterans that monitors current events related to the Vietnam and Laos wars, mainly via a Usenet Newsgroup known as "TLC," for "Thailand, Laos, Cambodia." Thompson also disseminates articles via e-mail to various players: a *Sunday Times Magazine* article on former CIA man Tony Poe; a *Washington Post* piece by freelancer Arthur Allen on April Oliver, CNN, and the discredited Tailwind documentary; the four-part *TV Guide* series on the Tailwind media debacle; and STRATFOR, Inc.'s "Global Intelligence Updates." Before he agreed to talk to me and to vouch for me with other members of the expat veteran community in Thailand, he "checked me out" via the Internet and stateside contacts. I was deemed "legit" in the vetting e-mails he distributed. The noble conceit is that it is up to expatriate veterans to correct biased misconceptions about the Indochina wars because so many stateside vets have been forced to retreat from public discourse to the bunker.

In each expatriate veteran there is a palpable sense of not

belonging in the United States. Ironically, however, wherever they live expat veterans still fall into distinctly American categories. Holthaus with his computers for kids, Taylor with his development and missionary work, Richter with his largesse and his plans to start a charitable organization, Searcy with his prostheses for mine victims—all these men are Rotarians abroad. There is more than a little of the forward-looking American can-do spirit in the lives of Sauvageot, Searcy, and Herter and of the hard-work ethic in Mike Byrne. Jeff McLaury is a rugged individualist. In the finest blue-collar tradition, the Air America boys took risks for their country, and now reap their just rewards: comely and unliberated women, cheap housing, elevated social status, and a small community of people with whom they share their fondest memories of days gone by. If the quintessential American ideals are independence, material comfort, and camaraderie, then the Air America alumni are living the American dream.

THE VALUE OF A LOST WAR

Vietnam veterans remain an unacknowledged part of the American narrative. Yet the war looms as large for them as did World War II to its vets. Stan Karber cannot shake the memory of the two Green Beret heroin addicts he had to identify; one ate his .45, and five minutes later the other squeezed off seven rounds of a CAR-15 and took off half of his own face and the top of his head. Glenn Holthaus cannot suppress the sight of the Marine in the tree next to him with his chest blown out, just as Greg Kleven imagines unrelentingly the men in his platoon who died as he writhed wounded on the ground and killed NVA, just as Mark Smith relives Loc Ninh, just as even former REMFs hear sappers and blade-slap and see again aluminum coffins on loading pallets.

Missing from the post-Vietnam generation's cultural memory is a true appreciation that Vietnam soldiers were people asked to do more than most others ever have. The post-Vietnam generation embraced the revitalization of the country's prestige under Reagan and Bush superficially—as if the wounds of Vietnam had healed and "that war" in Southeast Asia could be written off as a moral and political aberration. Yet that resurgence of American pride, culminating in the Gulf War, was unearned for most of us. The honor of war is not only about the glory of victory; it is also about sacrifice in and of itself. But because we choose to view the Vietnam War as a wholesale calamity, we tend to think that Vietnam veterans have nothing to teach us. In this warp, the vets have been lost.

There are positive features of the prevailing skepticism about military adventures: the United States is a little less arrogant in its assessments of the world's problems, less chauvinistic in the solutions it proffers, less presumptuous in its use of force. At the same time, a May 2000 Gallup Poll indicated that 70 percent of Americans considered it important for the United States to be number one in the world militarily. But, whereas the British in the First World War and the Americans themselves in the Second ascribed victory to the national moral virtue that permeated individual soldiers, Vietnam and technological advance muted that functional brand of patriotism. Nowadays people are inclined to attribute national success to the superiority of American military and economic *machines.*

Vietnam veterans fall between the cracks of the "greatest generation" vintage World War II, and the civilian epoch personified by Bill Clinton, the first nonveteran to become president since Franklin Delano Roosevelt. That the Vietnam Memorial on the Mall is the most visited war remembrance site in the United States may demonstrate that America has come around to a belated mourning for lives lost for the sake of a discredited policy. It does not change the fact that those lives are considered wasted and little more. The proclamations of pundits like Edward Luttwak, who argues that we have entered a post-heroic military epoch in which sound management and the "revolution in military affairs" rather than duty and the will to fight determines strategic outcomes, may be comforting to those who are disinclined toward military service. They may prefer to think, after Kosovo, that a few pilots and bombardiers and standoff weapons, and lots of REMFs and pogues, are what we need to win a war.

Pete Peterson—the former Air Force pilot imprisoned for six and a half years at the "Hanoi Hilton," who served as U.S. Ambassador to Vietnam from 1996 to 2001—identifies a gap in the knowledge of post-Vietnam Americans: they see the consequences of Vietnam, but fail to appreciate what brought them about. "Regardless of whether one served there or was just born yesterday, his or her life will be different because of the conflict. American politics, American policy, American engagements, American influence, standards for the integrity of public officials—everything, even American products, have changed because of the Vietnam War. The standoff weapons we're using today in Iraq were designed because we were taking too many losses on single targets in Vietnam. Everything's changed. But I doubt seriously that people are thinking about that. Now we're into a no-loss policy. We can't engage in a conflict for fear of a loss. You have public support until you have a loss, and then you've got to measure whether you can stay. The Iraqi war was an immense success because of the lack of loss. Had there been more, I'm not so certain the public support would have been there long-term. You have to go to the public for support before you engage. On the whole it's positive because it forces us to think through [prospective actions] more clearly and evaluate the data more accurately, but at the same time there may be a reluctance by individuals to stand out on the point of leadership when it's ultimately in our best interests regardless of consensus. And there are times when one has to do that."

In post-Vietnam America, military service is still widely considered something a person does when there is no other equally remunerative civilian alternative. From 1997 through 1999, only the Marine Corps reserves attracted sufficient numbers to meet the requirements of military planners; the Army, Naval, and Air Force reserves failed to meet their recruitment targets. Americans younger than their mid-forties have never confronted the prospect of conscription—of being compelled involuntarily to depart our homes, families, job, or schools for a controlled military environment of strict discipline and then for some hostile, distant place where they would risk violent death. The volunteer force, the professional army, so far has proved more than adequate, and it makes little sense to reinstate the draft. Yet the draft, during the Civil War, the two world wars, and the Korean War as well as the Vietnam era, imparted to fledgling adults better than any book or movie or civics teacher could the idea that able people who derive benefits from their nation are obliged to defend it, and more generally that living right means recognizing your responsibility to your entire citizenry as well as to your friends and family.

It would be silly to wax nostalgic for an era when boys were pressed into service and war brought mass casualties. And certainly nobody should deny the ugly realities of the Vietnam War. What is equally a mistake, though, is to repudiate the courage that even bloody, ill-conceived wars produce. Just as the pleasant rustic allusions of the First World War poets did not shield memory from the horror of trench warfare, neither would the measured celebration of Vietnam heroism redact the abominations of that war. In a perceptive comment on the sociology of war in *Vietnam: The Necessary War,* Michael Lind writes: "Pacifists often claim that glorifying soldiers means approving of the evils of war. But honoring doctors has nothing to do with celebrating the diseases or accidents that unfortunately provide the occasion for doctors to demonstrate their expertise and their personal virtues." In that Americans are inclined to avoid discussions about the war that dare to be anything but tendentiously negative or presumptively ashamed, Vietnam veterans have been the victims of the kind of illogic that Lind identifies.

Senator John McCain's account of his long captivity in North Vietnam, in his 1999 memoir *Faith of My Fathers,* is a war story particularly well aimed at American men and women complacently far removed from the prospect of serving one's country at risk. Inspired by his father and grandfather, both four-star admirals and "proud heroes of an epic war," he flew attack bombers in Vietnam, was shot down in 1967, and spent more than five torturous years as a prisoner of war. Early in his captivity, after brutal beatings, he momentarily confessed to war crimes. Thereafter he never broke again. He ascribes his steel not just to some individualist strength but more to his compulsion not to disserve his heritage or the fellow soldiers who had shown themselves to be stronger than he. His story is meant to show that no matter how dubious the cause—and he suggests the Vietnam War was "better left unfought"—fidelity to blood, to country, to ideal, matters. Why? McCain explains that "faith in myself alone, separate from other . . . allegiances, was ultimately no match for the cruelty that human beings could devise." He makes a strong argument not for war, but for the humility, honesty, and loyalty that emerge from it—and, paradoxically, are required to wage it. Merely maintaining military expenditures at $300 billion a year, in its bloodlessness, is insufficient to sustain us as a nation.

The suicide attacks on the World Trade Center and the Pentagon on September 11, 2001, horrifically drove home this point to an arguably complacent and indisputably unaware American people. Any nation must anticipate war and therefore prepare some of its citizens to descend into its hell. The suppression in cultural memory of the sacrifices of soldiers, many of whom still live among us, is no way to fill this need. At any moment, we may need patriots ready to make sacrifices rather than just to talk about them. Indeed, the events of September 11 illustrated that, as the lone superpower in a unipolar world, the United States inspires antagonists who are in fact harder to deter and less afraid to strike our homeland than were Cold War foes. Those events also portray fanatical enemies who themselves are ready to give their own lives and cannot be thwarted absent Americans' willingness to take the ultimate risk. Now is preeminently a time to extol rather than decry military sacrifice.

As for the Vietnam War itself, history should neither sanitize it nor caricature it. The U.S. military has arguably managed to avoid both. But the wider social legacy of Vietnam has been the diminishment of the soldier-hero as an American icon. This result is unfair to Vietnam veterans and casualties.

The cultural decline of the military hero is a dangerous trend. Imagine the consequences for the world had the British, after losing 800,000 in World War I, abandoned faith in the virtues of soldiering in 1939. Virtually all Britons regard the Great War as a logic-defying waste—what Siegfried Sassoon called "a dirty trick which had been played on me and my generation." Yet the memory of that generation of men who suffered and perished in that war resonates proudly through contemporary British culture. Historian Niall Ferguson writes: "That my grandfather fought on the Western Front was, and still is, a strange source of pride. If I try to analyze that pride, I suppose it has to do with the fact that the First World War remains the worst thing the people of my country have ever had to endure. To survive it was to be mysteriously fortunate. But survival also seemed to suggest great resilience." Ferguson's pride is unimpeded by his professional conclusion that World War I was "something worse than a tragedy" and "nothing less than the greatest *error* of modern history."

In the United States, World War II provides pride in abundance. The sons (literal and figurative) of Vietnam veterans may well wish they could feel the same way about their fathers' service in Vietnam. But they don't. Their cultural embrace of the Vietnam War is halfhearted, our vision of its extremes truncated. They absorb the trauma that some of our soldiers endured but not the transcendence of circumstance that many of them achieved. Romance over wars may have rightly ended, but it need not entail the effacement of those who fight them. If Americans could choose a war to fight, most would not select the one in Vietnam. Yet, from one perspective, there is something especially honorable about having survived a bad war. All the more reason to be grateful to the hundreds of thousands of Americans who carried forward and preserved the idea of duty to country.

If the American people have sought to escape from the Vietnam War and its fallout, the expat vets in many ways have sought to escape America's suppression of the war's memory. This makes them very "patriate" indeed. Their lives, as extended war stories, do justice to the Vietnam experience by uncovering, in Paul Fussell's words, "a part, and perhaps not the least compelling part, of our own buried lives." In the spirit of that exhortation, Vietnam veterans should be remembered not under the pall of a futile war, but as part of a valorous heritage that has cost soldiers dearly in every war Americans have fought—and will fight.

ACKNOWLEDGMENT

This project benefited from the generous financial support I received from the John-Christophe Schlesinger Writer-in Residence Fund of St. Paul's School in Concord, New Hampshire.